**DATE DUE**

# THERAPEUTIC
# PRESENCE

# THERAPEUTIC PRESENCE

## A MINDFUL APPROACH TO EFFECTIVE THERAPY

Shari M. Geller
Leslie S. Greenberg

AMERICAN PSYCHOLOGICAL ASSOCIATION

WASHINGTON, DC

Published by
American Psychological Association
750 First Street, NE
Washington, DC 20002
www.apa.org

To order
APA Order Department
P.O. Box 92984
Washington, DC 20090-2984
Tel: (800) 374-2721; Direct: (202) 336-5510
Fax: (202) 336-5502; TDD/TTY: (202) 336-6123
Online: www.apa.org/pubs/books
E-mail: order@apa.org

In the U.K., Europe, Africa, and the Middle East, copies may be ordered from
American Psychological Association
3 Henrietta Street
Covent Garden, London
WC2E 8LU England

Typeset in Goudy by Circle Graphics, Inc., Columbia, MD

Printer: Maple-Vail Book Manufacturing Group, York, PA
Cover Designer: Berg Design, Albany, NY

The opinions and statements published are the responsibility of the authors, and such opinions and statements do not necessarily represent the policies of the American Psychological Association.

**Library of Congress Cataloging-in-Publication Data**

Geller, Shari M.
Therapeutic presence : a mindful approach to effective therapy / Shari M. Geller and Leslie S. Greenberg.
    p. cm.
  ISBN-13: 978-1-4338-1060-2
  ISBN-10: 1-4338-1060-3
  1. Mindfulness-based cognitive therapy. 2. Psychotherapy. 3. Interpersonal relations.
I. Greenberg, Leslie S. II. Title.

  RC489.M55G45 2012
  616.89'1425—dc23
                                    2011018593

**British Library Cataloguing-in-Publication Data**

A CIP record is available from the British Library.

*Printed in the United States of America*
*First Edition*

doi: 10.1037/13485-000

# CONTENTS

# THERAPEUTIC
# PRESENCE

# INTRODUCTION

Scholars have increasingly recognized the importance of discovering the core qualities that enhance the therapeutic relationship and the working alliance, since differential therapeutic outcomes may only be minimally attributed to specific techniques (Duncan & Moynihan, 1994; Lambert & Ogles, 2004; Lambert & Simon, 2008; Martin, Garske, & Davis, 2000; Norcross, 2002, 2011). Although a great deal has been written about the therapeutic relationship and the working alliance as contributing to positive therapy process and outcome (e.g., Bohart & Tallman, 1998; Greenberg, 2007; Horvath, 1994; Horvath & Greenberg, 1986; Horvath & Luborsky, 1993; Martin et al., 2000; Norcross 2011; Watson & Geller, 2005), researchers still have not identified all the specific therapist and client factors that contribute to the development of a therapeutic relationship, to a working alliance, and to successful psychotherapy. Hence we are still left with two important questions: What makes for a successful therapeutic relationship? And how can therapists cultivate the qualities that lead to successful therapeutic relationships?

There is a vast amount of empirical support for the importance of therapist qualities and the therapeutic relationship originally proposed by Carl

Rogers (1951, 1957, 1980, 1986; Norcross, 2002, 2011). Rogers focused on certain attitudes, or *therapist-offered conditions* (TOCs), including empathy, unconditional positive regard, and congruence, as important in providing a facilitative and growth-enhancing environment for clients. In his later writings, Rogers focused on a more central quality, which he called and has been understood by later client-centered authors as *presence*. He suggested that this is a quality that in and of itself can release the growth potential in clients (Rogers, 1980, p. 129). Rogers also suggested that presence is the foundation of the TOCs (Baldwin, 2000, pp. 32–33). In a posthumous publication (Baldwin, 2000), Rogers noted:

> I am inclined to think that in my writing I have stressed too much the three basic conditions (congruence, unconditional positive regard, and empathic understanding). Perhaps it is something around the edges of those conditions that is really the most important element of therapy— when my self is very clearly, obviously present. (p. 30)

Buber, in his theory of relationship, also placed presence at the center of the I–Thou relationship. Following the deaths of Rogers and Buber, the characteristics of presence have been explored further (Bugental, 1987; Hycner & Jacobs, 1995; Schneider & May, 1995; Thorne, 1992), and presence has been proposed as a possible underlying contributor to a positive therapeutic relationship (Geller, 2001; Geller & Greenberg, 2002; Schmid, 1998; Thorne, 1992, 1996). Our research concurs that therapeutic presence is a central contribution to the development of the therapeutic relationship and the working alliance (Geller & Greenberg, 2002; Geller, Greenberg, & Watson, 2010).

Although the concept of presence has been theoretically discussed or alluded to in the literature (see Chapter 1 of this volume for a more thorough literature review), to date few published studies have been conducted on therapeutic presence (Geller & Greenberg, 2002; Geller et al., 2010). Prior to our previous publications, there was little rigorous theory or research on the experience of therapeutic presence or the relationship between presence and the therapeutic alliance, the TOCs and outcome. This book is grounded in and expanded from our initial research findings, which help in understanding the components of therapeutic presence and suggest that therapeutic presence is an essential ingredient in the development of a positive therapeutic relationship and therapeutic working alliance.

Our first study on therapeutic presence was qualitative and involved master therapists who have either written about or discussed presence as an important aspect of their therapeutic stance (Geller & Greenberg, 2002). Accounts from expert therapists from different disciplines (including humanistic, emotion-focused, Adlerian, and cognitive–behavioral) suggested that therapeutic presence is a necessary condition for a good therapeutic relationship and, hence, a positive therapeutic process and outcome for clients. Based on results from this study, we developed a working model that explains three aspects of therapeutic presence: (a) how therapists prepare for presence both presession and in general life (i.e., "preparing the ground for presence"), (b) what activities therapists engage in when being therapeutically present (i.e., "the process of presence"), and (c) what in-session presence feels like (i.e., "the experience of presence") (Geller & Greenberg, 2002). This model of therapeutic presence is summarized in Exhibit 1 and elaborated in Chapters 4 through 6.

EXHIBIT 1
Model of Therapeutic Presence
_____

**Preparing the Ground for Presence**
*In Life*
- Philosophical commitment to presence
- Practicing presence in life and relationships
- Meditation and spiritual practice
- Personal growth
- Ongoing attention to personal needs and concerns

*In Session*
- Intention for presence
- Clearing a space
- Letting go of self-concerns and issues
- Bracketing (theories, preconceptions, therapy plans)
- Attitude of openness, acceptance, interest, and nonjudgment

**Process of Presence**
*Receptivity*
- Open, accepting, allowing
- Sensory/bodily receptivity
- Listening with the third ear
- Inclusion
- Expanded or enhanced awareness
- Extrasensory level of communication

*Inwardly attending*
- Self as instrument
- Increased spontaneity/creativity
- Trust
- Authenticity and congruence
- Returning to the present moment

*Extending*
- Accessible
- Meeting
- Transparency/congruence
- Intuitive responding

*(continues)*

EXHIBIT 1
Model of Therapeutic Presence     *(Continued)*

**Experience of Therapeutic Presence**
*Grounding*
- Centered/steady/whole
- Inclusion
- Trust and ease

*Immersion*
- Absorption
- Experiencing deeply with nonattachment
- Present-centered
- Aware/alert/focused

*Expansion*
- Timelessness
- Energized/flowing
- Spaciousness
- Enhanced awareness of sensation and perception
- Enhanced quality of thought and emotional experiencing

*Being With and for the Client*
- Intention for client's healing
- Awe, respect, love
- Absence of ego involvement or self-consciousness

*Note.* From "Therapeutic Presence: Therapists' Experience of Presence in the Psychotherapeutic Encounter," by S. M. Geller and L. S. Greenberg, 2002, *Person-Centered and Experiential Psychotherapies, 1,* p. 76. Copyright 2002 by PCCS Books. Adapted with permission.

Our second empirical study focused on the development of a measure, the Therapeutic Presence Inventory (TPI), which is based on the model in Exhibit 1 (Geller, 2001; Geller et al., 2010). Two versions of the measure were created, one from the therapists' perspective and the second from the clients' perception of their therapists' presence. Our third study explored the reliability and validity of the TPI. Our research indicated that therapeutic presence is a foundation for the development of a positive therapeutic relationship and working alliance, as well as positive session outcome across person-centered, process-experiential, and cognitive–behavioral therapies (CBTs; Geller et al., 2010).

## PURPOSE OF THIS BOOK

The purpose of this book is to conceptualize therapeutic presence by presenting our empirically based model and to provide a theory of relationship based on therapeutic presence as well as practical and experiential approaches for cultivating presence. We discuss empirical research indicating that therapeutic presence is a necessary condition for both a good therapeutic relationship and a working alliance, and we provide explanations as to why therapeutic presence is a helpful stance in understanding the client and responding in a therapeutic manner. We also immerse you in mindfulness and experiential exercises to cultivate presence, and we invite you to develop your own definition, process, and experience of therapeutic presence.

Training in psychotherapy is often focused on intervention, on "what to do" and "how to respond" to a client in distress. A vast array of approaches can facilitate client change, and these range from exploring underlying childhood issues to modifying behavior to restricting cognitive schema or transforming emotional schemas that contribute to unhealthy functioning. We have learned a great deal from each of these approaches, and current thinking and practice often incorporate an integrative approach that is geared toward the client's personality, issues, and individual needs. Although much has been written on technique and client change, this book is distinct in that it focuses less on what to *do* and more on how to *be* with clients.

## WHAT IS THERAPEUTIC PRESENCE?

From our empirical research, we derived the following definition: *Therapeutic presence* is the state of having one's whole self in the encounter with a client by being completely in the moment on a multiplicity of levels—physically, emotionally, cognitively, and spiritually. Therapeutic presence involves being in contact with one's integrated and healthy self, while being open and receptive to what is poignant in the moment and immersed in it, with a larger sense of spaciousness and expansion of awareness and perception. This grounded, immersed, and expanded awareness occurs with the intention of being with and for the client, in service of his or her healing process. The inner receptive state involves a complete openness to the client's multidimensional internal world, including bodily and verbal expression, as well as openness to the therapist's own bodily experience of the moment in order to access the knowledge, professional skill, and wisdom embodied within. Being fully present then allows for an attuned responsiveness that is based on a kinesthetic and emotional sensing of the other's affect and experience as well as one's own intuition and skill and the relationship between them.

Therapeutic presence can also be viewed as a way that therapists monitor their own experience in therapy. Through an enhanced sensitivity to the client's experience, therapists can use their selves and their attuned bodily awareness as tools in understanding and responding to the client as well as in sensing how their responses are facilitating the client's therapeutic process and the therapeutic relationship. The therapist's bodily sense of the client's experience is a reflection of an inner synthesis of the client's expressed and felt experience with the therapist's own lived experience and his or her professional expertise. The therapist's presence and consequent in-the-moment physical, emotional, and cognitive awareness are a reflection of the client's multilevel expression and act as a receptor and a guide to the process of therapy.

## RELEVANCE TO VARIOUS THERAPEUTIC APPROACHES

We propose that therapeutic presence is transtheoretical in that it can optimize both therapists' and clients' functioning across a variety of theoretical approaches. Although presence is based on humanistic principles, it is in no way limited to humanistic therapeutic approaches. Rather, presence is a helpful stance in many therapeutic approaches, including psychodynamic therapy, emotion-focused therapy, gestalt therapy, cognitive therapy, behavioral therapy, and group therapy.

All therapeutic approaches, whether humanistic, analytical, cognitive, or behavioral, involve a direct human relationship. Human interactions are highly complex and dynamic processes, and therapists need to attend to what is occurring in the moment, which allows them to adapt what they do in relationship to where the client is and what the client is doing. This includes the therapists' contact and reading of their own experience in the moment as well as contact and attunement to the client, so that therapists can provide interventions that are based on what the client needs rather than what the therapist thinks the client needs.

Humanistic and relational approaches have long recognized the role of the therapeutic relationship as a change mechanism. For example, person-centered therapy (Rogers, 1957, 1980; Schmid, 2002), emotion-focused therapy (Greenberg, 2007; Greenberg, Rice, & Elliott, 1993), existential therapy (Bugental, 1987, 1989; May, 1994; May & Yalom, 2005; Schneider & Krug, 2010; Schneider & May, 1995), gestalt therapy (Perls, 1970), and dialogical approaches (Hycner, 1993; Hycner & Jacobs, 1995) place the foundation of effective interventions in the therapeutic relationship and recognize therapists' presence as a central contribution to the relationship and change. Current psychodynamic approaches have also broadened their approach to recognize the importance of the relationship in the therapy encounter (Mitchell, 2003; Stern, 2004; Stolorow, Brandchaft, & Atwood, 1987). More contemporary relational approaches emphasize that the therapist–client relationship is at the center of the change process (Gelso, 2011; Messer & Warren, 1995) and reference relational connection and special present moments as central ways that change can occur (Mitchell, 2003; Stern, 2004).

It is true that certain therapeutic approaches are more technical than relational in their approach, such as CBTs. However, more recently these therapies have also identified that the development of a therapeutic relationship or rapport is important and helpful in facilitating the use of cognitive–behavioral techniques and can increase treatment efficacy (Gelso, 2011; Goldfried & Davila, 2005; Holtforth & Castonguay, 2005; Kanter et al., 2009; Leahy, 2003; Lejuez, Hopko, Levine, Gholkar, & Collins, 2006; Linehan, 1993a; Wadding-ton, 2002). Furthermore, although the primary focus in CBT is on changing thoughts and behavior in relation to the world "out there," current perspectives have begun to emphasize the present moment in the therapeutic relationship as an active component of change (i.e., Castonguay et al., 2004; Kanter et al., 2009; Leahy, 2001; McCullough, 2000). However, research indicates that few cognitive–behavioral therapists actually focus on the present moment in the clinical encounter, despite recognizing the value of the approach (Kanter et al., 2009). This may be due to a lack of training in developing presence and cultivating a positive therapeutic relationship.

Therapeutic presence is not a replacement for technique, but rather can provide a foundation for different theoretical orientations, primarily as it is an essential way of meeting the client that can enhance listening and attunement, enhance accurate responding, as well as remain free of therapists' judgments and preconceptions. Therapeutic presence also allows for the development of a healthy and profound therapeutic relationship, one that supports optimal use of therapists' interventions and includes clients in the healing process.

## PRESENCE AND THERAPIST WELL-BEING

Therapeutic presence is not only beneficial therapeutically for the client and the therapeutic relationship but is also healthy and growth promoting for therapists. Presence practice provides therapists a way to release the residue of taking in the client's pain and experience. From this perspective, the commit-ment to presence can help therapists maintain energy and a positive flow of experience to prevent burnout. By feeling in contact with their own vitality, therapists can maintain a sense of health and inner connection, including greater well-being, decreased burnout, greater self-care, improved interpersonal relationships, decreased anxiety, and heightened vitality.

### Personal Well-Being

Although we emphasize that the psychological health and well-being of the therapist are essential to the cultivation of therapeutic presence, the process is also reciprocal whereby therapeutic presence promotes greater health and well-being. Furthermore, we know that therapists' emotional health and well-being are associated with their professional effectiveness (Coster & Schwebel, 1997). Successful outcome in therapy and a positive therapeutic alliance have been related to therapists' well-being and psychological adjustment (Beutler et al., 2004). Therapists in our study also noted that attention to their self-care and personal well-being improved their presence and ultimately improved their effectiveness as therapists. This concurs with Henry, Schacht, and Strupp (1990), who found that therapists who are high in negative emotion, which suggests a deficiency in well-being, were shown to elicit negativity in their clients. Although personal well-being is key to effective therapy, we propose that cultivating presence helps to enhance well-being as well as spiritual and interpersonal connection.

## Prevention of Burnout

Being a therapist can be taxing and can lead to emotional exhaustion and disconnection and hence to less satisfaction in work and ultimately to burnout. Burnout can arise from the accumulation of stress that is associated with doing intensive caring work with people (Maslach, 1986). Research indicates that therapists experience significant levels of burnout (Ackerley, Burnell, Holder, & Kurdek, 1988). In fact, Hannigan, Edwards, and Burnard (2004) found that four out of 10 practicing psychologists were experiencing clinically significant psychological distress, which supported the notion that many psychologists find their work stressful and emotionally draining. Feeling burned out can affect therapists' satisfaction with their work and contributes to personal distress and reduced well-being, and ultimately it can compromise their overall satisfaction in life and engagement in their personal relationships.

The emotional exhaustion that leads to burnout emerges in part from a lack of life–work balance, a lack of self-care, and inability to release the stress and difficult emotions that accompany hearing the depth of clients' suffering. We propose that cultivating and sustaining therapeutic presence forces therapists to take responsibility for life–work balance and their own personal growth and self-care, which can greatly reduce stress and burnout. Furthermore, a commitment to the experience of presence in life and in session helps therapists learn to take in the fullness of their clients' experience and let it go, moment to moment. In fact, therapists who experience high levels of presence in session report a sense of energy, vitality, positive feeling, purpose, and fulfillment (Geller, 2001). This supports findings that suggest that job satisfaction is associated with higher self-esteem and positive feelings toward clients (Garske, 2000). Hence, cultivating therapeutic presence is a sustaining process that can increase job satisfaction, increase personal wellness, and offer prevention against burnout and vicarious traumatization.

There is more recent recognition in the literature of the value to therapists of learning to cultivate a deeply present state of awareness for personal and professional health and sustainability (Bien, 2006; Epstein, 2001; May &

O'Donovan, 2007). Being deeply present, which includes being grounded, receptive, immersed, nonjudgmental, and with and for the client, can help therapists to be with uncomfortable emotions and situations with understanding and acceptance rather than becoming burdened or overwhelmed by the intensity of client's emotions (Fulton, 2005).

Therapists' self-awareness, a key aspect of therapeutic presence, may contribute to prevention of burnout. For example, being aware and attuned with one's self encourages therapists to know when they are emotionally drained or overwhelmed and hence can then respond to their needs appropriately. The commitment to presence and self-development supports therapists' acting on that awareness to meet and care for their own needs.

## Self-Care

The cultivation and deepening of presence, for both novice and seasoned therapists, demand that therapists have a high level of self-care, self-awareness, and self-compassion. This ensures that time is committed to reducing stress, being in nature, being present in life, laughter, exercise, and attention to personal relationships. Hence, cultivating presence means a commitment to one's self and one's own growth. This is not only a benefit but also provides a feedback loop to the development of therapeutic presence. To deepen our sense of presence with clients, we need to be present in our daily lives. The more we tune our vessel, ourselves, through cultivating presence in life, the greater our capacity to be present with clients.

Presence also demands that we work through unfinished business or issues that keep us stuck. We cannot expect our clients to develop any further than we have in our growth process. The idea that we can help our clients to resolve their issues and lead a healthier life simply by using proper techniques is misleading. We emphasize in this book that presence is not about letting go of techniques, as techniques can be helpful; however, techniques will have minimal impact if they are facilitated by someone who is detached or absent. To develop and sustain this quality of presence, therapists must commit to working through their own issues so that those issues will not interfere in the therapy process and so that therapists will be clear and open vessels who are accessible and attuned to the client, without personal interference.

Presence opens up the potential for happiness and joy now. If we are ruminating or expending mental and emotional energy on past hurt or future longings, we miss the preciousness of this moment. This level of present-centered attention demands constant attention to care for and to bring ourselves back to this moment, where the treasures of contentment, experiencing, openness, and inner peace are possible.

## Decreased Anxiety

A focus on present-centered awareness helps to decrease and modulate anxiety. In exploratory therapies, such as psychodynamic and humanistic or experiential therapies, there is a high need to trust in the process and in the moment as a guide to the unfolding of clients' experience. There are moments when it is unclear what will emerge, and the skill of following the moment and tolerating uncertainty and the unknown is highly important. In manual-based therapy, such as CBT, therapists tend to have less anxiety, as more of a structure to which therapists are expected to adhere exists. However, modulating therapist anxiety still is relevant in manual-based therapies because anxiety can cause therapists to rely too heavily on the provided structure without attending to the clients' current needs or experience or adapting to the clients' moment-by-moment response.

Present-centered attention, in one's personal life as well as with clients, helps avoid following anxious thoughts or sensations into a pit of despair. Personal practice in bringing one's attention back to the moment helps to develop a state that calms the nervous system, activates the parasympathetic nervous system, and invites a sense of calm or at least prevents the exacerbation of anxiety (Hanson & Mendius, 2010). Therapeutic presence is more than just a way of being: It is a philosophy of life that recognizes the inherent value of not allowing our ruminative tendencies and unresolved issues to lead us down a path of anxiousness or despair. Modulating anxiety is not only valuable in the life of the therapist but also important in sustaining a present-centered openness and connection with the client.

## Vitality

Cultivating presence helps to generate and sustain the vitality and joy that experiencing the moment offers. Research has indicated that presence-based activities, particularly practices that are characterized by flow and engagement with the present moment, result in heightened enjoyment and an experiential sense of vitality (Csikszentmihalyi, 1990; Deci & Ryan, 1985). The vitality that emerges from presence practice as well as spiritual practices helps to counter emotional fatigue and burnout. Furthermore, deep engagement in a relational encounter, particularly one that is characterized by presence and mutuality, heightens energy and vitality (Krug, 2009). Through the experience of relational therapeutic presence and the practices associated with cultivating presence, therapists experience a heightened sense of vitality that can transcend the therapy encounter.

## PRESENCE VERSUS MINDFULNESS

Recently, references to mindfulness have exploded in the literature (Baer, 2003; Bien, 2006; Cole & Ladas-Gaskin, 2007; Germer, 2005; Germer, Siegel, & Fulton, 2005; Hick, 2008; Linehan, 1993a, 1993b; Mace, 2008; McKay, Brantley, & Wood, 2007). We see therapeutic presence and mindfulness as distinct in two important ways. First, *mindfulness* refers to a practice or meditation technique that reflects a deep philosophical orientation toward Buddhist ways of dealing with "problems of the mind." This differs from therapeutic presence, which is a state of being with the client (not a technique) and is not necessarily rooted in Buddhism. Nonetheless, mindfulness is a powerful practice that can help to cultivate therapeutic presence. For example, Surrey (2005) noted that "mindfulness practice cultivates an expansive awareness in the therapist, which is implicitly or explicitly extended to the patient" (p. 96). We therefore refer to therapeutic presence as "a mindful approach" in the title of this book and devote Chapter 10 to the use of mindfulness in developing therapeutic presence.

Second, mindfulness approaches to therapy, such as CBT or mindfulness-based therapy, are primarily presented as an approach to work with clients and as a "mindful therapy" based on teaching and practices such as mindful meditation. In contrast, therapeutic presence does not necessarily involve teaching clients to be mindful, but instead focuses on the *therapist* being mindful. Furthermore, research on therapists using mindfulness is often concentrated on the effects of mindfulness for the client and rarely attends to the therapists' presence. Rather than the use of mindfulness as a technique for clients, this book focuses on the importance of therapists' presence and suggests that mindfulness is one way that therapists can cultivate being fully in the moment with a client (see Chapter 10), which can enhance a particular way of being with clients regardless of therapeutic approach or technique.

## ORGANIZATION OF THIS BOOK

This book is organized into four major parts. Part I presents the background and theoretical basis for therapeutic presence. Chapter 1 presents the theoretical basis for presence across different therapeutic approaches. Chapter 2 describes our qualitative and quantitative research on therapeutic presence, including the development of the TPI. Chapter 3 explains our theory of relationship, based on our empirical studies of therapeutic presence.

Part II presents our model of therapeutic presence, which we developed from our empirical research. Excerpts and quotations from therapists interviewed in our qualitative study (Geller, 2001; Geller & Greenberg, 2002) are embedded in these chapters. Chapter 4 describes how therapists "prepare the ground" for presence (i.e., practices, in general and before sessions, that promote presence during sessions). Chapter 5 describes the process of presence (i.e., what therapists do when in therapeutic presence). Chapter 6 describes the in-body experience of therapeutic presence.

Part III provides additional perspectives on therapeutic presence. Chapter 7 presents an applied approach to therapeutic presence, which includes viewing presence in levels. Chapter 8 presents challenges that therapists may face when practicing therapeutic presence with different populations. Chapter 9 presents a neurobiological perspective on therapeutic presence.

Part IV presents theory and exercises for cultivating therapeutic presence. Chapter 10 presents mindfulness approaches, and Chapter 11 presents experiential approaches. Both of these chapters stem from particular theoretical bases, and the exercises in these chapters stem from the respective theories. Chapter 12 offers individual and group exercises that are grounded in theory, like those of the previous two chapters. However, unlike Chapters 10 and 11, Chapter 12 does not emphasize theory. This chapter is intended to be a practical, user-friendly resource for teachers, trainers, or individual therapists who want to cultivate therapeutic presence without a focus on understanding the theoretical underpinnings.

The book concludes with an epilogue highlighting key points and suggesting directions for future research and practice. We hope that this book will not only provide a deeper understanding of therapeutic presence as a foundation for effective therapy but also allow opportunities to experience presence in your own life and with clients from the array of exercises we have provided. Becoming more present more often to your clients will enhance your therapeutic practice and outcomes and provide a new sense of vitality in your sessions and possibly in your life.

# I

# THEORETICAL AND EMPIRICAL BASIS OF THE MODEL

# 1

# HISTORY OF PRESENCE ACROSS THEORETICAL APPROACHES

Our true home is not in the past. Our true home is not in the future. Our true home is in the here and now. Life is available only in the here and now.

—Thich Nhat Hanh (2011, p. 65)

Theoretically, presence has been deemed the groundwork for good therapy (Hycner, 1993; Moustakas, 1969; Rogers, 1986). Certain qualities of therapist's presence have been described at a theoretical level. For example, the therapist's presence has been described as bringing one's whole self to the engagement with the client and being fully in the moment with and for the client, with little self-centered purpose or goal in mind (Craig, 1986; Hycner, 1993; Hycner & Jacobs, 1995; Moustakas, 1969; Robbins, 1998; Webster, 1998). Therapists are seen as using the essence of themselves as an instrument in understanding and responding to the client (Clarkson, 1997; Keefe, 1975; Kempler, 1970; Lietaer, 1993; Robbins, 1998; Shepherd, Brown, & Greaves, 1972; Vanaerschot, 1993). The general literature on presence also suggests the importance of therapists' self-development as part of their capacity for presence (Keefe, 1975; Lietaer, 1993; Shepherd et al., 1972; Webster, 1998). Commitment to one's own personal growth has also been seen as allowing a greater capacity for presence (Webster, 1998). The therapist needs to be aware of and to work on his or her own issues so those issues will not be brought into therapy sessions (Lietaer, 1993).

Rogers referred to presence as the essential underlying process in therapeutic relating (Baldwin, 2000; Rogers, 1980). Typically, presence has been deemed central to humanistic perspectives. However, present-focused attention has been suggested historically in different theoretical traditions. This chapter focuses on a brief overview of how aspects of therapists' presence have been suggested historically across different therapeutic approaches.

## FREUD AND THE PSYCHOANALYTIC APPROACH: THE ORIGINAL VOICE OF PRESENCE?

Original references to aspects of presence, particularly in the analyst as opposed to the client, can be seen as early as Freud's original work. For example, Freud emphasized the value of therapists' "attention." Furthermore, Epstein (2007) provided a good history of Freud's notion of "evenly suspended attention" (p. 101). Epstein referenced Freud's perspective of the value of being void of critical judgment combined with giving impartial attention to all that occurs in the field of awareness. Freud highlighted an aspect of what we call presence, *receptivity*, and described it as emerging from an impartial, nonjudgmental, evenly applied attention. Freud (1912) noted that the doctor "must turn his own unconscious like a receptive organ towards the transmitting unconscious of the patient. He must adjust himself to the patient as a telephone receiver is adjusted to the transmitting microphone" (p. 115). Although the therapist is seen as a receptor, presence in the therapeutic relationship is not valued. The therapist is to be receptive to his or her own unconscious, yet an extension of one's personal presence to the other is contrary to the objective position of the analyst or doctor.

This state of evenly suspended attention suggests a broad detachment yet openness so that analysts can pay attention in the moment to what they see and hear, without getting emotionally involved. This is an important aspect of presence but not the complete picture, as it is devoid of an actual present-centered awareness that is inclusive of emotional connectedness, both within the therapist and between the therapist and the client. Freud's "poised state of mind" portrays a present-centered focus and calm mental state, which can portray the typical objective and distant therapist noted in traditional psychoanalytic perspectives. However, the aspect of therapeutic presence that includes being in tune with the therapist's own authentic experience as a real and equal human being, as well as touching and being touched by the humanness in the client, is not a part of this approach.

Freud's concept of the analyst's evenly suspended attention was expanded by Reik (1948), as reflected in his book *Listening With the Third Ear*. Reik described "free floating attention," where he discarded the notion of even or poised attention and instead suggested a mind that is actively roaming the present for any clues of insight from the analysand. The analyst, in Reik's view, was to maintain an intellectual attention that oscillates between the analysand's projection of experience and "trial identification" of material (Epstein, 2007). While Reik saw attention as including a revolving searchlight, Freud's attention reflected more of a pendulum, "evenly encompassing everything within its two poles of existence" (Epstein, 2007, p. 117). In this vein, the analyst's impartial attention allows for an openness as well as attentiveness to all that is relevant, which in turn provides an ease in interpretation that is correct in timing and content.

Freud instructed psychoanalysts that the most important method was to just listen without bothering to keep anything particular in mind (Epstein, 2007). Freud did not want his analysts to listen with a preconceived agenda. Instead, he preferred therapists to listen with their "third ear" rather than with their thinking minds, so that they could make intuitive leaps rather than cognitive analytical statements (Epstein, 2007).

An aspect of presence, *spaciousness,* can also be rooted in Freud's concept of the "oceanic feeling" noted in the opening pages of *Civilization and its Discontents* (Freud, 1930). Freud seemed to have taken this term from Rolland, who was interested in having Freud examine the meditative experience and religious feeling from a psychoanalytic perspective (Epstein, 2007). While Freud was excited about the concept, he admitted to not having this feeling. In fact, Freud reduced the oceanic feeling to a sense of helplessness and powerlessness against fate and the need for a father figure (God) for guidance and a feeling of significance. Rolland believed that people do in fact have an oceanic feeling, which in his view is the basis of religion. He characterized it as a feeling of eternity, in which individuals feel connected to something much larger than themselves. Freud recognized this concept and even noted that it reflected a sense of boundlessness and oneness with the outside world and something larger, even though he reduced the understanding as stemming from an ego ideal and a longing for parental protection.

Epstein (2007) noted that in contemporary discussion of psychoanalytic technique, the emphasis is more on the cognitive processing of the analyst, as opposed to maintaining a disciplined and open state of awareness. Although there is some suggestion of the cognitive processing of present material expressed on both the conscious and the unconscious levels of expression, traditional psychoanalytic approaches focus on an observing therapist who is detached, calm, and even. This state promotes the ability to make interpretations as well as identify countertransference responses. However, analysts often see this state of awareness, originally posited by Freud, as infeasible and perhaps even impossible. For example, Reich (1951) described how difficult it can be to "listen in this effortless way" (p. 25). Consequently, the cultivation or discipline around cultivating this state of attention is not emphasized in psychoanalytic literature. Epstein (2007) noted that "the loss of reliance on evenly suspended attention has deprived psychoanalysis of one of its most potent tools" (p. 118).

Modern interpersonal psychodynamic approaches (Mitchell, 2003; Stern, 2004), however, focus on the present interpersonal contact between client and therapist. When treating patients, relational psychoanalysts stress a mixture of waiting and authentic spontaneity. They eschew the traditional emphasis on interpretation and instead emphasize the importance of creating a lively, genuine relationship with the patient. Overall, relational analysts feel that psychotherapy works best when the therapist focuses on establishing a healing relationship with the patient, in addition to focusing on facilitating insight. They believe that in doing so, therapists break patients out of the repetitive patterns of relating to others that they believe maintain psychopathology.

Stern (2004) emphasized that psychotherapy needs to be reexamined through the lens of present moment experience. He suggested that the therapeutic relationship is composed of present moments that are a critical starting point for therapeutic exploration. He asserted that the present moment has been traditionally neglected in psychoanalytic and psychodynamic approaches, and it is through the subjective lens of individual moments that therapeutic progress can be made. This way of thinking values the lived experience of each moment, shared between therapist and client. The subjective and lived experience invites the therapist to be opened and changed by the experience of the moment as it is happening, rather than viewing the client's experience through an intellectual lens of understanding.

Stern (2004) suggested that in psychoanalysis there is a rush toward meaning, leaving the present moment behind as opposed to experiencing something deeply. The present moment is seen as the lived experience from which verbal symbols and representations are all derived and has the potential for revealing the world "in a grain of sand." He described three groups of present moments: regular present moments, now present moments, and moments of meeting. The *regular present moment* is the envelope of time in which we chunk our lived experience and experience what is happening, whereas the *now present moment* is an experience that suddenly pops up in the moment, highly charged with impending consequences, heavy with presentness and the need to act. The *moment of meeting*, on the other hand, occurs when two people achieve an intersubjective meeting, each becoming aware of what the other is experiencing. Probably the moment of meeting is most similar to what we mean by presence. It highlights *mutual* presence and focuses on peak moments of this experience, which reflects our concept of therapeutic relational presence (see Chapter 3).

## GESTALT THERAPY AND THE DIALOGICAL APPROACH: PRESENCE EMERGING IN THE BETWEEN

Gestalt therapy is a present-centered approach in which the therapist increases sensory, affective, and cognitive awareness (Yontef, 2005). Through mindfulness and embodied awareness and the use of here-and-now experiments, the therapist is able to foster self-realization and balance. Perls (1970) wrote, "To me, nothing exists except the now. Now = experience = awareness = reality" (p. 14). Present moment awareness is thus central in gestalt. Some gestalt therapists have related the use of directed and focused awareness to the term *mindfulness*. For example, Fodor and Hooker (2008) explored the value of mindfulness practices, which feature focused awareness training. Stevens (1977) described the mindfulness concept and suggested that the attainment of fulfillment occurs "when you stop emptying yourself by trying to fill yourself and simply let the world fill you" (p. 269). Polster and Polster (1999) stated that "in moments of good contact, there is a clear sense of oneself and a clear sense of the other." Yontef (2005) described how the therapeutic relationship facilitates the healing process and states that "change happens through the contact between the therapist and patient. The emphasis is on 'meeting' the patient, on contact without aiming" (p. 95).

Gestalt therapy adopted Buber's I–Thou relationship as one of its foundational pillars (Perls, 1969). A dialogical form of gestalt therapy, which is an integration of the basic principles of gestalt therapy and Buber's I–Thou, has also brought the notion of presence, along with meeting and encounter, into the foreground (Hycner & Jacobs, 1995; Watson, Greenberg, & Lietaer, 1998; Yontef, 1998). An examination of Buber's I–Thou relationship indicates the centrality of presence in the depth of the deep meeting or relationship (Buber, 1966; Friedman, 1985, 1996; Heard, 1993; Hycner, 1993; Hycner & Jacobs, 1995; Korb, 1988). Dialogic approaches focus on the immediate dialogue and meeting of the therapist and client as the basis from which healing can emerge (Heard, 1993; Hycner & Jacobs, 1995; Yontef, 1998).

The dialogical approach takes place in the "between" and incorporates Buber's two polar stances—the I–Thou and the I–it—two primary attitudes that a human being can take toward another (Buber, 1966; Hycner & Jacobs, 1995). The *between* is Buber's name for the common ground that is created by two people who are in relationship with one another. The between is greater than what each person brings and is different from each person's separate existence (Heard, 1993).

The I–Thou is the natural connection that occurs when a person becomes fully present to another. I–it involves approaching another from a distance and is more of a separation and objectification of the other. The I–Thou relationship begins with a turning of one's whole being to the other (Hycner, 1993). It cannot be forced, but its emergence can be prepared for. I–Thou involves openness, directness, mutuality, and presence (Buber, 1966).

The I–thou and I–it encounters are both important and functional in the therapist and client interaction. I–it in therapy is different from I–it in distant relating. I–it is meaningful and essential, mostly at the beginning and end of therapy, to establish goals, to gather information, or to close and summarize (Korb, 1988). It becomes a base from which trust can be built and the I–Thou is made possible.

Buber (1958) believed that "all real living is meeting" (p. 11) and healing emerges from the meeting that occurs between the two people as they become fully present to each other. The purpose of presence, from this perspective, is the power it has in allowing one to meet and hence understand the other, for the purpose of healing (Friedman, 1985, 1996; Hycner, 1993). Genuine dialogue and encounter can only occur if approaching a person with presence (Friedman, 1996).

Inclusion is another part of the I–Thou encounter and is closely linked to presence because it involves being in direct and immediate contact with another person without losing contact with one's self (Friedman, 1985, 1996; Purcell-Lee, 1999; Rotenstreich, 1967). Buber (1988) called inclusion a bold swinging of one's whole being into the life of the other. Buber was quoted in Rotenstreich (1967): "Certainly in order to be able to go out to the other you must have the starting place, you must have been, you must be with yourself" (p. 127).

It is the therapist's challenge to be able to fully and deeply appreciate (take in) the client's experience and to maintain a sense of centeredness, even in the midst of difficult or conflicting experiences (Hycner, 1993). Centeredness is an expression of personal integration, a unity of body and mind. Centeredness carries the paradox of detachment and involvement; we need to be open and detached first in order to experience the fullness of the other (Clark, 1979). From this perspective, therapy needs to proceed from the whole and centered person.

Presence is a part of the dialogical attitude of the therapist and a preliminary step to being in an I–Thou relationship with the client (Hycner & Jacobs, 1995). Being in presence means staying moment by moment with whatever emerges. Presence involves the suspension of chronological time, the passing away of future and past (Rotenstreich, 1967). Presence also involves having full awareness of all the levels of communication (Friedman, 1996).

From a dialogical perspective, the therapist needs to suspend judgment as to what clients should bring up or even how therapy should go (Hycner, 1993). Presence implies experiencing and appreciating the uniqueness of the other and being fully present to the other with little self-centered purpose or goal in mind (Hycner & Jacobs, 1995). Dialogical traditions also highlighted receptiveness as an aspect of presence (Hycner, 1993; Robbins, 1998). Receptiveness involves a willingness to take in the full experience of the client without judgment and with full acceptance (Hycner, 1993; Moustakas, 1985).

Presence involves an emptying out of self, of knowledge, of experiences and opening up to the experience of the client (Clarkson, 1997).

> Much like Zen, it is only when I empty out my self that the ontological crystal clarity of the other can truly be seen. When I empty out my self, I permit a creative void within which allows me to be filled by the other's experience . . . [Presence means] to set aside my own neediness, vulnerability, and injuredness and to be able to touch the injured and disowned parts of another. If I am too full of myself there is no room for the other, there is no healing. (Hycner & Jacobs, 1995, p. 49)

Dialogical traditions describe *availability*, an aspect of presence, as a way of listening that is also a way of offering oneself to the other (Hycner, 1993; Purcell-Lee, 1999). Marcel (1956, cited in Purcell-Lee, 1999) noted that the most attentive listener may not really be present at all because there is a way of listening that involves refusing oneself. *Unavailability*, to Marcel, involves hearing the experience of the other and not really feeling much inside. Hycner (1993) noted that availability and wholeness of the therapist's self are crucial in the healing process, much more so than the therapist's theoretical orientation.

Dialogical therapists note that to be present and open to the uniqueness of the client, the therapist must also "bracket" or suspend presuppositions, biases, general knowledge about people and psychopathology, diagnostic labeling, and theories (Hycner & Jacobs, 1995). The therapist needs to enter each session openly "with an eye to discover what will be required of me in this relationship, during this particular time of this particular person's existence" (Craig, 1986, p. 23).

In this suspension of judgment and being with the now, we are "hallowing the everyday," according to Buber, which allows space for the numinous and spiritual dimension to emerge (Hycner, 1993). The spiritual dimension reflects the belief that we are part of a larger whole existence, in which the therapist and client can connect on a level that is larger than each individual. The spiritual dimension or spirituality also can be viewed as the subjective experience of the sacred that "appears to connect the personal to the transpersonal and the self to spirit . . . it implies awareness of our relationship to the transcendent, to each other, to the earth and all beings" (Vaughan, 2002, p. 18).

## Levinas and the Primacy of the Other

Buber argued for the I–Thou relationship in which it is in the meeting that healing takes place. Levinas went beyond Buber, arguing that the encounter of the Other through the face reveals a certain quality of humanness, which forbids a reduction of the Other to nonunique sameness and, simultaneously, instills a responsibility for the Other in the self. Levinas (1985), concerned with justice and morality, saw looking into the eyes of another as central to human compassion and justice. He offered the idea that the human face comes with a built-in "ought" of which the ultimate demand is "Thou shalt not kill me." Seeing the face of the Other thus demands that we care for the Other and creates a sense of ethical responsibility for the Other's well-being. Although Levinas's account of the face-to-face encounter bears many similarities to Buber's I –Thou relation, the major difference is Levinas's asymmetrical view of the face-to-face encounter, slanted as it is toward responsibility for the Other's well-being. For Buber, ethical relating meant a "symmetrical co-presence," whereas Levinas considered the relation with the Other as something inherently asymmetrical.

According to Levinas (1985), the face, actually the whole person of the Other, puts one under a tremendous obligation. Even without saying a word, fully encountering another person with presence speaks volumes. In this view faces are information centers, the location for the expressions and emotions that indicate character and manifest the soul. We know that talking face to face with people is much different from reading their e-mails or letters or speaking by phone. What is it about a face? For Levinas, the face of the Other sanctions the moral law even before reason comes into the picture. The face is meaning all by itself, and it leads you beyond your self-interest. The face of the Other encounters me directly and profoundly. Face-to-face encounter with the Other discloses the Other's weakness and mortality. Naked and destitute, the face commands: "Do not leave me in solitude." Looking at the face of the Other is thus central to human relating, dialogue, and presence. To this emphasis on the face, Levinas (1985) added that language originates and takes place in our efforts to transcend the foreignness of the Other. It is language, he argued, that establishes a universal connection and relatedness among individuals. It is through speech that we make the world common as we exchange thoughts and create community.

For Levinas, coming face to face with the Other thus is a nonsymmetrical relationship in which I am responsible for you without knowing that you will reciprocate. Thus, according to Levinas, I am subject to the Other without knowing how it will come out. In this relationship, Levinas found the meaning of being human and of being concerned with justice. This is the type of relationship created by presence in therapy: a relationship in which I am being there for the Other without knowing how the Other will respond.

## Bugental and Existential Therapy:
## Presence as an Intention for Engagement

Direct declarations of presence as a central principle are inherent in the existential literature (Bugental, 1987; Cooper, 2003; May, 1958; Schneider & May, 1995). Bugental (1978, 1983, 1986, 1987, 1989), a leading thinker in existential traditions, highlighted three aspects of presence: an availability and openness to all aspects of the client's experience, openness to one's own experience in being with the client, and the capacity to respond to the client from this experience. There is a sense of aliveness in presence, having more vitality or spirit, which is, in part, a function of being open to the many facets of inner and outer experience (Bugental, 1989). "Presence is a quality of being in a situation or relationship in which one intends, at a deep level, to be as aware and as participative as one is able to" (Bugental, 1987, p. 27).

Existential theorists emphasize presence as a major factor in their therapeutic approach and as a contribution to the "real relationship" that exists between therapist and client. May (1994) noted that with presence, the therapist is not just a shadow or reflector of the client "but an alive human being who happens, at that hour, to be concerned not with his own problems but with understanding and experiencing as far as possible the being of the patient" (p. 156).

Presence involves learning as much as one can learn about therapy and then letting it all go at the moment of meeting the client. May (1958) discussed further the nature of presence in relation to technique by likening it to the creative process of an artist:

> The therapist's situation is like that of the artist who has spent many years of disciplined study learning technique; but he knows that if specific thoughts of technique pre-occupy him when he actually is in the process of painting, he has at that moment lost his vision; the creative process, which should absorb him, transcending the subject–object split, has become temporarily broken; he is now dealing with objects and himself as a manipulator of objects. (p. 85)

For May (1958), technique follows naturally from presence and understanding. May concluded that technique without presence can fall flat or even be in the client's disservice.

Schneider and May (1995) described presence as the "sine qua non of the experiential liberation" (p. 111). While experiential therapists see presence as both the ground and the goal of therapy work, they also note that more can be gained from being present with a client than from any standardized assessment (Schneider & May, 1995). In this vein, the role of presence is viewed as a silent mirror that can hold or illuminate the poignant features of the client's experience and the therapist–client interaction. A therapist's presence can also inspire presence in the client. Schneider and May (1995) emphasized presence as one of the essential healing conditions of therapy.

In a tribute to Jim Bugental, Hoffman (2004–2005) described one of the paradoxes of presence in existential therapy: It can bring client's vulnerability and pain to the surface and with that the anxiety and fear that accompany that vulnerability. Presence is something that cannot just be discussed, but is "a way of being" that needs to be fully experienced. Hence, presence from an existential view needs to be cultivated by the therapist and not just conceptually learned.

## Rogers's Relationship Conditions: Presence as an Underlying Condition?

Rogers (1951, 1957) asserted throughout most of his life that the therapist's ability to be congruent, unconditionally positive and accepting, and empathic—what he called *therapist-offered conditions* (TOCs)—was necessary and sufficient for psychotherapeutic change. What follows from the TOC is the creation of a safe and supportive environment that allows for the emergence of the client's actualizing tendency and optimizes the client's potential for growth. More recent person-centered literature has reflected presence as either a fourth condition to the TOCs or as an underlying foundation to the therapist conditions (Geller, 2001, 2009; Geller & Greenberg, 2002; Geller, Greenberg, & Watson, 2010; Schmid, 1998, 2002; Thorne, 1992; Wyatt, 2000).

Presence has sometimes been equated with the concept of congruence (Corsini & Wedding, 1989; Evans, 1994; Kempler, 1970; Webster, 1998). While the quality of congruence does not incorporate all the subtle aspects of presence, the state of presence includes therapist authenticity in feeling and expression (Greenberg & Geller, 2001). Grafanaki (2001) noted that congruence was present during moments that the therapy was experienced as flowing and the therapist (and client) was deeply involved. This suggests that congruence emerges from a state of presence; congruence does not precede and is not equivalent to presence.

Presence also includes the quality of acceptance, an aspect of unconditional positive regard. Moustakas (1985) stated that presence requires recognizing the client "as a human being, in the moment, without judgment, with full support and unconditional valuing of everything that appears, of everything that is offered in words and silence" (p. 2). Receptivity and openness precede acceptance and prizing of the other as well as emerge from them.

*Empathy* is an active process of desiring to know the full present and changing awareness of a person and of reaching out to receive the other's communication and meaning and translating the important and meaningful aspects of the experience back to the client (Barrett-Lennard, 1981). Presence is more of a calm and receptive alertness that includes a letting go of self-concerns and needs and feeling empty and open inside so one can clearly tune in and receive the client's communication and felt experience. Presence allows therapists to be clear to receive the client's experience in an untainted form so therapists can hear, feel, and understand what the client is saying and experiencing. In this line of thinking, presence then prepares the ground for a therapist to be empathic and to respond to the client in an efficacious manner.

The idea of presence as a preparatory condition for empathy was affirmed by Barrett-Lennard (1981) in his comment that to achieve maximum empathic understanding the therapist is required to be receiving and allowing of clients' experience. Those receptive and allowing states are central aspects of presence.

A deeper spiritual or intuitive process to presence was suggested in Rogers's later years as he began writing about "one more characteristic" that exists in the realm of the mystical and spiritual (Rogers, 1979, 1980, 1986). This "characteristic" (Rogers, 1980, p. 129) has been referred to by client-centered writers as presence and as a possible fourth condition equal in merit to the three core conditions of congruence, unconditional positive regard, and empathy. Before his death, Rogers began to refer to presence as more of a spiritual dimension that allowed a greater healing to occur. The following passage is from Rogers (1980):

> When I am at my best, as a group facilitator or as a therapist, I discover another characteristic. I find that when I am closest to my inner, intuitive self, when I am somehow in touch with the unknown in me, when perhaps I am in a slightly altered state of consciousness, then whatever I do seems to be full of healing. Then, simply my presence is releasing and helpful to the other. There is nothing I can do to force this experience, but when I can relax and be close to the transcendental core of me, then I may behave in strange and impulsive ways in the relationship, ways in which I cannot justify rationally, which have nothing to do with my thought processes. But these strange behaviors turn out to be right, in some odd way: it seems that my inner spirit has reached out and touched the inner spirit of the other. Our relationship transcends itself and becomes a part of something larger. Profound growth and healing and energy are present. (p. 129)

In a posthumous article (Baldwin, 2000), Rogers suggested the value of presence as a process goal of or adherence to therapy:

> Once therapy is under way, another goal of the therapist is to question: "Am I really with this person in this moment? Not where they were a little while ago, or where they are going to be, but am I really with this client in this moment?" This is the most important thing. (Baldwin, 2000, pp. 32–33)

Unfortunately, Rogers did not have the opportunity to develop the understanding of presence, as it was only beginning to unfold before his death. It is also possible that he was not yet willing to refer to a powerful and spiritual domain that may have overtaken or changed his original contentions.

In a discussion on presence, Rogers noted a lot of active energy flowing from him to the client and described using his intuition and the essence of himself (Baldwin, 2000). As noted in his interview with Baldwin, Rogers stated: "Over time, I think that I have become more aware of the fact that in therapy I do use my self. I recognize that when I am intensely focused on a client, just my presence seems to be healing" (2000, p. 29). Rogers viewed caring and the ability to really listen with acceptance and nonjudgment to be a part of the quality of presence. He also discussed totally surrendering the self to the process and intuitively responding from an unknown terrain of being in the moment with the client. Presence just began to be a concept that partly suggested a spiritual domain in person-centered psychotherapy.

The relational aspect of presence is suggested in current person-centered literature in the term "relational depth." Cooper (2005) defined *relational depth* in therapists in a qualitative study as profound and consistent levels of empathy and acceptance toward the client, and the client's consistent acknowledgment of such. Self-report descriptions of therapists' experiences with relational depth include high levels of empathy to *all* aspects of the client's experience, greater perceptual clarity, high levels of congruence, feeling a resonance with the client's experience, deep acceptance of the client, immersion in or engagement with the client, being free from internal or external distractions, immersion in the moment, and feeling alive. Cooper (2005) described mutual or coacceptance as the fulcrum of the relational depth experience, wherein the therapist provides acceptance of the client and the client also acknowledges the therapist's acceptance of him or her. He suggests further study on relational depth, possibly framed within the terms *copresence* or *coflow* between therapist and client. Current person-centered perspectives on the relational aspect of presence are also reflected by Schmid (2002), as he pointed out that presence is like "joint experiencing with the client" (p. 65).

## Greenberg, Gendlin, and the Experiential Approaches: Presence in the Body

Experiential therapists note the centrality of the body for both the therapist and the client, as the body is viewed as a container and as an expression of primary emotions (Gendlin, 1978, 1986; Greenberg, Watson, & Lietaer, 1994). For example, therapists' contact with bodily experience helps them to be attuned to the experience of the moment within the self, with their clients, and in the relationship. Furthermore, inviting clients to pay attention to their own body helps clients to contact their in-the-moment self-experiencing. This concept of bodily awareness has been extended briefly to therapists in relation to presence, as therapists can access their own bodily experience of the client as a reference point, or barometer, in understanding the client. Lietaer (1993) described the understanding of the client's experiential world as personal for the therapist. Even though the focus is on the client, it is the therapist's own bodily experience of what the client is telling him or her. Vanaerschot (1993) used the term *active receptiveness* (p. 49) to describe the therapist's process of opening and receiving what is coming from the client and then looking for referents in the therapist's self that are similar to perceived feelings. An expressive arts therapist, Robbins (1998) described therapeutic presence as including an identification and understanding of the client through his own bodily messages about what is occurring. With personal presence the therapist uses the self as an interactional barometer in understanding the other.

Emotion-focused therapy (EFT; Elliott, Watson, Goldman, & Greenberg, 2004; Greenberg, 2002; Greenberg & Watson, 2005), an integration of humanistic, client-centered, and gestalt therapies, sees bodily experienced emotions themselves as having an innately adaptive potential that, if attended to, provide orientation and guide adaptive action and also can help clients change problematic emotional states or unwanted self-experiences. EFT views the therapeutic relationship as central in helping gain access to clients' emotional experience. The relationship in EFT is characterized by the therapist's presence and attunement to affect as well as by the communication of empathy, acceptance, and unconditional regard (Greenberg, 2007). EFT recognizes that to establish a positive therapeutic alliance, therapists must first be fully present to their clients (Greenberg, 2007). It is the therapist's presence that helps clients to feel received and safe and to be able to access their own emotional experience. Therapists' presence from an EFT perspective includes being real with the client and being aware of one's own emotional world, and it also involves continued self-development. Presence and the therapeutic relationship form the basis of EFT; emotion-focused tasks such as role plays, empty chair, and focusing techniques are added, but these require the therapist's ongoing presence and attunement.

Focusing is an experiential technique originally proposed by Gendlin (1978, 1996) that helps clients access their bodily felt experience as a source of information and inner awareness. Focusing therapists must first be comfortable with the technique of focusing and being present with their own bodily experience to facilitate clients' process. Cornell (1996) noted that a central aspect of focusing is the "radical acceptance of everything" and showed how all our experience, no matter how difficult or unpleasant, needs to be respected and listened to in the wider space of presence. Presence of the therapist is central to clients who are learning to listen to their own emotional experience. The more deeply the facilitator of focusing can contact his or her own felt sense and stay in presence, the more spacious and resonant the listening will be (Jordan, 2008). Cornell (1996) also referred to an attitude of not knowing, which includes qualities of presence such as curiosity, openness, and interest, as an essential precondition to approaching a felt sense in focusing. Welwood (2000) described the relationship between focusing and presence:

> As Focusing is commonly practiced, there is often a bias toward unfolding meaning from a felt sense, toward resolution, toward looking for a felt shift. In this way, it can become a form of "doing" that maintains a subtle I/it stance towards one's experience. The bias here can be very subtle. Wanting our experience to change usually contains a subtle resistance to what is, to nowness, to what I call *unconditional presence*—the capacity to meet experience fully and directly, without filtering it through any conceptual or strategic agenda. (p. 116)

Cole and Ladas-Gaskin (2007), in their experiential training, emphasized the therapist's intending presence: "Within a session, the therapist intends to be an attuned presence, a source of emotional nourishment, and an unimposing guide" (p. 26). An atmosphere of compassionate presence by the therapist helps to facilitate the client's body-centered exploration and awareness. These authors also describe how the attitude of compassionate or loving presence is nourishing and sustaining for the therapist.


## MINDFULNESS-BASED THERAPIES: SUPPORTING THE CULTIVATION OF PRESENCE

Presence has been referred to as equal to or interchangeable with mindfulness; however, as noted in the Introduction to this volume, we see them as different. Mindfulness is often referred to as a practice (i.e., mindfulness meditation) for calming the mind, and it can aid in the cultivation of presence (although it is sometimes also used to mean being aware in the moment; Linehan, 1993a). Therapeutic presence, on the other hand, is more of a state of being present with the client. Chapter 10 expands on mindfulness as a way of cultivating the state of being present.

Mindfulness meditation is the basis of insight meditation and the primary technique for insight in Buddhist philosophy (Geller, 2003; Germer, 2005; Killackey, 1998; Rosenberg, 1998). Although mindfulness practice began as an actual technique, it evolved into a way of being in the world (Hahn, 1976; Kabat-Zinn, 1994). We would argue that this "way of being" is the quality of presence that develops from practicing mindfulness. Even though mindfulness and presence are often confused in the literature, recent writings are beginning to tease out the distinction. For example, Hick (2008) noted that mindfulness is both a "technique and a way of facilitating therapeutic presence" (p. 1).

Mindfulness is derived from the Pali term *satipatthana*, with *sati* generally meaning "attention" or "awareness" and *patthana* meaning "keeping present" (Germer, 2005; Thera, 1973). To be practicing mindfulness is to be aware of the full range of experiences that exist in the present moment, with acceptance and with compassion (Marlatt & Kristeller, 1999). Mindfulness practices help to develop the capacity to observe and be with experience without becoming overwhelmed. An expansion of self and a sense of luminosity or spaciousness are benefits of practices of mindfulness (Epstein, 1995; Welwood, 2000).

Santorelli (1999) defined mindfulness as "our willingness to see, to hold ourselves closely just as we are" (p. 20). Mindfulness practices have also been described as focusing attention, being aware, without judgment (Hick, 2008). Practicing mindfulness involves a willingness to come close to our pain and discomfort without judgment, striving, manipulation, or pretense. Mindfulness meditation helps to develop a gentle, open, and nonjudgmental approach to being with our experience (Germer, 2005; Salzberg, 1999; Santorelli, 1999; Welwood, 1996). Mindfulness meditation can also provide a way to let go of judgment and the avoidance of pain and discomfort so that we can be with the other's experience from a place of presence.

Another distinction between mindfulness practices and therapeutic presence emerges from this sense of being with self and being with the other. Mindfulness meditation and practices in general, as described in the Buddhist and psychotherapy literature, seem to focus on a way to open fully to a person's own experience, with acceptance, compassion, and nonjudgment. To enter fully into experience and the unknown with others, however, requires the comfort to be in this space with ourselves and with our own experience (Santorelli, 1999). By knowing our own experience and our own pain, we can be open and fully know and connect to the pain of others (Salzberg, 1999). Hence, mindfulness practices can be a helpful technique in cultivating presence within the self and within the client (Bien, 2008; see also Chapter 10, this volume, for an expansion of this point). The development of presence in both therapist and client can also help the therapeutic relationship to deepen and grow.

Mindfulness meditation facilitates a way of being with things as they are, or presence, which is healing in and of itself. From that place of nondoing, the right interventions and responses can emerge. Santorelli (1999) stated:

> Healing is always asking us to step inside the circle, not going forward or doing something that gets in the way of being inside this moment. When

we step inside and wait, the right action usually makes itself known. Everything becomes clearer; ourselves, others, and situations are seen just as they are. (p. 164)

Mindfulness meditation can be a powerful healing tool in developing presence because it allows us to move from the details of personality to a larger state of being, and from this comes the discovery of inner resources and wisdom (Welwood, 1996). As therapists tap their own inner resources, they can facilitate their clients in a much more effective manner and ultimately help clients access their own presence and inner wisdom.

## Cognitive–Behavioral Approaches: Presence of Mind

While presence is not a therapist's stance that cognitive–behavioral therapy (CBT) approaches have incorporated specifically, the recent interest in the role of the alliance and recognition of the possible role of the relationship in CBT (Gelso, 2011; Goldfried & Davila, 2005; Holtforth & Castonguay, 2005; Leahy, 2003; Lejuez, Hopko, Levine, Gholkar, & Collins, 2005; Waddington, 2002) reflect a shift in approach. Current thinking in CBT generally recognizes that optimal outcomes emerge from a combination of technique and the alliance (Goldfried & Davila, 2005; Holtforth & Castonguay, 2005; Leahy, 2003; Lejuez et al., 2005; Linehan, 1993a). CBT therapists, however, generally seem to focus more on the collaborative aspect of the working alliance than on the bond or the relationship in and of itself (Gelso, 2011). It is still unclear which factors contribute to a positive working alliance, and in fact research focusing on understanding what underlies a positive working relationship is encouraged (Goldfried & Davila, 2005).

Several approaches have recommended that an increased present-focus on problems as they occur in the therapeutic relationship or in relation to the live therapy process would improve CBTs and the working alliance (Kanter et al., 2009). Kanter et al. (2009) investigated this question by rating sessions from recent trials of CBT for depression and found that therapists rarely focused on the present therapeutic relationship and did not spend much time in present-focused intervention, despite recognition of its value in enhancing the therapeutic alliance. In addition, Geller, Greenberg, and Watson (2010) found that clients reported CBT therapists as less present, and CBT therapists reported themselves as less present than did either EFT or person-centered clients or therapists. This all indicates the need for a greater emphasis on the value of presence in CBT, as the utilization of technique with therapists' presence can ensure that each step of the procedure fits the clients' current state.

A number of cognitive-based perspectives have incorporated mindfulness into their approach. For example, mindfulness-based cognitive therapy

(MBCT; Segal, Williams, & Teasdale, 2002) has a particular focus on and success in preventing the relapse of depression. However, in this approach it is the technique of mindful meditation that is referred to. Interestingly, the cofounders of MBCT, after applying this approach, recognized that there is a necessary and previously missing aspect to the approach, which is the practice of mindfulness by therapists. In addition, in acceptance and commitment therapy (ACT; Hayes, Strosahl, & Wilson, 1999; Wilson & DuFrene, 2008), acceptance and mindfulness are seen as central to change. Therapists' commitment to a personal practice of mindfulness and an attitude of acceptance and present-centered focus are now prerequisites in facilitating this approach.

Although manual-based therapies, such as CBT, do not emphasize presence, the value of therapists' attunement to the moment can help to optimize therapists' efficacy, skill, and timing when intervening or challenging negative thoughts. ACT therapists Wilson and DuFrene (2008) described the value of therapists' presence in manual-based therapies:

> By increasing our own ability to focus on what's happening in the present moment, we can sharpen our clinical skills. Our interaction with clients is a sort of dance. We may lead, but we need to lead with flexibility, including the flexibility to know when to give over the lead. We need to determine when it's time to intervene and when we'll accomplish more by sitting back and listening. Sometimes we need to speed things up; at other times, slowing down is what the situation demands. In all of these cases, studied and practiced attention to the present moments is one of our greatest clinical resources. (p. 127)

ACT has incorporated mindfulness as a therapeutic technique. Aspects of presence are emphasized for ACT therapists, such as authenticity. For example, Roemer and Orsillo (2009) discussed the importance of therapist disclosure, when therapeutically relevant, in order to demonstrate the universality of the client's struggles. Other variations of mindfulness therapy have developed, such as mindfulness-based relapse prevention for substance abuse (MBRP; Marlatt, Bowen, Chawla, & Witkiewitz, 2008; Witkiewitz & Marlatt, 2007; Witkiewitz, Marlatt, & Walker, 2005), with each approach emphasizing the need for a personal awareness practice of the therapist and facilitator.

Linehan's dialectical behavior therapy (DBT; Linehan, 1993a, 1993b; McKay, Brantley, & Wood, 2007) is an early example of the recognition of the quality of attention of the therapist as well as the clients, as DBT emphasizes an integrated approach with both mindfulness and behavioral components for people with borderline personality disorder.

Basic tenets of mindfulness-based CBTs include the value of self-development and personal practice, which are a part of cultivating therapeutic presence. Mindfulness approaches generally require therapists to have a mindfulness practice, both to encourage a level of self-understanding of the advantages and pitfalls of facing one's own experience with acceptance and to better respond to clients' experiences. Some approaches, such as MBRP, emphasize the therapeutic alliance as a change principle, noting that the "non-judgmental curiosity and openness of the therapists towards group members provide a model for clients to develop a mindful, accepting, and compassionate approach to their own experience" (Marlatt et al., 2008). From this perspective, therapists' mindfulness practice helps develop qualities of therapeutic presence, such as a nonjudgmental therapeutic stance and an attitude of openness and curiosity toward one's own thoughts and feelings, and consequently an acceptance and deeper understanding of the client's thoughts and feelings. Roemer and Orsillo (2009) contended that in cultivating a present-focused therapeutic stance, in addition to mindfulness practice, research is clearly needed to guide recommendations for optimal training for therapists.

## Summary of the Literature on Presence: An Unfolding Story

The therapeutic stance of being calm, even, and present centered has been suggested throughout the history of psychotherapy. However, few perspectives have focused on the essentiality and the ways of cultivating this state of being, as well as the personal growth of the therapists themselves that is central in cultivating a close, connected, and yet respectful healthy therapeutic relationship. Freud and the psychoanalytic approach emphasized the importance of the analyst maintaining an even and calm mental state; however, this was underemphasized in psychoanalytic training and literature, perhaps because of the difficulty in attaining this personal level of calm and self-awareness in the face of patients' complex emotional difficulties. Furthermore, this was based on more of an intellectual exercise than a heart-based connection.

Paying attention to and being with the client on a level beyond just the intellect were introduced by dialogical and humanistic therapists who recognized that healing can occur through a deep meeting of therapist and client. Although this relational perspective is valued by current psychodynamic writers more than in the past, there is still an underemphasis across all traditions on the how, what, why, and complexity of cultivating the present-centered, grounded, and open-hearted attention and connection that are demanded in good and effective psychotherapy. Even though humanistic therapists espouse the value of presence, they have not clarified *how* to be fully present. Recently, CBTs have recognized the value of the therapeutic alliance in relationship to outcome, and psychotherapy research has indicated that therapeutic effectiveness of techniques is enhanced when they are delivered in the context of a positive therapeutic relationship. Suggestions have been made that present moment focus may enhance the therapeutic relationship and working alliance, although it is minimally practiced in actuality. Some CBT perspectives have also incorporated mindfulness traditions and have recognized the value of personal mindfulness practice in heightening therapists' acceptance and presence. Nonetheless, even in mindfulness traditions, there is recognition of the gap in understanding what composes an effective therapeutic stance. Although there is some recognition of the value of presence across different therapy traditions, the gap in research on understanding or measuring therapists' presence led us to conduct the series of studies described in Chapter 2.

# 2

# EMPIRICAL RESEARCH ON THERAPEUTIC PRESENCE

Believe nothing, no matter where you read it, or who said it, no matter if I have said it, unless it agrees with your own reason and your own common sense.

—The Buddha

In Chapter 1, we noted some interesting and powerful theoretical conjectures on presence in the historical literature across different approaches. However, there is a gap between the rich conjectures of presence and the lack of empirical study on presence. We believe that both conceptual and empirical knowledge are necessary for understanding presence. Therefore, we have conducted two empirical studies of therapeutic presence—one qualitative and one quantitative. In this chapter, we begin by reviewing some earlier unpublished studies and studies with a small number of participants that helped to provide the context for our research. We then present our empirical studies in greater depth, as well as related studies on therapeutic presence. First, however, we introduce pause moments as a way of integrating your own personal experience of presence with the research on presence.

## PAUSE MOMENTS: TOUCHING YOUR OWN SENSE OF PRESENCE

To honor the conceptual understanding of presence and simultaneously evoke your own personal understanding of being fully in the moment, we invite you to sporadically stop, pause, and check in with yourself. We label these breaks for internal reflection as *pause moments*, which include an intention for reflection about an aspect of presence or nonpresence. They are placed through-out subsequent chapters and allow you an opportunity to connect to your in-the-moment, body-focused experience. We invite you to use these pause moments to stop reading and allow for an internal resonance and experience of presence in your life to take form within you.

- Take a moment to rest your eyes, and reconnect to your bodily experience of breathing. Rest your awareness inside, in the center of your body or in rhythm with your breathing.
- Pay attention to your present experience, sensations, feelings, and any awareness of internal events. In addition, be aware of what is occurring in your outer awareness—sounds, sights, and touch, and anything else in your zone.
- Breathe and allow yourself to be absorbed in the moment and feel the expansiveness of being in the moment.
- Now ask yourself what presence means to you. What aspects of your own bodily experience let you know when you are fully present? What feelings or bodily experiences accompany presence?
- Allow each breath to take your awareness further into your bodily experience of presence. What does it feel like to be fully present with another human being? Allow yourself to recall a recent experience where you felt fully present with someone in your life. What did it feel like? How did it affect your relationship in the moment with that person?
- What does it feel like to be fully in the moment with a client? How is it similar to or different from being fully present with someone in your own life? Ask inside.
- Allow yourself to take a few minutes to arrive into this moment and to ask for and receive your own personal and professional understanding of presence.

Whether you are a therapist, a counselor in training, or in another health-related profession, you already have your own sense of what it means to be present or not present in your own life or with your colleagues and clients or patients. As you read this book, compare your own personal understanding of presence with what our research has revealed. Before we describe our research in greater detail, we review the few unpublished studies that have been conducted, as they helped to provide a clinical context for the development of our own research on therapeutic presence.

## PREVIOUS STUDIES AND MODELS OF PRESENCE:
## THE BEGINNING OF UNDERSTANDING

There are a few qualitative studies on presence, yet much of this research remains unpublished. For example, Pemberton (1977) observed and interviewed five recognized and influential therapists who were considered to have a powerful sense of presence. Pemberton concluded that therapists with presence had *awareness*, *acceptance*, and *appreciation* of who they are in relationship to others, particularly family and intimate relationships. These people were in tune with the present, which contributed to their state of presence. They were not focused on past or future except in how one or the other enhances the present, and they were accepting of experience and rooted in the now. They were personal in their sharing, not detached (objective) or immersed (subjective), but instead were ready to be transparent with others. Pemberton moved from his initial conception of viewing presence as interpersonal and occurring in relationships with others to viewing presence as personal and individual and having more to do with the therapist than the therapeutic relationship. According to Pemberton, presence is defined as knowing the totality of oneself in the moment.

Pemberton's (1977) study revealed that although presence cannot be ensured and there are always mysterious factors contributing to it, certain functions in the process of psychotherapy can lead a person toward presence. First, there is a clear *commitment* to being oneself and with the client. Then the therapist needs to activate forces that generate presence by focusing, extending, and enfolding. *Focusing* is a way to clear one's mind, connect to one's center, and prepare for whatever might happen. *Enfolding* is the "ultimate act of receptivity" (Pemberton, 1977, p. 96). Combined with focusing, it means that therapists actively bring the client into their being. Enfolding encompasses the skills of empathy, unconditional acceptance, and understanding. *Extending* involves a process whereby therapists actively extend their boundary out to the other and to their surroundings.

Pemberton (1977) also described the healing element that arises when presence occurs for therapists as "self experiencing oneness with the self" (p. 98). Presence involves a sense of integration and aliveness and results in authenticity, centeredness, clarity, purpose, and autonomy. Although Pemberton's study was a good first step in the investigation of an ineffable quality such as presence, it had limitations, as there was a lack of any prescribed qualitative methodologies. This may be a consequence of the underdeveloped stage of qualitative methodology at the time that the study was conducted (1977).

A later unpublished study by Fraelich (1989) began explicating a thematic model of presence, which he likened to a hub with a central structure and related structures radiating from this central cluster. He interviewed six psychotherapists in a phenomenological investigation of presence. Four major themes emerged from this research: (a) presence as spontaneous occurrence, (b) immersion in the moment, (c) openness of being, and (d) living on the cutting edge. Related themes or structures radiate from this central hub. They include self-sacrifice, interest, the psychotherapist's expression of self, immersed participation in the client's world, connected relationship with the client, completeness and definition of self, presence as trust, and genuineness and authenticity with self and others.

In contrast to Pemberton, Fraelich (1989) saw presence as an interdependent experience and defined presence as "an intense and richly lived moment." He used this study to exemplify that presence does indeed exist and suggested that it may have significant implications for outcomes in existential psychotherapy. He suggested that presence may be a key factor in therapy outcome and that further research was needed to reach conclusions about the significance of presence in psychotherapy.

Phelon (2001, 2004) incorporated several methodologies into what she deemed an "intuitive inquiry" to study the concept of healing presence, including hermeneutic study of texts, observation of clinicians who had experienced presence in the role of the client, and qualitative interviews with groups and individual therapists. She eventually came to see healing presence as a core concept in psychotherapy and that it can be understood as processes within the therapist's self rather than a list of qualities.

Phelon's (2001, 2004) final model included four groupings of concepts related to healing presence. The first grouping pertained to the therapist's development and growth (seasoning, commitment to personal growth, integration, and congruence), the second included therapists' integrated spiritual practice and belief, the third pertained to the therapist's awareness (attentional ability, inner awareness, and kinesthetic aspects of presence), and the fourth included qualities that pertained to the alliance between the therapist and client (alignment with the client, receptivity).

Phelon (2004) noted that "inner awareness," or an ability to attend to one's own inner experience and to work with inner resonances within a session, is essential to healing presence. She also noted that exemplary clinicians emphasized the value of an integrated spiritual practice (vs. an unintegrated practice, which could be detrimental to the development of presence), although spiritual practice is not essential to cultivating presence. These clinicians also emphasized the importance of continued self-work on the part of the therapist in the development and maintenance of a "healing presence."

In summary, these early studies provide preliminary support for the importance of the concept of presence and provide some description of presence as well as the interplay between presence and the therapeutic relationship. Some aspects of presence began to unfold through this research; however, much of it remains unpublished and not empirically driven, and this leaves a gap in a clear definition of presence and the relationship of presence to the therapeutic relationship and alliance. We sought to fill this gap by conducting both a qualitative study to gain a clear definition and model of presence and a quantitative study to develop a measure of presence and to study the contribution of therapeutic presence to important therapeutic processes. We describe these studies in the next sections.

## QUALITATIVE STUDY

The model of presence briefly described in the Introduction to this book emerged from a qualitative study with experienced or master therapists who had written about or discussed presence as an important aspect of their therapeutic stance (Geller & Greenberg, 2002). Seven experienced therapists who had been identified as authors or proponents of the concept of presence were interviewed about their experience of presence. All seven had a minimum of 10 years of experience in practicing psychotherapy and had an active therapy practice at the time of the interviews. Four therapists were from a humanistic/experiential theoretical background, one from a cognitive–behavioral therapy (CBT) perspective, one an Adlerian/transpersonal perspective, and one an Eriksonian background.

Therapists were contacted via phone or e-mail and asked to participate in the study. They were then provided a basic definition of presence via e-mail, which was based on the literature:

> Presence, an aspect of Buber's I–Thou relationship, refers to the quality of a therapist to be fully with the client in the moment, empty of thoughts of future or past, and unattached from ideas that she or he may have on what the client's issues are and even of the desire for the client to change. Clarkson (1997, p. 66) refers to this state as inherent in the "transpersonal relationship" and posits that it is a "letting go of skills, of knowledge, of experience, of preconceptions, even of the desire to heal, to be present."

We then asked the therapists to reflect on their own experience of presence following their therapy sessions over a period of a couple of weeks before we conducted a more in-depth interview. A general interview format was followed in the meeting, in which therapists were asked about aspects of their own experience of presence, such as the physical, emotional, and cognitive elements.

Transcriptions of the audiotaped interviews were used in a qualitative analysis and interpreted according to a method combining condensation and categorization of meaning (Kvale, 1996). This approach entailed extracting the key components of presence from the transcripts and compressing them further and further into meaningful but briefer statements of presence. Themes were then extracted and specifically examined in terms of understanding presence. Themes with similar meaning and understanding with respect to presence were placed under a higher level categorization reflecting these commonalities. In the final stage, the essential, nonredundant themes and categories were tied together into yet another higher level of categorization. After much thought and consultation, three higher order categories were generated that subsumed all of the descriptive categories. These three higher level categories formed the foundation for a model of therapeutic presence.

The model of therapeutic presence that emerged was made up of three larger categories that are essential to understanding therapeutic presence (Geller, 2001; Geller & Greenberg, 2002) and that constitute the components of presence. One was labeled *preparing the ground for presence*, referring to the presession and general life preparation for therapeutic presence. Another described the *process of presence*, the processes or activities the therapist is engaged in when in presence. The third reflected the *actual in-session experience of presence*. The essence and aspect of each of these larger categories are elaborated in Chapters 4 through 6. The quotations in these subsequent chapters were extracted from the original transcripts from this study. The model describes a way of being to help therapists optimize their efficacy with clients.

It is important to note that separating the totality of the experience of presence into aspects or parts is an exercise conducted to understand and explicate the many presumed dimensions of presence. The so-called parts are intertwined and contain much overlap in meaning and experience. Our speaking of parts and wholes is a dialectical heuristic used to make meaning from the respondents' answers to queries about their experience of "presence." Specifically, aspects of presence that fall under one category may also qualify under a different category. For example, "openness" is presented as part of preparing the ground for presence and as part of the process therapists engage in when they experience presence.

Therapeutic presence is more than the sum of its parts. Therapeutic presence is more than just being congruent, more than just being real, more than just being accepting of the client, more than being empathic or attuned or responsive. It is a complex interplay of therapeutic skill and experience guided by the underlying intention and experience of fully being in the moment and meeting that experience with the depth of one's being. While presence is a holistic subjective experience that loses its essential nature when analyzed in an objective manner, our attempt to articulate such an ineffable quality is essential in gaining an understanding of and appreciation for the quality that we feel is essential for good psychotherapy.

# QUANTITATIVE STUDY

As a follow-up to the development of our model, we conducted a second study to develop a measure that reflected the process and experience of therapeutic presence (Geller, 2001; Geller, Greenberg, & Watson, 2010). There were four stages in the development of the therapist version of the Therapeutic Presence Inventory (TPI): item selection, item refinement, scale construction, and scale refinement/construct validity. Each stage built on the results and findings of the previous stage. A fifth stage involved the development of a preliminary measure of clients' perception of therapists' presence. This process resulted in the creation of two versions of the TPI: one for therapists about their own presence (TPI-T) and one for clients on their perceptions of their therapists' presence (TPI-C).

In the first stage (item selection), 150 items were generated (75 items for process of presence and 75 items for experience of presence) by extracting the central sentences and themes used in the development of the model of therapeutic presence.

In the second stage (item refinement), two expert raters (one male and one female) reviewed the list independently and eliminated items that were thought to be redundant, wordy, unclear, or difficult to rate in a questionnaire format. The result of their review was a revised list that consisted of 84 items. Two other experts reviewed this list and eliminated items that were unclear, which resulted in 32 items reflecting the core aspects of the process (16 items) and experience (16 items) of therapeutic presence.

In the third stage (scale construction), each of the 32 items was presented on a 7-point Likert scale ranging from *completely* to *not at all*.

In the fourth stage (scale refinement/construct validity), construct validity was explored by having nine expert raters, two women and seven men, review and rate the 32-item TPI-T in three separate tasks. Six of these experts practiced from an experiential perspective, two from an existential perspective, and one from a dialogical perspective. The experts were provided a brief definition of presence as well as the 32-item TPI-T. For Task 1, they were asked to rate items on a scale assessing how clearly the items related to presence or nonpresence. Items not rated as directly related to presence (or nonpresence in the case of negative items) were eliminated. For Task 2, the experts were asked to rate the original 32-item TPI-T after two sessions with two separate clients, one after a session in which they felt they were highly present and one after a session in which they felt they were not present. Scores on the TPI-T rated after high- and low-presence sessions were compared with each other by using a paired-sample *t* test. Findings indicated significant differences between high and low presence on all items except for three, one of which was identified in Task 1 as not representative of presence. Hence, a total of eight items were eliminated, six items from Task 1 and two items from Task 2, based on expert ratings. For Task 3, the experts were asked to provide general feedback on the items of the scale as a whole. An examination of the comments confirmed difficulties with four of the eight items eliminated from the first two tasks as difficult. Three additional items were identified as difficult, and also had a high overall mean rating on the first task and were eliminated, and one item was reworded.

Additional analyses confirmed that the remaining 21 items reflected therapeutic presence. Paired *t* tests on total scores indicated that sessions viewed as high in presence were rated significantly higher than sessions viewed as low in presence ($t = 9.92$, $p < .001$). The 21-item revised TPI-T consisted of 11 items written in a positive direction and 10 items written in a negative direction. The TPI-T was demonstrated to have good face validity as it is based on the model of therapeutic presence as well as expert comments and ratings.

The fifth stage involved developing a preliminary measure of clients' perception of their therapists' presence (TPI-C). The process of the development of the TPI-C involved two steps: first, generating items from the TPI-T and the model of presence that could be reflected in clients' experience, and second, refining the items into a measure that reflected the process and experience of clients' perceived presence of the therapist. The researchers initially selected a sample of 15 items that (a) reflected the model of therapeutic presence, (b) were reflected in the TPI-T, and (c) could be easily converted from a therapist-rated item to a client-perceived item. Three of the 15 items were chosen by the primary researcher and one expert rater for clients' perception of therapists' presence based on ease in rating as a perceived presence item and a clear reflection of the model. The three items were set to the same 7-point Likert scale used for the therapist TPI-T. The TPI-C has good face validity, as items chosen were based on the model of therapeutic presence as well as confirmation from expert raters.

## Exploration of Reliability and Validity of TPI-T and TPI-C

The pilot research on the measure showed good face validity and construct validity, as it was based on the model of therapeutic presence and expert ratings and comments (Geller, 2001; Geller et al., 2010). The reliability and validity of the measures were further explored by submitting these measures in two larger randomized control studies for the treatment of depression, one at York University (Goldman, Greenberg, & Angus, 2006) and the other at the Ontario Institute for Studies in Education, University of Toronto (Watson, Gordon, Stermac, Kalogerakos, & Steckley, 2003). These studies compared treatment effects of a 16-week trial of process experiential therapy (PET) and client-centered therapy (CCT; Goldman et al., 2006) and PET and CBT (Watson et al., 2003).

There were 25 therapists (21 female and four male) in the study (eight therapists offered CBT, four therapists offered only PET, and the remaining 13 offered both PET and CCT). The client sample consisted of 114 clients (33 CBT, 63 PET, and 18 CCT) who met *DSM–IV* criteria for major depression based on the *Diagnostic and Statistical Manual of Mental Disorders* (4th ed.; *DSM–IV*; American Psychiatric Association, 1994) and scored at least 50 on the Global Assessment of Functioning Scale of the *DSM–IV*.

Therapists completed the TPI-T after every third session (Sessions 3, 6, 9, 12, and 15) as well as a 40-item short form, therapist version of the Relationship Inventory (RI-MO40; Barrett-Lennard, 1973) after Sessions 6 and 12 to assess the relationship between therapeutic presence and the core conditions of the therapeutic relationship including empathic understanding, congruence, level of regard, and acceptance.

Clients completed the TPI-C after every third session (Sessions 3, 6, 9, 12, and 15) as well as a 12-item short form of the Working Alliance Inventory (WAI; Horvath & Greenberg, 1989). Clients also completed a postsession outcome scale, the Client Task Specific Measure (CTSC-R; Watson, Schien, & McMullen, in 2009), to assess the relationship between perceived presence and in-session change.

Items on the TPI-T (21 items; $N = 522$) and TPI-C (three items; $N = 364$) were subject to a principal-axis analysis to explore whether the scale reflected one or more factors. All the items loaded > .40 on both measures. On the TPI-T, 21 of the items fell under one main factor with an eigenvalue of 10.50, accounting for 50.01% of the variance with similar results when a factor analysis was conducted on each of the three therapy types (PET, CBT, CCT). Hence, the 21 items were viewed as composing a single score, called therapeutic presence, which further supported the construct validity of the measure. On the TPI-C, the three items resulted in one factor with an eigenvalue of 2.03, accounting for 67.59% of the variance, with similar results found across the three therapy types. These findings reflected a unidimensional measure with good construct validity. Hence, a composite score of the three items in the TPI-C was used in later analyses to reflect client's perceptions of therapists' presence.

Analyses were conducted to confirm the reliability and the relationship of the subscales in each of the additional measures used in the current study. The client measures, the WAI and CTSC-R, were included to assess predictive validity with the TPI-T and TPI-C, and the therapist-rated RI was used to explore construct validity with the TPI-T. Reliability was calculated by computing Cronbach's alpha (for TPI-T, $\alpha = .94$; for TPI-C, $\alpha = .82$), indicating good reliability that was also shown to be consistent across therapy types.

Concurrent validity was assessed by examining the relationship between therapists' ratings on the TPI-T and the TOCs of empathy, congruence, level of regard, and acceptance as measured on the RI. With regard to the total sample, the TPI-T correlated significantly with all four subscales of the RI. Significant regression coefficients were also found between the TPI-T and all of the therapist RI subscales; empathy, congruence, and unconditionality of regard, and level of regard. Wilks' lambda (converted to $F$) is $F(4, 271) = 30.29, p < .001$.

Predictive validity was assessed by examining the relationship between therapists' (TPI-T) and clients' (TPI-C) ratings of therapeutic presence and clients' ratings of the therapeutic alliance and client session outcome. A multivariate regression model was used to assess regression of the independent variables (IV = TPI-T and TPI-C) on the dependent variables (DV = WAI and CTSC-R), controlling for therapy types. Multivariate test results indicated that there was no significant relationship between therapists' self-reported presence (TPI-T) and clients' reported therapeutic alliance (WAI) and session outcome (CTSC-R).

With respect to clients' perceptions of therapists' presence, evaluation of bivariate relationships indicated that all three therapy types showed a positive relationship between the TPI-C and the CTSC-R and WAI. Multivariate test results indicated that there was a significant relationship between clients' report of therapists' presence (TPI-C) and their report of the therapeutic alliance (WAI) and session outcome (CTSC-R). Wilks' lambda (converted to $F$) is $F(5, 348) = 44.61, p < .001$. Significant regression coefficients were found between the TPI-C and session outcome and the therapeutic alliance. Hence, clients' reports of therapists' presence showed a significant relationship with clients' ratings of session outcome and the therapeutic alliance.

## Discussion of Results

A central finding in this research is that clients reported a positive change following a therapy session when they felt their therapist was present with them, regardless of the theoretical orientation of the therapy. Clients also rated the therapeutic relationship alliance as stronger when they felt their therapist was more present with them.

The current study found significant correlations between the subscales of the RI, which reflect previous literature suggesting a lack of independence between the TOCs. It has been suggested that the high correlations between the TOCs indicate a global therapist quality (Gormally & Hill, 1974). Perhaps therapeutic presence reflects this global quality that encompasses the TOCs yet goes beyond them. In this vein, the relationship conditions can be seen as a way that being fully in the moment is communicated to clients. This research is suggestive of Rogers's later postulations about the nature of presence as a possible overarching condition.

Another interesting finding is that CBT therapists rated themselves lower on presence, and their clients rated their therapists as lower on presence, than did CCT and PET clients. On the one hand, the difference in self-rated and client-perceived therapists' presence is consistent with the theoretical approaches, as presence is not viewed as highly integral to a CBT approach. However, the therapeutic relationship is valued in current CBT models, yet the relationship conditions of empathy, congruence, and positive regard were also found to be significantly lower as rated by CBT therapists in comparison with PET and CCT therapists. Yet, CBT, PET, and CCT clients who perceived their therapists as present rated the therapeutic alliance and session outcome as significantly higher than did clients who perceived their therapist as lower on presence. While we have shown that presence is an important predictor of the therapeutic alliance, these findings suggest that presence may be an important variable in more manualized therapies, such as CBT, even though it is not generally practiced or integrated into the approach.

An interesting finding with respect to therapists' self-rated presence was that therapists' perception of their own presence was not related to clients' session outcome or therapeutic alliance. Findings from the qualitative study mentioned earlier revealed that therapists describe their experience of presence, in interviews, as helping them to feel more connected to clients and more efficacious in their use of responses and technique. Yet findings in the second research study indicated that clients do not rate the session as more productive or the alliance as more positive when therapists report they are more present. It is likely that these interventions only affect clients if they are feeling the therapist present with them.

Note that the latter finding is reflective of psychotherapy research in general (Duncan & Moynihan, 1994; Horvath & Luborsky, 1993; Lambert & Simon, 2008). Clients' experience of the therapist has a greater impact than how therapists experience themselves. For example, Rogers came to the conclusion that the degree to which the client perceives the therapist as being unconditionally accepting, empathic, and congruent is the main factor for a good therapeutic outcome (Rogers & Truax, 1976). The findings of this study reflect this notion, that the degree to which clients perceive their therapist as present affects clients' session outcome.

One reason why therapists who rated themselves as present did not affect clients' ratings of the session or clients' ratings of the therapeutic alliance may be that although therapists may be experiencing presence within themselves, they are not communicating it or expressing it effectively. There may not be a one-to-one correspondence between what is experienced by the therapist and what is expressed behaviorally or experienced by the other. A second reason may reflect therapists' reporting on an experience of presence in themselves but not on relational presence. Here awareness is lacking both of where the client is emotionally and of the client's ability to receive the potential intensity of this state of being. The relational quality of presence implies that the therapist and client are somewhat matched in their ability to be present with each other. Clients may need to feel open to therapists' presence, or to some degree of presence within themselves, to fully experience the presence of the therapist.

Another important reason why a positive effect of therapists' self-rated presence was not captured in this study may lie in the way it was measured. Self-reports have limitations in capturing such a subtle and complex internal experience. It would be beneficial to try to capture therapists' presence through behavioral manifestations, such as videotape observations. This way we could both understand the qualities of therapeutic presence from a different vantage point and note whether there are ways therapists offer themselves or specific behaviors they are "doing" that trigger clients' feelings that the therapist is fully present with them.

In addition to not having a developed understanding of presence, the therapists in this study (mostly graduate students) may have been undeveloped in their understanding of presence and may have felt self-conscious or critical of themselves in anticipation of supervision. This suggests that presence is a quality that takes time and experience to fully understand and cultivate. The experience of presence is something that a person understands or is sensitive to only with practice in life and self-development, as indicated in the model and the literature (Geller, 2001; Keefe, 1975; Lietaer, 1993; Shepherd, Brown, & Greaves, 1972; Webster, 1998).


## RELATED THERAPEUTIC PRESENCE STUDIES

Following our research, there have been a few studies using TPI, in order to understand the relationship of presence with empathy and the therapeutic alliance further. Oghene, Pos, and Geller (2010) examined the relationship between therapists' presence, empathy, and the working alliance, using the TPI-T and the TPI-C as an indicator of presence. Findings revealed that clients' ratings of their therapists' presence early in the therapy process (Session 3) predicted the level and strength of the therapeutic working alliance 12 sessions later (at Session 15). Furthermore, clients' perception of their therapist being present was related to their perception of their therapist being empathic. Low presence also related to low empathy, suggesting the proposition that presence may be a precondition for empathy.

The TPI-T was also used in a study by Vinca and Hayes (2007), although these investigators adapted their own version to measure clients' perspective of therapists' presence. Whereas the current TPI-C developed by Geller et al. (2010) is a three-item measure, Vinca and Hayes (2007) developed an 18-item questionnaire based directly on a translation of the therapist measure. By translating items measuring therapists' experience on the TPI to a client perspective, these authors had to drop three items that were not translatable from a client's point of view. We will call the Vinca and Hayes (2007) 18-item measure the TPI-Client to distinguish it from our three-item TPI-C.

Vinca and Hayes (2007) asked clients ($n = 88$) referred by the University Counseling Center to fill out the TPI-Client, the Session Evaluation Questionnaire–Depth (Stiles & Snow, 1984), and the Barrett-Lennard Relationship Inventory–Empathy subscale (Barrett-Lennard, 1961, 1986) after a therapy session, and the Outcome Questionnaire (OQ-45; Lambert et al.,1996) prior to the following session. Therapists ($n = 42$; graduate students in counseling psychology and counselor education) completed the TPI after the same session. Findings revealed that the TPI and TPI-Client had good reliability (.93 and .87, respectively). They also noted that Geller et al.'s (2010) TPI-T demonstrated good predictive validity with session outcome, as measured on the OQ-45.

Vinca and Hayes (2007) noted that preliminary analyses indicated that therapists' perceptions of their presence were significantly related to client ratings of session depth and therapist empathy. Client perceptions of therapist presence were much more strongly related to the dependent variables given the likely monosource bias. Interestingly, client and counselor perceptions of counselor presence were virtually unrelated (.10), which was similar to our data (Geller et al., 2010).

## CONCLUSION

The data in the Geller et al. (2010) and the Oghene, Pos, and Geller (2010) studies, along with Vinca and Hayes (2007), supported the notion not only that presence is an important therapeutic principle but also that clients' sense that their therapist is present with them is associated with a better therapy session and a strong and positive therapeutic alliance across different therapeutic approaches. When we look further at these studies, both from a qualitative and a quantitative perspective, a relational approach to presence emerges. Although we started to see presence as an intrapersonal experience, we recognize that therapeutic presence is in fact an interpersonal or relational experience; hence, it is the shared and developed sense of mutual presence that is truly healing. We can see the emergence here of a therapeutic presence theory of relationship—that being fully in the moment with the client, and the client's being open and experiencing the gift of presence from the therapist, is fundamental to an optimal therapeutic and growth experience and may be seen as a common factor in relation to positive process and outcome. Chapter 3 describes this therapeutic presence theory of relationship.

# 3

# THERAPEUTIC PRESENCE:
# A THEORY OF RELATIONSHIP

What we are missing! What opportunities of understanding we let pass by because at a single decisive moment we were, with all our knowledge, lacking in the simple virtue of a full human presence.
—Karl Jasper (cited in Sonneman, 1954, p. 375)

As Kurt Lewin (1951, p. 169) stated, "There is nothing so practical as a good theory." In this chapter, we outline a presence-based theory of therapeutic relating. This theory, based on the results of our empirical studies described in Chapter 2, posits that although the experience of presence by the therapist is important, presence is healing only if the client *experiences* the therapist as being present. We provide a flowchart of the components that make up a presence-based therapeutic relationship. This is followed by a discussion about some of the paradoxical aspects of presence in psychotherapy. We then discuss what makes presence therapeutic, expand on the relational aspects of therapeutic presence, and explore relational therapeutic presence and intersubjective and reflective consciousness. Finally, we present our understanding of the relationship between therapeutic presence and Rogers's therapist-offered conditions (TOCs), the therapeutic alliance, and affect attunement.

## RELATING WITH THERAPEUTIC PRESENCE

Our therapeutic presence theory of relationship suggests that the therapist's ability to be present—*fully immersed in the moment*, without judgment or expectation, being with and for the client—facilitates healing. As we have said, therapeutic presence involves having one's whole self in the encounter with a client by being completely in the moment physically, emotionally, cognitively, and spiritually. Therapeutic presence involves being open and receptive to what is poignant in the moment, and this allows for an attunement to the other that is based on sensing the other's as well as one's own experience and the relationship between them. This is communicated nonverbally by such things as gaze and tone of voice and verbally by timing and pace.

In addition, we hypothesize that although the experience of presence by the therapist and its communication to the client are important, they are healing only if the client *experiences* the therapist as being fully there in the moment. It is clients' experience of their therapists as present and authentically engaged in a relationship with them that promotes the type of depth of connection and significance to the encounter that is therapeutic as well as greater presence in the client. This deepens the client's experience of self and deepens the relationship between client and therapist. A reciprocal relationship between therapists' felt and communicated presence—clients receiving and feeling therapists' as present with them, and both people developing greater presence within and between them—allows for the development of relational presence, for an I–Thou encounter between the two, and ultimately it is this mutual presence that leads to therapeutic change.

The theory of therapeutic relating that we present here, based on the importance of presence, thus proposes that therapeutic presence is the essential quality underlying an effective therapeutic relationship and that regardless of theoretical orientation or type of therapeutic approach, presence promotes good session process and outcome and enhances the therapeutic alliance. Our theory suggests that it is the therapist's presence that provides the therapeutic relationship with the types of depth and connection needed to help clients access their deepest feelings, meanings, concerns, and needs; provides the type of environment in which these can be most effectively attended to, explored, and accepted or transformed as needed; and promotes therapists' ability to respond in an attuned manner that best fits the moment.

The three major components of presence, as we have seen from the research-based model of presence (elaborated more fully in Chapters 4–6), are *preparing the ground for presence*, the *process of presence*, and the *actual in-session experience of presence*. The qualities of therapists' presence, described in the model, which include compassion, allowing, spaciousness, openness, acceptance, patience, and gentleness, promote the emergence of the others' inner core. Social roles are dropped as the client and therapist become engaged in the vital contact of seeing each other as they truly are in the moment. This meeting involves looking into each other's eyes, seeing the face of the other, and feeling the warm accepting embrace of the connection with another human being, alongside meeting the pain and vulnerability of the other.

This form of presence promotes an attuned therapeutic responsiveness, which facilitates actions by the therapist (responses and interventions) that are sensitive to and fit the moment. The actions are based on the therapist having access in the moment to what is occurring in the present and a resource base of skills and abilities. The ability to be present in the moment to self and other thus promotes attuned responsiveness and is crucial to being therapeutic. It is awareness of the moment that allows the therapist to synthesize a response that is attuned to and fits the moment. A response that fits the moment comes from a tacit understanding of what is occurring in the present moment in the context of past moments.

Thus, the therapist is ready to be present in the moment, and he or she shows this through facial expressions and other forms of nonverbal and attuned verbal responsiveness. However, if being there in this manner is overwhelming for the client, the therapist—being attuned to the other—can make adjustments (e.g., dropping the gaze downward), which can allow the other to feel safe to remain open and seen. This is where therapists' present-centered attunement to what the client feels and needs is essential. The type of mutual presence that arises from this kind of meeting provides a sense of connecting, of being seen, and of seeing as no other human experience does.

Our research (see the quantitative study described in Chapter 2) suggests that clients who experience their therapist as fully present form better alliances and experience better therapeutic outcomes, regardless of therapists' therapeutic orientation. We hypothesize that therapeutic presence, along with facilitating the client's healing process, is an important aspect of optimizing the therapeutic alliance. Although we understand that the therapeutic alliance is one of the nonspecific factors that contribute to good therapy process and outcome (Horvath & Greenberg, 1994), it is unclear what helps in alliance formation. We suggest that therapeutic presence contributes to the development of the therapeutic alliance.

In summary, a relationship theory based on therapeutic presence suggests that therapeutic presence will lead to the development of a synergistic relationship in which the client develops greater presence and a deepening of relational presence occurs. In the experience of therapeutic presence, therapists are grounded in their bodies, are fully open, and are listening fully to their clients in that particular moment. In addition, being present in this way is the most important guide to the synthesis of the next therapeutic response. From the state of presence, the therapist can fully optimize the process or doing of therapy. That is, from that place of receiving the client on a multisensory level, and integrating this tacitly with the therapist's own theoretical, learned, personal, tacit, and intuitive understanding of the client, a natural response, or direction, emerges from within the therapist. This natural state of flow (Csikszentmihalyi, 1990) in the therapist, as well as providing a sense of direction, encourages clients to feel open, safe, and accepting or present to themselves and with their therapists. The latter allows relational presence to emerge and leads to a deepening of the relationship between the therapist and client.

Figure 3.1 outlines the components of this theory. The components are presented in a sequential manner for ease of understanding but are in circular and dynamic relation to each other. The top part of the figure (Figure 3.1a) presents the components of the essence of being and relating with presence to capture the experience of the relational bond in presence as well as the deepening into relational presence as the therapist and client become more present within themselves and with each other. The bottom part (Figure 3.1b) presents the aspects of responding in presence, which emphasize the action or intervention aspects promoted by presence. These two diagrams can be seen

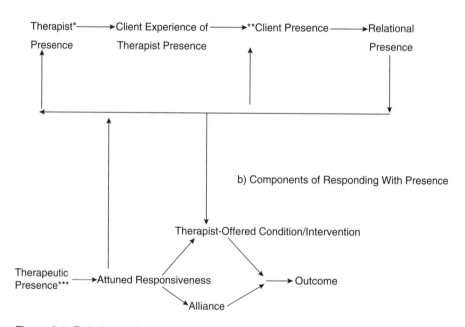

*Figure 3.1.* Relating and responding with presence.
*Receptivity, inwardly attending, and extending. **Deepening of client self-experience.
***Attuned responsiveness, therapist-offered conditions/intervention, and alliance can occur anywhere in the above process of relating with presence.

as intertwined rather than separate or sequentially related, and this conveys the multilayered nature of relating in which we each experience the other's way of being with us as we experience the things we do with each other. As we can see, the process of therapist presence involving receptivity, inward attending, and extending is communicated to the client through the expression of presence, and this increases the likelihood of clients experiencing therapists' presence, leading to client presence and a deepening of their own experience and ultimately to a reverberatory relational presence. All of these steps occur in the experience of being together. Then, in the domain of doing, the therapist responds in an attuned manner, communicating the TOCs and intervening in whatever way fits the moment. This promotes the formation of a good working alliance in which both the bond and the collaborative components of agreed-upon goals and perceived relevance of the tasks the therapist is engaging in with the client are formed. This all combines to promote better outcomes.

### Presence as a Paradox: Dual Level of Consciousness

Therapeutic presence involves a careful balance of contact between the therapist's own experience and the client's experience, while maintaining the capacity to be responsive from that place of internal and external connection. Robbins (1998) described presence as involving a "dual level of consciousness" (p. 11). Similarly, Hycner (1993) described this quality as "detached presence" (p. 13), and quoted Buber as saying "the therapist must be fully present and yet concurrently be able to reflect on what is experientially occurring at that moment" (p. 13). Therapeutic presence involves a process of shifting from internal to external, from self to other, from being open and receiving to being responsive.

It is clear that the felt experience of presence requires this dual level of consciousness, and hence many paradoxes occur in the felt experience of presence. For example, the dual level of consciousness requires therapists to balance the polar aspects of the subjective and the objective. Therapeutic presence requires the therapist to be deeply engaged and immersed in the client's experience, yet the therapist must maintain an appropriate objectivity by being centered, unshaken, and responsive to what is being experienced by the client.

Whether therapists are actually cognizant of themselves when they attempt to be in such a state of presence with all its subtleties and complexities is questionable. The complexity and intricacy of therapeutic presence can be seen in the following list of the paradoxical aspects of therapeutic presence:

- letting go of preconceptions yet offering the client facilitative responses as they emerge in resonance with the moment, responses that are based on understanding the client;

- letting go of beliefs and theoretical knowledge yet bringing this knowledge into the session and allowing it to inform intuitions and responses;
- feeling open and receiving yet maintaining consistent focus;
- feeling the intensity of the client's experience yet remaining spacious, calm, and centered;
- feeling intimate and joined with the client yet feeling a separate sense of self;
- feeling the depth of the client's experience yet being cognizant that these feelings are separate from one's own feelings and sense of self;
- letting go of a direction or plan for the session yet allowing a direction to emerge naturally;
- accepting the client in the totality of his or her experience yet offering new possibilities or an environment in which to make novel discoveries;
- being spontaneous but only as it directly relates to or benefits the client;
- keeping boundaries open and permeable yet maintaining contact with one's self as separate;
- being with the known (of theory, client) and the unknown (of experience, what is to emerge);
- maintaining a sense of openness, wonder, and intrigue toward the client and the experience emerging in session yet being a trained and learned professional with expertise;
- allowing one's personal self to be with the client yet letting go of personal concerns or issues; and
- allowing one's own emotions and wounds to be accessed and communicated if helpful yet not losing a sense of center or making the healing of the therapist's own self the focus.

Presence allows an openness and flexibility to be able to maintain multiple levels of awareness of the many dimensions of experience that are part of the therapy experience. This stems from therapists' receptivity and openness to clients and to their own experiences. Finally, whether a therapist feels she or he was in a high state of presence during therapy is not particularly relevant when the client does not sense this in the therapist.

### What Makes Presence Therapeutic?

Presence provides the therapist with the capacity to notice and be aware of different levels of what is poignant in the moment in the client's inner world. It also provides the type of relational encounter that infuses the client's moment-by-moment experience with significance. In being present, the therapist's way of being declares: "I am here with you." This state—of being able to be with whatever is, without judgment, agenda, preference, or prejudice— also helps clients to reveal their experience and the essence of themselves, to feel the importance of what they experience and say, and to feel that this is received, understood, and responded to in ways that meet the essence of the client and his or her suffering.

The therapist's presence helps clients feel seen, heard, attended to, and received. It breaks their sense of isolation. Therapist presence infuses in clients the sense that their experience is important and being attended to. Having lived in an experiential desert where they felt that their experience was not relevant, clients suddenly will begin to listen to themselves and take their experience as valid and as conveying something important. This allows clients to feel held and entrusted in the sanctity of the therapeutic relationship as well as respected in who they are.

As we saw in Chapter 1, Buber (1958) argued that in the I–Thou relationship healing takes place in the *meeting* between two people. Levinas (1985), however, went further and emphasized that in a meeting between two people, the relation with the Other is inherently asymmetrical, and the Other, as appearing, especially the face of the Other, takes priority over the self and demands a response. In meeting another, there is a demand to respond to the other. This puts each in the service of the other. For Levinas, such a demand occurs prior to any experience of the self and its desires, intentions, or plans. His view highlights the importance of the role of the response in encountering the Other. Being present places a demand on the therapist to respond. One cannot respond to the Other's experience without being present to it. The responsiveness that flows from presence is the essence of what makes presence healing.

A key aspect of the experience of therapeutic presence involves the intention of being with and for the client in a healing encounter. If therapists are present with their own experience and with the clients, then the decision to share their genuine experience must be guided by this intention. To be therapeutically genuine, therapists need to be present with and aware of their own experience and to be able to assess when their own issues emerge and need to be put aside temporarily or whether what is emerging could be of benefit to the client's healing process.

From this it appears that therapist presence is a precondition for therapist attunement and responsiveness because it allows for a particular kind of sensing, seeing, and listening that promotes a response that is attuned to the client's present moment. It is this type of attunement that creates a unique sense of connection that makes the client feel fully received and heard. Both the therapist's nonverbal experience of presence and the verbal communication result from this state are essential to the formation of a therapeutic relationship.

Being immersed in the moment and attending fully to the other promote attunement to what is happening in the other. Attunement to the other is probably seen most clearly in infant–caretaker interactions because of the nonverbal nature of the communication and interaction and the great sense of being with and for the infant (Stern, 1985). To respond to an infant in an attuned manner, one has to be present to the infant and sense what is occurring for the infant in the moment. Of course, one can ignore the infant, but as soon as one looks at the face of the infant one is drawn into an encounter in which the otherness of the infant demands a response. If one is not present to the other, there is no experience of the demand to respond. Attuned responsiveness thus is highly contingent on presence.

The second author of this volume (L. G.) conveyed the following vignette to demonstrate this sense of attunement and responsiveness:

> Thus as I sit with my client and she struggles to talk about her feeling over the week of having felt cut off, and having sunk into a type of despair that she hasn't felt for many years, I see her face and the pain of her aloneness. It communicates a sense of how isolated and unseen she feels and how painful this is. I respond with "just so alone, like I'll never be known and loved in the way I need." As I say this I feel compassion for the pang of painful aloneness that I feel as if I were her, by having entered her world and sensing what it feels like to be her in this state. I hear my voice as I respond and feel both soothing and soothed by my own feeling of compassion for this sense of universal pain. I see her face, her eyes look sad, and the corners of her mouth begin to drop and I say "so sad." She nods, and I say "let the tears come, you're not alone here." She weeps gently and says, "It hurts so bad." I nod and she sighs and continues, "I feel sad and so tired." I respond, "You are just so sad and tired, just stay with it, you sighed, can you breathe again?" For these few moments we are in mutual and relational presence. She then says, "I'm scared of my sadness, have been all my life so I keep pushing it away, it's exhausting." What flows from this is a reflection on her situation of having recently received some bad news related to her health and the creation of meaning that is now grounded in her body. This leads to a resolution to no longer neglect the messages her body gives her.

If the therapist had not been aware of the client's face in the moment, he would not have been able to respond to the pain of his client's aloneness. It is this type of moment-by-moment awareness that helps the client enter into the moment of meeting described in this vignette.

So presence is necessary for attunement and responsiveness. Being therapeutically responsive means responding in the right way at the right time in a manner that is therapeutic. Therapeutic presence thus promotes optimal responsiveness and optimal application of methods and knowledge. Therapists' timing of what they say and do is crucial to effective intervention (Greenberg, Rice, & Elliott, 1993). This is dependent on being in contact with what the client feels, needs, and says in that moment. The theory of therapeutic presence thus suggests that (a) the therapist's attitude and manner are more important than any technique, (b) the therapist's manner of using the technique is an important aspect of its effectiveness, and (c) the appropriate implementation of technique is dependent on timing, and presence promotes the use of technique as an aspect of responsive attunement. Technique can be helpful, but in the long run it is of little value if the therapist is not present because the technique will not be used in the right way, at the right moment, and in the right manner to optimize therapeutic growth.

Therapeutic presence thus creates a relationship of authenticity, trust, and responsiveness in which two people are able to encounter each other without pretense such that they feel fully accepted as they are in the moment and their interactions flow fluidly moment by moment. This involves a total lack of expectation that one should be or feel any particular way other than to be there as an experiencing other, plus the support to be able to be in the moment as one is. Presence is helpful because it facilitates a connection between two people that differs from conventional ways of relating. Therapeutic presence helps create the conditions for therapists' optimal understanding of and responding to the client, which in turn allows for the client to feel understood and responded to in a therapeutic manner. When clients feel that their therapist is there fully in the moment, they become more open to, present with, and accepting of their own experience, which deepens the client's therapeutic process and allows the client to feel safe to share further their experience as it is happening.

The more present the therapist is, the greater the opportunities clients have to become present and accepting with themselves, and the more present clients become, the greater the presence the therapist develops. Schmid (2002) described this sense of mutual encounter as *coexperiencing*. For example, if the therapist is present with the client's pain, yet not overtaken by it, he or she becomes more and more present to the multiplicity of experiencing. Therapist and client open more to hearing and sensing the client's experience at a deeper level with each encounter.

The inner state of the therapist strongly influences the response of the client. If therapists are in a state of presence that includes being open, receptive, accepting, nonjudgmental, grounded, and connected to self and other and with intention toward healing, they are more likely to invite clients into an open, accepting, and exploratory state in which they can experience feeling listened to on a deep and profound level. If the therapist is in a state of nonpresence, which includes rigidity, control, judgment, distraction, or defensiveness, the client is more likely to feel or respond in a defensive, protective, or closed way in which he or she feels judged or not fully heard.

Therapeutic presence thus involves listening deeply to the client on a multisensory level and to one's own self in response to the client and the evolving relationship. This complex state of attunement informs the therapist about what to do or say to facilitate the client's process. Attuned responsiveness involves a therapeutic response that is contingent on what is occurring in the client. It is driven by what is happening in the moment and it fits the moment.

The following vignette is an adaptation of the first author's (S. G.) experience with a client. It demonstrates how the therapist's resonance with the client's in-the-moment experience can inform the therapist about how to respond to a client.

> I was seeing my client, Lisa, when I became aware of how an inner emotional sense I was feeling of being overwhelmed was actually my inner resonance of the client's experience. Lisa had been in a traumatic car accident, was coping with trying to get through the many rehabilitation appointments. She began to discuss a call from her boss, who wanted to know when she would return to work, followed by her husband's stress over the extra financial burden and housework that he had to take on. She was describing these conversations in detail when I became fully present to her experience. I could see her face, sense her holding her breath, her voice was becoming higher in pitch, and I experienced all these without concept or symbol, but more like having them enter me, and I began to feel a sense of what it was like for her. I had this sense in my body of what it is like to feel an overwhelming feeling in one's chest. I became aware in my chest of a sense of what it is like to have a panic feeling and did not recognize it as anything familiar in my own experience. I noted that it was an internal resonance to the client's underlying experience, from which she was disconnected as she talked about it. I reflected, with a slight questioning tone, that I heard in her expression, feelings of overwhelm and panic. I reflected: "Just feeling so overwhelmed and panicky?" Tears began to roll down her eyes and she opened further about her deep fear and anxiety that she was never going to feel okay and about the vulnerability she felt in being dependent. This was an access point from which she began to express her earlier despair as a child when she felt disappointed by her father's inability to support her when she had broken her leg at 10 years old.

This was a critical moment in the therapy, where presence, or nonpresence, could have guided the unfolding of the session in two different directions. If the therapist had not been fully present, receptively opening herself to take in her client's experience, and if she had not been fully grounded and sensing in her own body, she would not have had access to this experience. In addition, if the therapist had not understood that her sense of what it was like to feel panic was a present-centered experience of resonance, she could have felt overwhelmed by and disconnected from or could have ignored the sensation in her body and actually shut down to the client. If she had not recognized her own body as a resonator, or if she had not had the tools to listen deeply to her own experience, she would not have helped the client gain access to her own deeper inner experience. In this example, however, the therapist allowed herself to trust her own bodily experiential resonance and risked sharing this intuitive sense of her client's experience. This reflected the therapeutic presence process in being open to receive the client while inwardly attending to her own bodily resonance and the emergence of this state in direct relational resonance with the client.

This relational and self-trusting experience of therapeutic presence allowed the therapist to respond in a way that deepened the client's contact with her own experience. Feeling heard and understood by the therapist, and the subsequent sharing and opening, can deepen clients' presence and healing within themselves. In addition, the therapist and client are meeting on a deeper level as both share the intention of a positive movement toward the healing of the client. This more fundamental point of meeting, where the essences of therapist and client are in direct contact with each other, while the therapist is in a grounded state of openness, emerges into a relational presence.

In this vein, we see presence as a reciprocal process that enhances the quality of each person's presence and deepens the connection to create a relational presence. This facilitates a deeper therapeutic relationship between therapist and client in which the client deepens his or her experience, revealing to him- or herself and disclosing to the therapists aspects of experience previously disclaimed or not previously acknowledged.

## Therapeutic Presence and Clients' Presence

A significant value of therapeutic presence is in the invitation to the client to enter into a more present state within. Clients' presence can be activated by therapists' presence through both being deeply met by the therapist as well as by intersubjective sharing. Schneider and Krug (2010) suggested that presence is enhanced in clients through the therapist's attuned listening and through the intensive quality of connection that occurs between the therapist and the client in moments of presence. Schneider and Krug suggested that therapist presence helps clients on four levels: (a) reconnects them to their pain, (b) promotes agency and responsibility, (c) attunes them to opportunities to transform their pain, and (d) allows for the developing of a safe therapeutic relationship that is growth promoting.

When clients experience presence, they begin to feel open, trusting, and more connected to their selves and their own experience. This inner connection, combined with being in a safe and supportive therapeutic relationship, allows clients to experience a healthy state and invites them to express their deepest pain and vulnerability in the service of healing. Welwood (1992) suggested that the therapist's unconditional presence is the most powerful agent of change because it facilitates the client's ability to experience presence and promotes a "vertical shift" in the client's awareness. This vertical shift invites clients into a more self-aware and self-compassionate state and allows for greater awareness of their experience and needs, and how to satisfy those needs, which can then lead to a sense of self-integration.

## RELATIONAL THERAPEUTIC PRESENCE

*Relational therapeutic presence* refers to the deepening of the state of presence that occurs as a function of two (or more) people being fully present with one another. The relationship is enhanced with a quality of being fully in the now, connected, open, and in touch with a larger sense of spaciousness that is opened in relationship to each other and the moment. This reflects Schmid's (2002) discussion on coexperiencing and mutual contact being the goal of therapists' presence. Cooper (2005) referred to the mutual state of presence that can ensue between therapist and client as *copresence*.

Deepening into presence through the process of touching and being touched by another human being is a beautiful and healing process in and of itself. To meet someone face to face, heart to heart, mind to mind, essence to essence, with openness, spaciousness, nonjudgment, and reflexivity, changes both the person meeting the other and the person being met. That deeply shared moment of presence attunes each person on a level that resembles a neurological mirroring. It is akin to Jung's (1959) collective unconscious and the notion that human beings are part of something larger—a larger ocean of energy, vitality, and knowledge. Perhaps it is something on a relational and spiritual level, a touching of a larger consciousness, an expansion of heart and mind that touches a field that is subtle and evolves from the deep presence within the therapist and within the relationship. It is the potential that opens up in each and both persons when they meet fully and deeply in presence together.

Thus, from a place of interpersonal safety, the possibility exists of accessing deeper parts of the psyche and the self. As the therapist deepens into presence, presence deepens into a relational experience that is healing within, between, and beyond the two individuals. Not only is the client changed in this process of deep relating but also the therapist is changed in each presence moment and each relational presence encounter.

## Relational Therapeutic Presence and Intersubjective Consciousness

To understand what happens in therapeutic presence that allows the therapist to access deeper aspects of experience and know how to respond with understanding and the capacity to facilitate the client's process, we need to look at the level of the shared reality or consciousness that exists in moments of relational presence. Stern (2004) introduced the concept of *intersubjective consciousness* to explain how the experience of the present moment in therapy is implicitly grasped in consciousness. Intersubjective consciousness develops when two people (i.e., therapist and client) are cocreating a shared present-moment experience: the consciousness of one overlaps that of the other. Thus, in the therapy dyad the client has his or her own experience as well as the therapist's experience of their experience as reflected in the eyes, body, face, vocal tone, and so on. While the client and therapist experiences are not the same, the reflection of the experience in a present moment allows for sharing the same landscape or an intersubjective consciousness. Stern (2004) proposed that when one person in the dyad has an experience, when felt directly by the other, almost the same experience in the other is activated through intersubjective sharing. This creates a reentry loop between the two, which in a shared present moment gives rise to intersubjective consciousness.

## Reflective Consciousness and Feeling Felt by the Therapist

On a social level, inward attention or consciousness is a collective experience of the entire body (physically and mentally) and an engagement with other people's minds, the culture, and the social world of the time (Siegel, 2007; Stern, 2004). With respect to dialogue, reflective consciousness only occurs in the presence of another witnessing that experience. While this can include witnessing one's own experience from different parts of the self, in psychotherapy it is the client's direct experience of the therapist's witnessing the experience that is helpful.

Hence, in the clinical situation, Stern (2004) argued that three types of consciousness are at play. The first is *phenomenal* consciousness, which reflects experiences that one is aware of only as they are happening. This rise and fall of events or moments in therapy is a reflection of the ongoing discourse in therapy. The second is *introspective* consciousness, which concerns conscious experiences that are reflected on, and a word or symbolic label becomes attached to the experience, enabling future introspective moments. In therapy, this is equivalent to "verbal consciousness" (Stern, 2004, p. 131) and reflects the majority of the content of what is discussed in a therapy session. The third is intersubjective consciousness, which reflects experiences that only happen in intense interactions in therapy and comprise special present moments or what we call relational therapeutic presence. The experience in this case is cocreated by therapist and client: The experiences of both are intermingled yet separate, and what is experienced in those moments is long lasting and creates impressions that then create intrapsychic and social change when meaning is attached. A negative form of intersubjective consciousness, a failure in reflection or matching of experience, also exists where what is locked into consciousness in that moment is separation or absence of connection.

So how can therapists optimize intersubjective consciousness and the fertile ground of the present moment experience? Stern (2004) described the ancient Greeks' term *kairos*, which is a moment of opportunity in the moment, where events have come together to provide an opportunity to act or respond in a way that could change the course of one's destiny, either for the next moment or a lifetime. In psychotherapy, therapists' attention to the fertile ground of the present moment (Schmid, 2002), to the visible and invisible expressions of the client's experience, offers an opportunity to respond in a way that the client recognizes that he or she has been deeply seen or understood. This level of attention demands the therapist to be in contact with his or her deep inner world and attend to what is being experienced and expressed in the moment, without agenda or preconception and with flexibility and openness. This calls on a deep trust in the sometimes unformed and unclear bodily sensations, images, or words that may begin to arise within the therapist. Through recognizing and attending to these fertile moments of opportunity in the self and the client and responding in a way that emerges from his or her own present-centered attention, an optimal possibility for growth occurs. With this level of sensory perception and detailed attention to the present moment, the therapist capitalizes on a potential opportunity for kairos. In fact, both Stern and Schmid proposed that all present-moment experiences, when recognized and given deep and sensory attention, are moments of kairos.

## THERAPEUTIC PRESENCE AND ROGERS'S THERAPIST-OFFERED CONDITIONS

Therapeutic presence has been proposed as the underlying contribution to a positive therapeutic relationship in client-centered therapy (Bugental, 1987; Schmid, 1998; Thorne, 1992, 1996). This view is paralleled by client-centered theorists (Bozarth, 2001; Segrera, 2000; Wyatt, 2000), who view presence as a precondition to or foundation for the other conditions. Schmid (2002) referred to presence as "the proper term for the 'core conditions' in their interconnectedness as the way of being and acting of the therapist" (pp. 81–82). According to Rogers, being present is an embodiment of the therapeutic conditions (Baldwin, 2000).

This connection between presence and the TOCs of empathy, unconditional positive regard, and congruence was supported in both our qualitative and quantitative analyses of the therapist's presence. In the qualitative study (Geller & Greenberg, 2002), therapists emphasized that presence was the larger experience and the necessary receptive position to allow for greater empathic understanding and responsiveness. The close relationship between presence and empathy was supported in the quantitative study (Geller, Greenberg, & Watson, 2010) by a statistically significant relationship between therapists' self-reported presence assessed in the Therapeutic Presence Inventory (TPI-T) and therapists' ratings of the relationship conditions of empathy. The therapists also described the importance of presence in gaining a sense of genuine, accepting connection with the client, and this was supported by a statistically significant relationship between TPI-T and congruence, and unconditional positive regard on the Barrett-Lennard Relationship Inventory (RI), suggesting that presence underlies the core conditions of a positive therapeutic relationship. This is exemplified by looking at the conditions individually in relation to therapeutic presence.

Presence is an important precondition for empathy to occur, and although the two concepts are similar, they are not equivalent. Therapeutic presence was described by therapists' interviewed as the underlying experience or foundation that allowed them to comprehend and experience the client's experience but was not equal to the whole experience of presence itself. For example, one therapist (Geller & Greenberg, 2002) noted that "it does require presence, to have empathy with another person. There has to be some presence there to allow yourself to feel the feeling and to understand it." Another said, "I need to be present in the moment in order to be empathic."

The more presence therapists experience, the more they feel they are accurate in empathic understanding and responding. This is partially understood as presence allowing an expanded perception and sensitivity to, as one therapist stated, "many more dimensions of the patient's being," which in turn allows the therapist to understand the client on a deeper level.

We understand that to be empathic to others, one must first be able to be present with the other. However, there is an additional step that often gets missed in psychotherapy training: To be fully present with a client demands that therapists cultivate a sense of presence within themselves first. This involves a practice of empathy and understanding with one's self. To practice empathy within one's self, one must be interested in, willing, and able to revisit or experience an event and its associated affect with acceptance and nonjudgment.

Being in therapeutic presence also means being grounded in one's self. Inclusion, in particular, which is Buber's (1958) term for a more broadly based conception of empathy, was more clearly articulated with respect to presence in that therapists feel centered and strong in their own self while receiving and entering the experience of the other. The experience of being grounded in one's self supports the process of opening oneself up to receive the totality of the client's experience and to be open, focused, and clear in that process. One therapist in our study explained that

> the more you experience presence, the clearer you can be, or the more empathic or resonant you can be . . . really feeling everything, this is not being present, this is being swept by the wave. I do believe when one is very, very centered, the attention is very clear so you do notice, you are aware, you can be fully aware of the nature of the wave, of the nature of the client's experience.

The process of empathy is viewed as that aspect of presence that takes in the experience of the other and responds from the place of understanding within the therapist. The process of presence, which involves being receptive, inwardly attending, and actively using the self as an instrument in understanding the client, acts as a base for empathic experience. Being receptive is being a clear and open vessel for the other's experience to be taken in. Presence, then, is a necessary prerequisite for empathy to be experienced by the therapist. Barrett-Lennard (1981) proposed three major components of the empathic process. First, the therapist needs to receive, then resonate, and then communicate, and then the client needs to receive. This suggests that to achieve maximum empathic understanding, the therapist is first required to be receiving and allowing of clients' experience, a key component of presence.

Unconditional positive regard is also viewed as an aspect and natural manifestation of being therapeutically present. Support for this perspective from our study emerged from findings that therapists' presence was positively correlated with unconditionality ($r = .29$) and level of regard ($r = .34$). The correlations, however, are not high, which suggests some differences. In addition, therapists interviewed described therapeutic presence as involving qualities such as caring, warmth, love, respect, and acceptance, which are all aspects of unconditional positive regard and of the experience of therapeutic presence. Allowing the essence of the therapist to be in contact with the essence of the client, which is a part of therapeutic presence, elicits a deep warmth and acceptance toward the other. Unconditional positive regard thus is facilitated by presence, and presence, by virtue of being nonjudgmental, will result in being unconditionally accepting and respectful of the client and his or her experience.

As Levinas (1985) said, even more than acceptance, there is a sense of responsibility for the other to look and to see. Being present to experience also involves acceptance and nonjudgment of the therapist's own experience.

Some authors view presence as the same as congruence (Bozarth, 2001; Kempler, 1970; Webster, 1998). For example, Bozarth (2001) stated that congruence "can be identified as the therapist's presence in client-centered therapy" (p. 185). Our research demonstrated a significant correlation ($r = .41$) between therapists' ratings of presence and the RI Congruence subscale, suggesting a relationship between the two but also a difference (Geller et al., 2010). The factor analysis on the TPI-T and RI also suggests that presence and congruence are distinct from one another. Based on this, we believe that congruence differs from presence because congruence does not incorporate all the subtle aspects of presence, even though therapeutic presence includes therapist authenticity in feeling and expression. From an examination of the qualitative and quantitative analyses, therapeutic presence is viewed as preparing the ground for congruence and as a precondition of congruence, but involves more than congruence.

Congruence has both internal and expressive aspects, authenticity, and transparency (Lietaer, 1993). Being congruent means feeling, thinking, and expressing the same thing. The process of therapeutic presence involves inwardly attending and extending. We propose that therapeutic presence precedes congruence in that therapists first must be present and receptive to, and make contact with, the fullness of both the client's and their own immediate experience in order to understand what is being experienced and how to respond. Congruence, although it emphasizes being in touch with oneself, does not make explicit the need to be in the present to do this. In presence, the experience that is received resonates in the therapist's body and is experienced as a bodily sense or intuition in the form of feelings, words, or images. Becoming present in the moment at this point involves a moment of attending inwardly to that which is being presently experienced. Thus, being present is a key aspect of congruence that promotes being able to open to and be aware of one's ongoing flow of inner experiencing (Lietaer, 1993).

Therapeutic presence thus is viewed as the foundation of the TOCs, as supported by therapists' interviews (Geller, 2001; Geller & Greenberg, 2002) and the statistically significant correlations between the TPI-T and the RI (Geller et al., 2010). The "in-the-moment" receptive position that presence offers allows the therapist to take in the experience of the client, to not impose his or her own agenda, to be open to what is presented in the moment, and to provide the framework for which more alert and attuned hearing and kinesthetic sensing of the client can happen. Receptivity is viewed as a necessary component for being open and attuned to what is being experienced within the therapist's own self and with the client. What therapeutic presence appears to add to empathy, congruence, and unconditional regard is the preliminary necessity of receptively being empty and open to receive the totality of the client's and one's own experience.

Presence could be seen as the larger condition by which empathy, congruence, and unconditional regard came to be expressed. Perhaps TOCs are the way that being fully in the moment is communicated to clients. It is possible that empathic communication, for example, is the therapist's way of saying "I hear you" and "I am open to whatever it is that you want to express." Similarly, the transparency component of congruence can be an expression of "I am open and connected to what I am experiencing in relation to you and respecting you enough to share it." These responses also communicate that "I am here for you in this moment, I am here to be in healing encounter with and for you."

This view that presence is a precondition of the TOC is supportive of Rogers's later postulations about the nature of presence. In an interview with Baldwin (2000), Rogers wondered, "Perhaps it is something around the edges of those conditions that is really the most important element of therapy—when my self is very clearly, obviously present" (p. 30). Therapists' presence thus can be viewed as the receptive condition that allows the TOC to emerge.

## PRESENCE AND THE THERAPEUTIC ALLIANCE

In the Introduction to this volume, we discussed research evidence on the relationship between the therapeutic or working alliance and therapeutic change (Bordin, 1976, 1979; Horvath & Greenberg, 1986; Lambert & Bergin, 1994). Horvath and Greenberg (1986) briefly summarized Bordin's (1979) three aspects of the alliance (goal, task, and bond) as follows. *Goals* refer to the client and the therapist agreeing on and valuing the desired direction or outcome that therapy is working toward. *Tasks* are the substance of therapy, what occurs in the session that is perceived by client and therapist as relevant and effective, and reflect what is done in therapy to reach the client's goals. *Bond* encompasses the relationship aspects of therapy that contribute to a positive attachment between client and therapist and include mutual trust, confidence, respect, and acceptance. This relational component is posited to be healing for clients in and of itself (Bordin, 1979; Bugental, 1987; Horvath & Greenberg, 1986; Hycner & Jacobs, 1995; Lambert & Simon, 2008; Rogers, 1957).

A gap in knowledge on which factors contribute to the development of a therapeutic alliance still exists (Horvath, 1994). Some findings that have emerged focus on client factors, such as degree of submissiveness, isolation, or friendliness (Wallner Samstag, Muran, Zindel, Segal, & Schuman, 1992), and on clients' ability to engage in exploration of the here and now of the relationship (Safran, Crocker, McMain, & Murray, 1990). While the model of the alliance is interactional, understanding the therapist's role and contribution to a positive alliance is of vital interest (Horvath, 1994). One model that comes from Safran et al. (1990; Safran & Muran, 1996) identifies three key features of the therapist that affect a positive alliance. These are the therapist's recognition of here-and-now relationship problems as they occur, use of the alliance rupture to explore clients' negative experiences and feelings, and the therapist's ownership of his or her own struggles in the therapeutic relationship and how this contributes to clients' negative experiences and feelings. The research on both client and therapist factors involves a focus on the here-and-now relationship.

Therapeutic presence allows the therapist greater sensitivity to here-and-now aspects of the therapeutic alliance, including possible ruptures. With presence, the therapist is using the body as a sensor of what is occurring in the therapist and the client and in the relationship itself. The therapist can then use this inner sensitivity and knowledge to identify possible relationship difficulties, explore them with the client, and share the awareness of his or her own contributions to the alliance rupture.

The contribution of therapeutic presence to building and maintaining a strong therapeutic alliance is supported by our findings (Oghene, Pos, & Geller, 2010), which demonstrate that clients' perception of their therapist as present was predictive of a positive therapeutic alliance (Geller et al., 2010). We theorized that with presence, therapists are able to attain greater attunement to clients' experience, and this allows clients to feel heard and understood and trust that their therapists are working with them as allies in their healing process. In this way, presence supports the development of a relational bond and safety in the therapeutic encounter.

Bordin (1980) viewed the alliance as not just a relational process but also a vehicle that facilitates counseling techniques. Therapeutic presence can provide the opportunity for the therapist to hear and respond to the poignancy of what the client is experiencing, which helps develop tasks and goals for therapy that emerge directly from the client's deepest needs and experiences. The more present the therapist is, the more the techniques and goals that emerge are in direct relationship to what is present and poignant for the client.

Presence is thus important to building a therapeutic alliance because it allows a bond to develop between the therapist and the client. The therapist is a human witness of and companion to the client's painful and challenging journey of self-discovery. The more the therapist is fully there with the client in his or her experience, the safer the client can feel in opening up to his own experience and trusting that the therapist will accompany him in his journey.

Being there with the client in the way that presence entails also provides the opportunity for the therapist to really hear on a deep level what the client is experiencing and hence develop a focus and goals for therapy that emerge directly from the client's deepest needs.

## PRESENCE AND ENHANCED AFFECT ATTUNEMENT

Therapeutic presence involves having an open and sensory-receptive experience of the client that allows for an enhancement of attunement. Intersubjective theorists see attuned responsiveness by the therapist as central to the healing aspect of transference (Stolorow, Brandchaft, & Atwood, 1987). In this view, it is assumed that affect attunement is an antidote to early caregivers' malattuned responsiveness and serves a reparative function enabling the resumption of the growth process. The concept of affect attunement has grown out of the study of infant–caretaker interaction (Stern, 1985) and has been taken up by interpersonal theorists and emotion-focused therapists as a central aspect of dealing with emotion.

Affect attunement is a particular sort of relatedness that makes interpersonal communion with the client possible. According to this view, this is accomplished by the therapist when he or she verbally or nonverbally succeeds in matching aspects of the patient's ongoing internal feeling state, and affect attunement stands in contrast to those therapist-response modes whose purpose is to influence, change, or guide the patient. Several therapist factors facilitate affect attunement. First, and probably most fundamental, the therapist must relinquish any intention of changing the patient's thoughts, beliefs, feelings, or behavior. Such intentions may prevent the therapist from being with the patient in the here and now and entering the patient's experiential world. Second, the availability of therapist attention is a prerequisite for optimally attuned responses. Preoccupations, for example with the therapist's own personal life or the patient's current problems, may distract the therapist's attention to such an extent that the material, which should be the focus of the therapist's attuned response, is lost. The attuned therapist focuses on the patient's ongoing affective experiences that are being sensed from moment to moment by the therapist through subtle or less subtle verbal or nonverbal patient displays. Therapeutic presence allows for greater sensory perception of the client's experience and hence enhances emotional attunement.

The emotional availability of the therapist, a key aspect of presence, is viewed as another crucial factor in facilitating affect attunement. The manner in which therapists make their availability known is through attentive listening, displays of interest, or a soft, responsive voice. The therapist's ability to be moved by the client's feelings is another aspect of affect attunement. As the therapist is able to access a variety of his or her own affects and experiences, the better he or she is placed to acknowledge a variety of feelings in clients. Authenticity of response is an integral part of optimal attunement and is experienced by the client when the therapist is sincerely and wholeheartedly engaged in interactions with the client. The capacity for authentic responses is also related to emotional and attentional availability. Empathic listening is often seen as a precondition for entering the experiential world of the client (Basch, 1983; Schwaber, 1981, 1983).

We have argued that therapeutic presence is a precondition to empathy and hence to affective attunement. Although the concepts of affect attunement and empathy at first glance may bear some resemblance, a number of factors render them distinct clinical concepts (Stern, 1985). First, as far as type of therapist activity or process of presence goes, affect attunement is primarily a response mode that is a particular kind of emotional responsiveness. According to Basch (1983), Fosshage (1997), Schwaber (1981), and Trop and Stolorow (1997), the concept of empathy refers to an investigatory stance of the client's experiences and not to forms of therapist responsiveness. In this tradition, empathy thus refers to a specific form of listening that views the client's experiences as its primary referent. Second, the subject matter of affect attunement includes those feeling states that are displayed verbally, facially, vocally, or behaviorally by the client in the here and now or in connection with a past incident. The subject matter of empathy, on the other hand, may include other phenomena such as motives, intentions, defenses, desires, or longings in addition to feeling states. Third, affect attunement and empathy also differ as to their primary clinical aims. By recognizing and recasting the client's feeling, the therapist aims through affect attunement to achieve interpersonal communion with the client. The aim of empathy, however, is for the therapist to come to know the world of the client, to understand what it is like to be the client under a variety of circumstances (Bohart & Greenberg, 1997). While affect attunement is more spontaneous and immediate and based on perception and action, the empathic process is more complex because it regularly involves cognitive operations such as reflection, conceptual analysis, the search for analogues, and role taking. In the process of empathy the therapist must "perceive what the client is feeling, attempt to understand their communications, imaginatively enter their world, and engage in a complex process of comprehending what it is like for that person to be that person" (Bohart & Greenberg, 1997, p. 444). To summarize, the process of affect attunement involves the therapist's accurate reading of the client's feeling state, followed by the matching of aspects (e.g., intensity, duration) of this feeling state (Stern, 1985). This type of affect attunement is enhanced by therapeutic presence.

# CONCLUSION

The essential purpose of this volume is to understand therapeutic presence in depth, to understand how to create the conditions for it, and to see it as a development of relational presence as well as an underlying and essential aspect of good psychotherapy. We propose that therapists be trained in self-development and the development of personal presence and relational presence, which are of equal value and perhaps even provide a foundation for learning particular therapy skills. Furthermore, seasoned therapists need to allow ongoing self-care and self-development and enhancement of their own presence in their personal lives to maintain a sense of presence with clients. The next section focuses on providing an enhanced exploration of the model of therapeutic presence to deepen understanding of these distinct aspects of therapeutic presence. Chapters 4 through 6 explore the three major components of our model of therapeutic presence in greater depth: the preparation, process, and experience of therapeutic presence.

# II

# THE MODEL OF THERAPEUTIC PRESENCE

# 4

## PREPARING THE GROUND FOR THERAPEUTIC PRESENCE

In the beginner's mind there are many possibilities, but in the expert's there are few.

—Shunryu Suzuki (2006, p. 1)

The first major category that emerged in our qualitative study of therapists' presence was *preparing the ground for presence* (Geller & Greenberg, 2002). This chapter elaborates on what this important aspect of presence entails and includes quotations from the original transcripts (Geller, 2001). Presence is not something that can be forced, but we can create the conditions to optimize the potential for presence to be experienced. The subcategories that emerged from our research with respect to the preparation for presence included *in daily life* and *prior to* or *at the beginning of a session*. In this chapter, we discuss practices and processes that therapists can go through, in life and in the therapy room, to enhance their sense of presence that emerged from research.

### PREPARING FOR PRESENCE: IN LIFE

At its core, presence involves a triad of relationships: being in connection with self, with others, and with a larger spaciousness. To heighten the ability to listen and connect to one's self, therapists need to create time for self-care and self-nourishment activities, such as relaxing and meditating, engaging in hobbies or activities that are fulfilling and creative, spending time in nature, or

75

pausing to listen within. The focus on self-development has been described by therapists in Orlinsky and Rønnestadt (2005) and is aligned with our findings (Geller & Greenberg, 2002). To allow for a healthy depth of connection with clients, therapists must cultivate presence in their own personal relationships, paying attention to and spending time with friends and loved ones and being with others in a way that allows for nonjudgment, acceptance, and deep listening. To access a sense of spaciousness, therapists benefit from engaging in practices that develop a solid foundation in the self in order to go beyond the self and ego, through activities such as meditating and spending time in nature, engaging in spiritual practice, or developing awareness of and thoughtfulness about compassionate values. Ceaseless efforts toward personal growth are necessary for therapists to be attuned to their baseline tool—an integrated sense of self.

### Attention to Self-Care

The baseline of and ongoing attention to self-care, personal relationships, and developing and nurturing a spiritual or value-based practice are often not taught in graduate schools or in clinical training programs. Yet programs often reference the importance of present-moment awareness in some form or other. Despite this recognition, there is little emphasis and perhaps appreciation in psychotherapy training regarding the time and ongoing commitment needed to cultivate therapeutic presence and therapists' greatest tools—their selves and their personal, relational, and spiritual way of being in the world.

The focus on techniques during training offers an easy way to learn skills for being an effective therapist. However, without a primary focus on the person of the therapist, techniques will fall flat because they are often prescribed in a rigid way. Emphasis on the development of therapeutic presence helps in the development of the person of the therapist, which will allow techniques to be offered from a deeper sense of contact with self and other, and hence there will be more flexible responsiveness in interventions as they result from awareness of the unique person and moment that the therapist is working with.

It is not just one's experience of presence that needs cultivation, but the awareness of obstacles to presence and a developed ease in recognizing and removing those obstacles. Obstacles to presence in life could include stress, fatigue, burnout, lack of self-care, overwork, unresolved personal issues, lack of presence with others in daily life, and excessive busyness. Obstacles to presence prior to entering into session or in the session itself could include preplanning the session; not taking time to prepare oneself; excessive or analytical thinking; lack of self-awareness, noisy office space or interruptions; attachment to a particular perspective on the client or what a good outcome is; and feeling ungrounded, anxious, or depressed. The cultivation of self-care and relational and spiritual values requires a high level of attention and commitment outside of the therapy room.

The Dalai Lama is a recognized figure of compassion and present-moment awareness. His fundamental values include care and compassion and harmony in one's self and in all relationships—personal, social, and political. It just takes a few moments in his presence to feel how he naturally exudes compassion and equanimity. Most people think it is his nature that exudes such calm and natural harmony and wisdom. However, a walk through a day with the Dalai Lama reveals his commitment and dedication to cultivating the values of presence and compassion. He devotes hours (at least 8 hr a day, starting at 4:30 a.m.) to meditation, learning, or discussion. Calculated over 50 years, that is 146,000 hr, which does not count all the retreats and meditative practice in his daily life!

Gladwell (2008), in his book *Outliers: The Story of Success*, reveals that it takes 10,000 hr to gain mastery in any given activity or state. How can we obtain mastery in our ability to be fully present in a helpful way for clients and in therapy without spending time to cultivate these basic yet essential qualities of therapeutic presence? The Dalai Lama has over 140,000 hr banked and is still working on it!

PAUSE MOMENT. We invite you now to pause and consider your own commitment to the time and space for the cultivation of your self and presence:

- Take a moment to stop, gently lower your eyes.
- Take a deep breath and allow your awareness to move to your belly breathing.
- Reflect on what needs greater attention in your self-care and self-development or in your personal relationships.
- State an intention as to how or what you want to pay attention to in your week, within yourself, or in your relationships. What has been neglected that is calling out for your attention? How can you bring that care and attention in, even in a small way, each day?

We now expand on the aspects that are a part of the in-life preparation for presence.

### Philosophical Commitment to Presence

A philosophical commitment to presence includes a willingness to go beyond a cognitive understanding of what it means to deeply meet another human being. This commitment involves facing ourselves and others directly, with openness, and without judgment. It also involves listening in a present-centered way not only to what is said but also to what is felt in our own bodily experience from this receptive, grounded, and open state. This includes going beyond the stories to instead paying sharp attention to our bodily felt experience, including our needs, experience, and deeper wisdom.

We often view the world through the lens of our concepts, with our thoughts constantly racing by. As therapists and academics who genuinely want to understand how to best help others, we need a level of cognitive understanding of how to be more effective. Yet when we limit our understanding of the world to what we see through a conceptual lens, we miss a keen sensitivity to all the dimensions of experience. This is equally true with our clients—if we listen only to their stories and do not attune to their in the moment experience, we miss the essence of who they are and what they feel and are trying to express. Instead, listening to their stories with a keen ear and connecting with a bodily resonance will help us to know them. This commitment to presence then includes a commitment in daily life to cultivating groundedness, acceptance, nonjudgment, openness, deep listening to ourselves and others, and attending to our bodily felt experience.

To acquire a deeper understanding of the multidimensionality of presence, we need to constantly expand and restructure our daily or weekly schedules to incorporate time to listen to our deepest self. Real knowing ultimately has to include contact with our present-moment bodily felt experience. A commitment to the philosophical value of presence includes a commitment to strive to live with the fundamental values of being receptive, open, compassionate, grounded in self, spacious and aware, and connected to self and others in service of healing and actualization.

A commitment to presence also involves holding the basic value of presence as a healthy and growth-enhancing state. Therapists interviewed for our qualitative study on presence (see Chapter 2) understood the ability to be present with clients as stemming from their valuing of presence in all aspects of life, as well as their own growth as individuals, and acknowledged the need to be aware of and involved in practices in their own lives that help to deepen and allow for the experience of presence.

## Practicing Presence in Life and in Relationships

One of the basic principles in medicine and health care in general is reflected in the famous quotation "Physician, heal thyself." This is especially true for therapists who need to engage in ongoing self-healing and "knowing thyself" to directly meet their clients and to help them to heal and directly face and accept who they are. Knowing one's self and going beyond the veils of self-illusion involve daily commitment to and practice of presence with one's self.

We cannot be fully present with others until we can be fully present and at home with ourselves. Among the most important aspects of such "coming home" is to pause and be aware of our own selves as well as to take time for cultivation of presence in life. Brach (2003) called it "waking up out of trance," as we often get in a trancelike state, such as when we are in modes that are automatic, caught up in negative or busy thoughts, or trying to get comfortable and pushing away discomfort. Waking up from trance is only possible when we pause and listen to what is really true inside, rather than living by an idea of who we are or what we feel. We cannot see or hear who others actually are or what they feel unless we are at home with ourselves and not living behind a veil of self-deception or ego.

A therapist interviewed in the presence study talked about her ongoing work to pause and to know herself by practicing presence in her own life. This allowed her to access presence with greater ease in session:

> And so calling on your presence takes practice too. And so I practice. I meditate and . . . I do things that help me to recognize presence. Well, meditation, yoga, anytime I do craniosacral work . . . those are things I would say that teach me on a regular basis to call on my presence. And practicing presence with others, not in a therapeutic setting. So practicing presence with my partner, for instance.

To be fully in the moment with another person, we need to develop and maintain comfort in being present with others in our world. Being fully present with our intimate relationships is sometimes a challenge. We often can feel more present and engaged with our clients than we do with people in our intimate lives. The therapy room can be a safer and more controlled environment in which we can let ourselves be open without revealing too much of ourselves. Yet there is a limit to how deeply we can know our clients and allow them in when we keeping those barriers in our own relationships.

There are a lot of overt and subtle levels and ways of keeping intimate others at a distance. For example, we spend a lot of energy controlling the other people in our lives as we often have an agenda for what the other should be. There are various reasons this happens—our need to be liked, to be in control, or to deflect our own vulnerability.

Being willing to look at where we sustain distance from others, through judgment or blame or protection from our hurt and pain, is integral to removing the obstacles to fully meeting another. When there is hurt in our own relationships, we often blame others for what we feel, hiding behind an illusion of self-protection. This can lead to a push-away response to protect ourselves from being hurt and in pain. We easily move into blame and judgment when something happens that causes us discomfort or pain, and every time we blame, we are distancing ourselves from others.

When we judge and blame, we are living in a contracted state of who we are and who others are. One practice, such as focusing, involves stopping, softening, and checking in on what we are feeling in our body anytime there is judgment or blame.

PAUSE MOMENT. Let us now pause to explore going beyond barriers and bringing presence to our relationships:

- Where are you carrying resentment right now in your personal relationships? Be aware of a relationship where there is conflict and resentment. Reflect on what the story is that led to you feeling this resentment, judgment, or blame. Be aware of what your thoughts are around this resentment or violation.
- Now reflect: If you had to let go of your angry or resentful thoughts, what would you have to feel that would be difficult? Sense what might be there . . . is it vulnerability, shame, deep wound, grief, fear, loneliness, despair? Take a quiet moment to feel those emotions in an accepting, nonjudgmental way.
- When you are ready, return to the breath with an awareness of softening around your inner experience.

It is often easier to hold on to our blame than to forgive. To forgive or soften our heart means feeling and moving through painful and vulnerable emotions. Yet to allow for comfort and steadiness in that vulnerability is to allow for the possibility of deeply meeting and being present with another.

## Meditation and Spiritual Practice

Therapists interviewed in the qualitative study discussed having a formal or informal practice of pausing and being attentive to the moment. Some therapists found solace in a daily meditation practice, which they described as helping to support the development and sustenance of therapeutic presence. A cognitive–behavioral therapist interviewed noted, "I do know that by far the main thing that correlates with increasing presence for me is regular meditation practice." Another therapist described the experience of therapeutic presence as being akin to a meditative state or being aware or mindful, which is a key aspect of *vipassana* or mindfulness meditation in Buddhism. In this vein, presence with the client in session is similar to "meditating with another person," and presence emerges through the present-centered relational contact.

There has been an increase in theories proposing that meditation (including practices from mindfulness, concentration, Zen, and zazen traditions, and yoga) is helpful in enhancing therapists' attention, empathy, concentration, compassion, nonattachment, equanimity, energy, and expansion of awareness, which are all important components of presence (Fulton, 2005; Sweet

& Johnson, 1990; Thomson, 2000; Tremlow, 2001; Valentine & Sweet, 1999). Gehart and McCollum (2008) proposed a training protocol for trainee therapists, using mindfulness meditation specifically, to invite therapeutic presence. The authors claimed that meditation practice helps therapists in training to reduce stress and to readily calm one's self in the face of difficult emotions so that they can access their equanimity and knowledge.

Therapists' experience with meditation can support familiarity with the experience of presence, and hence they can move more easily into being fully in the moment with a client. Meditation can also help to develop a method to recognize when they are distracted or involved in a self-focused emotion or something that is detracting from the moment. This practice, or awareness training, can help therapists to recognize with ease the source of these inner distractions, ascertain their usefulness (in cases of countertransference) or their detraction (in cases of absorption in self), and to return to the moment with greater ease. More readily calming anxiety and stress, both obstacles to presence, is an additional benefit of meditation in the cultivation of therapeutic presence.

Meditation is one particular form of a present-centered practice; however, spiritual practice or readings that support the basic values of presence are also a part of the cultivation process. In a separate study on "healing presence," exemplar therapists noted that an integrated spiritual practice is supportive for the development and sustenance of healing presence but that spirituality is not an essential component and, in fact, an unintegrated spiritual practice may be detrimental (Phelon, 2004). It is the ability to have a strong inner awareness, however, that is central to developing a healing presence.

PAUSE MOMENT. We invite you to reflect on your core and spiritual values:

- Take a moment to stop, breathe, check in.
- What are the core values that guide your decision making and relationships in life? What spiritual or humanistic principles define what you believe in?
- Reflect on what you do in your life to cultivate your values or your own sense of spirituality (e.g., time in nature, meditation, travel, reading).
- Where are you now, in your life, with respect to care and sustenance to practice the spiritual or humanistic values that are basic to your existence?
- Where is the gap between what you believe you need and your actual daily practices? How can you alter your current life to allow for even 10 more minutes a day of awareness or cultivation of these basic principles of life?

Whether it be with meditation, spiritual practice, value-based readings, or self-development, psychotherapists must continuously work on themselves to optimize presence in the therapeutic experience.

## Personal Growth

Accessing a sense of therapeutic presence, particularly qualities such as centeredness, groundedness, or feeling whole and integrated, which are parts of the presence experience, requires a level of personal growth. In particular, accessing a steadiness inside may be challenging for people who have had an insecure attachment; were brought up in a family of loss, fighting, divorce, or abuse; or perhaps experienced emotional neglect or absence. Inner stillness, groundedness, and openness are not familiar or natural places for some therapists, especially therapists in training. The truth is many therapists are drawn to help because of deep loss or pain they may have experienced in their early or adult life. This personal understanding of conflict or trauma is a gift for a therapist if there is a commitment to working and resolving these issues as well as continuing a path of growth and self-optimization. However, when the issues are unresolved, they will inevitability be triggered, in or out of therapy, and create a greater obstacle to truly being present and being a good clinician. Hence, the work of cultivating presence is based on an ongoing commitment to personal growth and self-awareness, not just in training but also in the life of the therapist.

Expert therapists interviewed described having an ongoing commitment to their own personal growth as a key aspect of preparing for and sustaining the ability to be present. Ongoing attention to their inner conflicts and relationships and adapting to change, therapy, or supervision, or just to facing directly the issues that are unresolved in their own life, are all a part of therapists' commitment to their own growth. One therapist in our study commented that presence is easier to maintain when "minimizing distraction . . . taking care of life, taking care of my own life. Ensuring that there aren't . . . unnecessary loose ends" (Geller, 2001). It is through self-care and an ongoing commitment to working through personal issues that therapists continue to tune their greatest instrument, their selves, in order to optimize effective and deep therapeutic work.

Commitment to ongoing self-development and growth occurs in the professional world of the therapist, too. Therapists change in who they are, as they are shaped moment to moment by life events and life experiences, and this in turn influences their ideas about therapy. Furthermore, new developments and ideas about human nature, psychotherapy, and change occur all the time, and it is therapists' responsibility to continue to challenge and grow their own ideas through engagement with literature or participation in workshops. Personal growth requires revisiting and aligning with therapists' own core values, enhancing these values, committing to ongoing professional workshops, and shaping ideas in the field. Therapists of all ages and experience need to recognize that their ideas and approaches to effective therapy may change as they change and develop as individuals. Time and attention are helpful in reflecting on core values, so that therapists can be in alignment with them and attain a sense of inner integration and wholeness. Hence, when therapists bring their whole selves to the therapy encounter, they include their changing ideas, experience, and professional and personal knowledge and wisdom.

Investing in personal growth to cultivate a sense of personal presence is helpful. Personal growth also enhances therapists' confidence and self-worth, which are key to being fully integrated persons who are there for the client in the healing process. Therapists' self-care enhances therapeutic presence and is a model for the client for the acceptance of the reality and challenge of being human and the commitment to looking at and moving through one's wounds to find a calm inner place that is authentic and whole.

## Ongoing Attention to Personal Needs and Concerns

By connecting with their own emotional worlds and attending to their personal needs and concerns on an ongoing basis outside of sessions, therapists enable therapeutic presence to occur in session. An interesting example comes from one therapist who was interviewed in the qualitative study. He described how having a low level of distress or sadness in his own life allowed him to show up fully in session with the client, perhaps bringing more humanness into the moment (Geller, 2001). Being connected to his own emotional experiencing was key for him to being real and fully himself in the moment with a client:

> I get nervous every time I have to see a new client. I mean I am always aware of the anxiety and so on so that there is a lot of emotional preparation that is going on before I see somebody. And I essentially experience myself as feeling very vulnerable . . . and I think that is important somehow. . . . If I didn't allow myself to feel vulnerable then I wouldn't be bringing myself into therapy.

Care of one's own self, needs, and concerns includes the satisfaction of basic daily needs. For example, having enough rest is important for the emergence of presence for one therapist in particular:

> When my energy is really low it is going to be hard for me to be present, there is no question about it, or maintain it. Because it requires energy, it energizes, and also it requires energy . . . because when I am tired and I don't have a lot of energy it is much more difficult to be present or certainly to maintain it.

This includes attending to one's own mental and physical health, for example, having good sleep hygiene, reading, exercising, and so on, and not neglecting these important facets of self-care.

Overall, there are certain conditions that make it easier for therapists to be therapeutically present with clients. Practicing presence in life and in intimate relationships, meditation or a spiritual or value-based practice, personal growth, and taking care of one's own issues and needs contribute to the ease with which one can experience therapeutic presence in session.

## PREPARING FOR THERAPEUTIC PRESENCE PRIOR TO OR AT THE BEGINNING OF A SESSION

Time for self, commitment to being still, to being present, to pausing to connect with ourselves and others—these are essential aspects of the first stage of the model of therapeutic presence. The preparation or cultivation of therapeutic presence occurs not only in life but also prior to sessions, which is the second subcategory in preparing for presence.

The first author (S. G.) had a recent supervision session with a therapist in training, which exemplifies the effect of preparing for presence prior to session:

> The supervisee spoke of his difficulty connecting with a particular client. He was feeling frustrated and uncertain of what was really going on for the client. We talked of his feeling of disconnection and difficulty attending in session. When I asked him what he does between sessions, he noted that he spends those few precious moments checking e-mail, catching up on messages, etc. Each moment was filled with busyness, until he rushed to the door to greet his client. He recognized his lack of preparation and settledness in welcoming the client. I invited him to spend the next week taking those few moments in between sessions to reconnect to himself and to prepare for presence by being still, stretching, doing a brief receptivity or grounding meditation, and briefly connecting to the client before they came in, either by reviewing notes or just visualizing the person as they prepare to welcome and receive that person, in that particular moment. The next week this supervisee came back and he was struck by the depth with which he was able to connect, understand, and respond to his client, just by eliminating the busyness just prior to session and instead taking a few moments to be still, to pause, and to set the intention to open and receive his client.

### Preparing to Be Present With the Client

Preparing for presence involves taking the time to clear one's self of personal issues, self-needs and concerns, judgments, preconceptions, plans, and conceptualizations so that the therapist can create room inside to take in the experience of the client. It involves emptying out from the self unwanted distractions so that the therapist can enter freely into the session with the client. To enter into the session in this way allows the therapist to discover the unique experience of the client at that particular moment in time.

PAUSE MOMENT. We invite you to take a moment to reflect on your own preparations when approaching the therapy session:

- Take a moment to stop, breathe, check in.
- What is your normal practice at the beginning of a therapy day or between sessions? What activities do you do? How do you spend time in those few precious moments?
- How much stillness or ritual for preparedness do you engage in?
- How can you add in 1 to 5 minutes before or between each session to enhance your sense of stillness or receptivity?
- Pay attention in the next week as you try adding in a few minutes at the beginning of the day and between sessions. Conduct a personal investigation and notice if your state of presence is enhanced. If so, notice how being present affects you, your client, and the relationship between you and your client.

## Intention for Presence

Therapists' commitment or intention, prior to session, to bringing all of their self to the client's healing experience is an integral part of preparing the ground for presence. One therapist in our study discussed his intention when engaging with a client:

> I think I have an intention to be connected, I have an intention to be involved in their healing process. I have an intention to be nonjudgmental, to be present with them, to . . . facilitate whatever process I know how to facilitate. I think I bring an intention into it.

For the most part, therapists do not accidentally or spontaneously become present, although it can happen, especially in the face of clients' strong emotional experiencing. Generally, to optimize the conditions for presence to emerge, the therapist approaches each session with an intention to be there, fully, with his or her self, with the client, and with whatever arises in session. This may involve a moment to breathe and be still prior to session. It also may include focusing one's attention and intention just moments prior to the session on being as present as possible for the client.

Another therapist interviewed in the presence study described using her breath as a focal cue to bring herself into presence. Focusing on her breath is akin to her meditation practice, the method by which she practices presence in her daily life. She describes her awareness of breath as her aid in moving inward into presence:

> Well, the breath is really taking a deep breath with total awareness. So focus on the breath, and that just anchors me. And then I'm in, in a sense. So I am totally in my body and not out somewhere. I'm in my body but I'm open at that point.

For therapists, the inner intention for presence can involve self-coaching. For example, one therapist interviewed stated, "I invite it. I invite it. I ask for it . . . when I sit down with a client I call on my presence. I take deep breaths, I call on my presence." Another therapist discussed his process of engaging in brief cognitive encouragement to bring him into presence: "A mental set I mean, and one I can just sort of just prepare myself and say, now I am going to just be here and then that works relatively well." This therapist acknowledged how the therapy room represents another external cue to help bring him into presence. By using the focal cues in the therapy room, by looking at an object or even attending to one's own body in the chair, one can invite the self back into the moment.

Returning to presence during a session when there is inner distraction or distance can also be facilitated by simple conscious intentions such as "return to the moment" or "back to my breath." Conscious intention can help restore presence, but one needs to explore whether the distraction was the therapist's disconnection or resonance with a client's sense of disconnection. Hence, a conscious intention to return to the moment is not only beneficial just prior to session but also during the therapy process. This is based on the assumption that there is familiarity with the experience of presence in one's life as well as ongoing personal and professional growth.

## Clearing a Space

Another common component mentioned by the therapists interviewed involves the act of clearing a space by putting aside personal concerns, needs, and experiences from one's daily life. This idea is similar to a first step in Gendlin's (1981, 1996) focusing process, wherein one imagines emptying out inside to create room for contact with inner experiencing. Clearing a space involves visualizing a space inside to allow the experience of the client to enter in. This allows the therapist to approach the session ready to receive the experience of the client fully without feeling distracted by other concerns that may take away from the moment of meeting the client.

One therapist described feeling a sense of "positive emptiness . . . like I am a container ready to be filled." He described actively taking time before or in session to clear a space inside:

> I would leave aside 5 minutes before a session to just meditate and clear myself . . . it's a little bit like clearing a space in focusing . . . there are dif-

ferent things, being aware of the different things that are with me and just mentally imagining or putting them aside and creating a sense in myself of openness with the client.

Another therapist described his method of clearing a space:

When I start a session with a client, I often have a sense of having to deliberately put away, put aside things that I have been doing. And I unplug my telephone, put up my *do not disturb* sign . . . sometimes I will even say to clients, "Give me a minute to set aside the things that I've been in the middle of so that I can be with you."

Preparing to meet a client through clearing a space inside is a helpful in releasing thoughts or emotional distractions and inviting one's self into the present. As noted earlier with the supervisee, we forget that these moments just prior to entering into a session can shape the direction of the therapy. The stronger the foundation the therapist has in establishing the conditions for presence prior to session, the stronger the possibility that the emergence and contact with therapeutic presence will happen.

### Letting Go of Self-Concerns and Issues

Therapists interviewed discussed specifically letting go of self-concerns or issues prior to and during a session, an extension of clearing a space (Geller & Greenberg, 2002). Again, this involves putting aside personal concerns, needs, demands, or other issues that are not related to the client's therapy process. For example, one therapist acknowledged bringing her whole person to the session with the client but leaving behind her personal "stuff" or issues. This allowed her attention and focus to be fully available to the client and the therapy process.

While putting aside personal needs and concerns can occur as part of clearing a space, it also can occur as a separate process in the session if distractions of a personal nature arise. This entails actively attending to interfering emotions or internal distractions by noting them and putting them aside to return the focus to the client and the therapy process.

Putting aside personal emotions before and during therapy does not mean ignoring emerging emotions that are relevant to understanding the client. On the contrary, awareness of one's own emotional experiencing is key to presence. However, being aware of and letting go of what is not relevant for the client and is predominantly about the self are helpful in the active process of leaving therapists' unresolved issues out of the therapy encounter. One of the therapists interviewed elaborated: "It isn't like I block off any of my internal emotions . . . but when they come up, they come up, and I am aware of them and [it's an] 'Okay, file it away' kind of thing." This therapist discussed how, at times, her own issues and concerns need to be actively put aside and how she used her awareness to return to presence:

> If I'm feeling in my own body what [clients] are experiencing and I start to experience my own grief over a death or something . . . that would not be an appropriate time to really investigate that. But it's something to file away "oh, this, this is something there for you" and then stay present with whatever is going on here. Sometimes I may feel that incredible grief, and yes I have incredible grief, too, but it is not triggering anything for me.

If an issue such as the grief mentioned earlier is mostly resolved, then we may recognize our own grief and not be overwhelmed by it.

The ability to let go of personal concerns and issues prior to and in session is built on a strong inner foundation of self-awareness and inner stability in one's own personal life as well as a commitment to dealing with personal issues on an ongoing basis.

## Bracketing

Another way that therapists actively prepare the ground for presence is by putting aside expectations, beliefs, preconceptions, categorizations, theories, and plans concerning how the session should go to enable them to approach the client with a sense of openness and curiosity about how the session will unfold. This concept is termed *bracketing* or *suspension* in the literature (Hycner, 1993; Hycner & Jacobs, 1995; Senge, 2008). As one therapist noted:

> The theory helps as long as you're not attached to it. In some way. It helps inform me but I have to remain unattached to it because if I become attached to it then I think I lose my presence.

Bracketing does not suggest an absence of learning or studying theory or using technique in therapy. Bracketing allows learned theories to be a part of the therapist's knowledge base but does not allow these theories to dictate the direction of the session, before it has occurred, without having been in contact with what is true and real in the moment for the client.

In therapeutic presence, responses may be informed by theories, but these responses emerge naturally and in resonance with the client's in-the-moment experience. As one therapist noted, the theories become a part of one's "cellular structure but not driving you to be or act in a certain type of way":

> I have a lot of working hypotheses and models in my head from previous experiences which are going in the session but I don't attach them to that person. They may inform me in that moment about my responses but that's it. That's as far as it goes. I don't actually grab hold of the person and try to pull them into that space.

This experience of suspending theories, preconceptions, and therapy plans involves openness to the client and to the therapy process as it changes and evolves. This means meeting the client as a person and not as a category of illness (e.g., depressive) and not expecting that person to act or feel a certain way based on preconceived experiences or notions. It also means letting go of the desire to control how the therapy process should unfold (e.g., "today we will speak about your father"). Instead, the therapy process unfolds moment to moment, as the therapist stays open and attuned to the client's experience and to his or her own internal experience. The process is guided by theory as well as presence, but it is the being-in-the-moment quality that allows aspects of theory, technique, or intervention to emerge in the conduit of the therapist as he or she is listening and responding to the client fully in the moment.

### Attitude of Openness, Interest, Acceptance, and Nonjudgment

The overall approach to the session focuses on being with what is real and most alive in the moment for the client. Nonpresence with respect to this quality occurs when the therapist enters the session with a particular agenda and does not allow space or an openness for the emergence of what is important to the client. By creating an environment for presence in session, the therapist meets the client in a clear and receptive state, with an attitude of openness, interest, acceptance, and nonjudgment rather than through the lens of preconceived knowledge or beliefs.

From the receptive position created by clearing a space and bracketing, the therapist can approach the unfolding session with a sense of curiosity and intrigue. One therapist described this openness as a gentle, nonjudging approach to the client's experience and the client as a person and found this nonjudgmental quality central to presence:

> I generally am present with a client in the sense that I go in without expectations, that I go in without judgment. That is, what they bring up is what they talk about. I don't judge their worth as a human being or whatever based upon how they dress or how they look or those other things. I go in with who I am and the intention to be involved in something that is a healing process for them.

According to another therapist, accepting the client as a person with a range of experience is central to presence. This acceptance is maintained throughout the session and is key to the experience itself:

> Somehow I see acceptance as a component of presence, more than empathy as a component of presence. I see that as very, very central because presence involves nonevaluative being there and just taking what is as is and taking it in and so on. So that I think presence involves nonevaluative "being with."

Some theorists have termed this quality *empty mind, beginner's mind,* or *Zen mind* (Hycner, 1993; Welwood, 2000). This means not having a particular agenda for the session but being open and accepting to whatever issues or feelings the client brings there, which in turn allows for a number of possibilities to unfold as the therapist is not fixed on one particular direction or way of responding.

Openness and acceptance imply that the therapist has a level of comfort with the unknown. Having a preconceived plan is in fact more comfortable than moving into the unknown with a beginner's mind. Yet with developed and intentional presence, therapists learn that when they can pause and be open, multiple avenues for healing emerge. This cultivation and trust of the beginner's mind is also helpful in session when there are moments of deep emotion or chaos amidst uncertainty. It is an opportunity for therapists to breathe, to return to that state of acceptance and curiosity regarding what is being experienced, and to trust that by listening deeply and responding to what is real in the moment a positive therapy direction will emerge. This state is akin to the artist who is open and empty and allows a picture to be revealed through the act of painting itself. It is through this attitude of openness, acceptance, curiosity, and nonjudgment that therapists can see the whole picture of the client and deep healing and wisdom can be revealed. This is equally true for manual-based therapies.

PAUSE MOMENT. Take a moment now to invite therapeutic presence:

- Breathe, close your eyes, and open to the moment.
- Check inside: What aspects of preparation for presence stand out to you as missing in your life or in therapy itself?
- Set an intention to add or take away what is needed within your life or therapy environment to allow for greater presence.

While we have spoken primarily of internal preparation, both in life and prior to the session, as part of optimizing for presence to emerge, attention to the physical environment or therapy room is also helpful to allow for presence to emerge. Consider the following exercise, adapted from an exercise called "Creating a Mindfulness Environment" (Silsbee, 2009, p. 234).

### Presence Exercise: Preparing the Physical Space

Take a few minutes to simply sit in your office or the physical space where you conduct therapy. Become aware of what it feels like, noticing what helps you to feel calm or present and what distracts your attention. Consider what you could do in the overall office environment to enhance presence:

- Simplify the environment and remove distractions—eliminate clutter, arrange or organize desk or office space more harmoniously, remove unnecessary piles of paper, used coffee cups, or distracting items.

- Surround yourself with beauty; include objects that reflect harmony and beauty, such as art and candles; clear window view; move therapist and client chairs so you are in view of these items or views. Minimize florescent lights, add accent lighting.
- Incorporate reminders of presence—either natural elements (e.g., plants, rocks, shells) or a symbol or object that reminds you to be present.

Consider what you could do prior to the session to enhance presence:

- Optimize a confidential and safe space—include a *do not disturb* sign, turn off phone ringers, turn off computer screens.
- Create a preparation space for clients in the waiting room: Ensure relaxing or introspective music, include books or items that encourage calm and inward attending. Try to place the chairs in waiting room to minimize the flow of traffic from colleagues, other clients, or courier or mail delivery people.
- Perhaps include a candle or object that you light or touch to support your preparation for presence before greeting your client.

Now take the time to make some of these changes. Keep attending to your physical environment and experiment with how it affects your sense of presence.

## CONCLUSION

Preparing the ground prior to or at the beginning of a session allows an optimal environment for presence to emerge. The aspects involved in preparing the ground, such as intention, clearing a space, bracketing, putting aside self-concerns, openness, acceptance, and nonjudgment, are also maintained throughout the experience of presence in a therapy session. The stronger the foundation therapists have in their own experience of presence, the more steady, open, and readily available they are to fully meet the client. This in turn can invite the client into his or her own state of presence and allow a deeper therapeutic relationship and relational presence to unfold. Next we will expand on the process of therapeutic presence while being in a present-centered therapy session.

# 5

# THE PROCESS OF
# THERAPEUTIC PRESENCE

Some stories don't have a clear beginning, middle and end. Life is about
not knowing, having to change, taking the moment and making the best
of it, without knowing what's going to happen next. Delicious ambiguity.
—Gilda Radner

This chapter focuses on the second major category in the model of therapeutic presence—the process—which reflects how therapeutic presence deepens through the therapist's and client's flow of contact and in-the-moment
awareness (Geller & Greenberg, 2002). The process of presence is what the
therapist *does* when allowing the session to be guided by therapeutic presence.
It can be thought of as the verb of therapeutic presence and reflects the therapist's intrapersonal and interpersonal process of deepening into each moment
with the self, the client, and the relationship.

The process of therapeutic presence reflects a synergy between complete
openness and connection to the other, to one's self, and to the larger relationship that is created between the two. The process involves a simultaneous
awareness of what the client is experiencing, the therapist's own in-the-
moment resonant experience, and the relationship between the two. Therapists' responses are directly informed by their receptivity and contact with the
in-the-moment experience of the client and the relationship, and how this
experience resonates in the body of the therapist.

In the process of presence, the therapist is open and attending to his or
her receptive experience of what the client is expressing. The resonance that

comes from deep listening and being with the client in the profoundness of the relationship between therapist and client is felt intuitively by the therapist, in a place where professional knowledge meets life experiences and in-the-moment poignancy. From that synergistic dance inside the therapist's awareness emerges a response that extends to the client, from the deep humanness and core of the therapist to the core of the client.

This dance of attending to self, other, and between is what the process of presence is about. It is what we *do*, when we are present, to facilitate a deepening of relational connection and self-awareness regardless of the particular theoretical vehicle we align with. We distinguish between the process of presence and the experience of presence. The experience of presence is the "being" state, what it feels like to be fully present, which we discuss in depth in Chapter 6. The process of presence is what we do when we allow the experience of presence to guide the therapy process.

In the qualitative study and model of therapeutic presence described in Chapter 2, three subcategories emerged from an analysis of the processes involved in therapeutic presence: *receptivity*, *inwardly attending*, and *extending and contact*. Throughout the session, the therapist experiences each of these aspects with different degrees of awareness depending on what is occurring at any given moment. There is no order in the experiencing of these aspects of presence—the therapist oscillates among them or simultaneously experiences all three. For example, in one moment the therapist may be in a more receptive state, open and deeply listening to the client's pain of watching her dying father. At the same time, the therapist is attending inside to his or her own bodily resonance of the client's grief and pain while listening to the place inside where that in-the-moment resonance meets knowledge and wisdom and comes together in an orginal response. This emergent response is then extended to the client in silence, words, or techniques and as an offering of the therapist's deepest compassionate self. In this chapter, we present the subcategories that emerged from the qualitative analysis along with examples of experts' statements about the process of presence (Geller, 2001; Geller & Greenberg, 2002). First, though, we invite you to pause.

PAUSE MOMENT. We invite you to generate an experience of shifting awareness that is key to the presence process:

- Take a moment to stop, gently lower your eyes.
- Take a deep breath and allow your awareness to move to your belly breathing.
- Become aware of the natural rhythm of your breath in this moment. Is it fast or slow? Deep or shallow? Just notice without changing what is there.

- Allow your awareness to be with the natural rhythm of the rise and fall of your belly as you inhale and exhale.
- Now take a moment and become aware of the sounds around you. Notice both the subtle and the loud sounds, as if you were non-judgmentally observing or listening to sound. Not reacting, just noticing.
- Allow your awareness to return once again to the rise and fall of your belly in synchronicity with your breathing.
- Allow your attention to vacillate between the feel of your breath and the hearing of sounds around you.
- When you are ready, open your eyes yet stay connected to your breath.
- Take a moment to look around the room and notice what is around you while staying connected to your breathing.

## RECEPTIVITY

At the core of therapeutic presence is the ability to be fully open and receptive, which is the first subcategory of the process of presence. Overall, *receptivity* involves fully taking into one's being, palpably and bodily, the experience of a session in a way that is kinesthetic, sensual, physical, emotional, and mental. One therapist expressed her experience of receptivity as follows:

> It's the difference between my looking out and seeing something and bringing back information and inviting whatever wants to reveal itself to me to come . . . that's the difference. And so when I say "letting it in," it's seeing, but not seeing only through the eyes. But seeing through all perceptions in a sense.

Another therapist expressed this receptive quality by opening up his hands widely as a symbol of his body. Yet another described her experience as being inviting and welcoming of whatever sensations arise from the client or within herself in relation to the client.

Receptivity implies a willingness and an ability to bring the client into one's being. It demands a conscious intention and commitment to remain open and receptive to all of the dimensions of whatever is inside and outside the self. The receiving of the other's experience takes place from a grounded and centered position within the self. The therapist hears, sees, feels, and ingests the depth of the pain and experience that is being expressed and felt by the client yet maintains contact with his or her own integrated self; this is inclusion. The therapist sometimes experiences a knowing or an understanding of the client's unsaid experience in a way that feels like there is extrasensory communication with the client. We now explore the aspects of receptivity.

### Open, Accepting, and Allowing

Receptivity involves being open to, accepting of, and allowing for the experiences that arise in a therapeutic session. Openness is an intricate part of therapeutic presence; the therapist not only enters into the session with it but also maintains or returns to openness throughout the session. The therapist is continuously clearing a space inside to open, accept, feel, and take into his or her being whatever new experiences emerge during the session. One therapist interviewed described this experience as follows:

> There's this space inside of me and I'm present with the person and that's what it's about . . . so this other stuff may play a part because it's part of me and it may come . . . and I do think about markers, and I think about even various kinds of steps and various kinds of processes but it doesn't [interrupt], it feeds the process. It doesn't, like, disrupt it or something. It's like presence and the process is kind of like the same thing . . . my availability, the process, it all kind of feeds itself. And I don't, sort of, get knocked out of being open or available.

This therapist described an allowing quality that is sustained throughout the session, and yet what is received in the process of presence further informs the response and the unfolding of the moment-to-moment in-session experience. The therapist allows the other's experience to flow through the body, as opposed to feeling threatened, worrying about the outcome of the experience, or observing the other's experience with a sense of emotional or clinical distance.

A therapist described this aspect of presence as "allowing whatever is happening to move through me, in a sense. So that I'm looking but I'm not, it's not a looking out, it's more an allowing in, in a sense." This aspect involves sensing, feeling, perceiving, intuiting, seeing, and accepting in the client, the self, and the relationship as it truly is at that moment in all its subtleties and dimensions.

> Not trying to do something with it or fix it or push it away, but just allowing it to emerge if there is something that wants to emerge. And the reason that becomes important when we're, when I'm with a client, is that whatever might be emerging might be really useful. And so that's where I get, that's where I check it out "is it or is it not [important]? No? Yes?"

The basis for being accepting to the other is to gather an acceptance of one's self and one's own experience.

## Presence Exercise: Crossing Over to Acceptance

Here is a simple yet profound exercise that can help to enhance a sense of self-acceptance:

- Find a comfortable place to sit or lie down, and allow yourself to relax your breath and into the moment.
- Imagine a difficult experience that has occurred in your life. It could be the loss or death of a loved one or a difficult interaction with a partner, friend, or colleague.
- Now imagine what it would be like to fully accept all of that experience. Notice the multitude of sensations and feelings that emerge and imagine saying a silent "yes" to each of those sensations and feelings.
- Notice what it feels like to fully accept all of that experience.

## Sensory and Bodily Receptivity

Openness often allows the therapist's and the client's experience of the session to occur on a sensory and bodily level. All the therapists interviewed reported experiencing in their body a resonance with what was occurring for the client in the session and that this bodily resonance became an important source of information for understanding and responding to the client. One therapist described feeling, sensing, and receiving in his body the other's experience:

> I will often get some sense in my stomach of what they are talking about. A sense of . . . some worry. Whatever the emotion is, I'll often get that in my stomach. I'll feel that in my chest . . . that is what I am looking for. I am looking for a sense in my body of the emotion that they are experiencing.

In therapeutic presence, the therapist's body is a receptor and a guide to the process of therapy. To take in the fullness of the experience, the therapist listens deeply to the client with his or her full sensory, cognitive, emotional, and physical being.

## Listening With the Third Ear

Presence involves listening to the client with all of one's senses and perceptions. This means more than just listening to the words stated by the client, but receiving and sensing what the client is expressing between sentences and beyond words. This was termed "listening with the third ear" by one of the experts consulted, a phrase that borrowed from the work of Reik (1948). This acute listening involves taking in all of the client's verbal and nonverbal experiences and expressions and allowing oneself to be touched by the depth of the client's experience. One therapist described this experience in the following manner:

> I think it's just not listening to the words, [it's] listening to the tone, listening to what the person's bodily experience is somehow. I know that sounds a bit funny, but somehow listening with my body to their bodily experience. I think that's crucial. I don't think you can be empathic in a fundamental way without that. That you can hear the words and you can tell them what the words are back. But if you're not really present with them, you're not still sort of getting it.

This process involves sensing and listening to what is occurring in the meeting between the therapist and the client as well as retaining a sensitivity to what is occurring within the therapist in being with the client. Another therapist spoke of this full sensory listening quality:

> I listen way more intensely, it's part of the increased sensitivity. I am not just listening to what they are saying, I am listening to how they are saying, I am listening to what they are feeling, to all kinds of stuff. And I am listening to, paying attention to images in me and hunches and intuitions. So way better listening, way better. Not necessarily at facts, like in an assessment I can hear, listen to the facts. I don't have to be so present. I can hear what they are saying, are they depressed and they are listing their symptoms and all that . . . But it is listening with all my senses.

To listen with the full sensory awareness that presence entails, therapists need to feel a sense of steadiness in their selves so they do not feel overwhelmed by the experience.

### Inclusion

To take in the fullness of the client's experience, the therapist openly enters while remaining centered in one's self, reflecting Buber's (1958, 1988) concept of inclusion. Inclusion is similar to the receptive quality of empathy, but with the added focus of contact with self. One therapist described the process of being fully receptive yet whole and centered within:

> So it's like being, feeling so steady so the client can go through all that and you are really aware of that terrible suffering, and the details of the suffering, but you feel so steady that it does not touch you.

Inclusion does not mean that the therapist is distant or absent from the client's experience; instead, he or she is taking in the fullness of the other's experience while staying grounded and connected to one's self. Although inclusion is a part of the grounding aspect of the experience of presence, which is discussed in Chapter 6, it is mentioned here because it is also an important aspect of receptivity.

## Expanded or Enhanced Awareness

Therapists also described being present in any given moment with an expanded or enhanced awareness, an additional component of receptivity. The therapist experiences bodily and sensory receptivity as an enhanced state, and what is being received has a richness and tone. This involves an expansion of awareness and includes rich images, words, bodily sensations, or other sensory experiences that emerge from an attunement to the moment. It is akin to being present to a sunset or to a beautiful piece of music. The more present you are with the sunset, the richer the colors appear. The greater stillness and receptivity you have while listening to music, the more distinct the instrumentation or voices are and the more the sounds come alive. An aliveness in sound and color is experienced when being fully receptive and present with clients.

## Extrasensory Level of Communication

Receptivity also includes an extrasensory level of communication occurring between the therapist and the client. A few therapists noted an ability to receive a client's experiences and feelings in a way that feels clear and vivid, yet they felt an inability to articulate any known or demonstrable origin for the information being received. One therapist discussed this experience as a kind of expanded or altered state of consciousness:

> I guess a sort of transcendental element in that this is an altered state, which is not a very altered state for me. I mean it's a common state that I have often throughout my life so it doesn't seem so different. But occasionally I wonder if there is something, if there is another level of communication going on . . . that is not one of our basic senses. If I am somehow picking up from a more, I can't think of the word, but extrasensory kind of level of communication. Well it's more like I don't know if it is that, but just sometimes there's sort of a sense of just being so with the other that it is as though we are kind of connected and I sort of know what is going on.

A therapist interviewed described a particular experience with a client wherein he knew and could feel what the client was experiencing even though there were no obvious clues that led him to this information. This therapist related his experience as emerging from a deep level of connection with the client:

> I was just so superconnected and there was something about her facial connection, there was something about the quality of her voice or something

about something . . . there was some empathic resonance with a place that she wasn't even expressing.

Another therapist understood this occurrence of feeling the client's unsaid experience as having emerged from a deep sense of sharing space:

> It, it also, in the present moment is the whole sense of, without the boundaries, of, you being as much a projection of me as I am of you and so, the meeting is somewhere in a much more profound, sacred space at that point . . . the feelings are, of course, shared.

A different description comes from a therapist interviewed as he described feeling like a "vessel of information . . . there's things sort of, again this is esoteric language, sort of moving through me and connecting to me." He acknowledged feeling connected to a "larger sphere of something."

PAUSE MOMENT. We invite you to pause for a moment to create an image of receptivity:

- Close your eyes and allow your attention to move to your breath.
- Become aware of what the experience of being fully open and receptive would look like in the body. Is it open hands? Perhaps it is a doorway into your heart or into some other receptive part of your body where you listen from.
- Allow your own personal image or phrase of what being fully receptive would feel like in the body.
- Spend a quiet moment with this image or phrase, really allow yourself a moment of presence to take it in so you can return to this image when you need to.

While therapists may be in a purely receptive mode, open and taking in the experience of the client at any given moment, to know, to understand, and to utilize this information require the therapist to connect with and attend to his or her own bodily experience of what is being received. This aspect of the process of presence is called *inwardly attending*.

## INWARDLY ATTENDING

The second subcategory in the process of presence involves being in contact with and inwardly attending to one's own flow of experiencing. For therapists to access their receptive experience in a way that is therapeutically beneficial, they need to be in contact with what is occurring in the flow of their inner experiencing. One therapist discussed his experience of inwardly attending to and utilizing his inner referent:

I attend to everything that's true that I experience inside of me. My own images, feelings, memories. All these things come up and they sort of inform me in the process . . . there are moments in which I'm present, I just listen to whatever arises in me.

Inwardly attending can help to identify the therapist's experience of what the client is sharing, insights, intuitions, responses, and barriers to being fully there with the client (e.g., countertransference responses, distraction, boredom, wandering attention). The barriers to presence inside the therapist can be either acknowledged and shelved for exploration at a later time (e.g., with countertransference reactions) or acknowledged as transition moments to invite one's attention back to the moment. Inwardly attending to therapists' experience takes skill and practice in self-awareness and the ability to discern what is therapeutically useful and what is a distraction from or an inhibitor of the relationship with the client and the therapy process in general. A main aspect of inwardly attending from a presence perspective is accessing one's self as an instrument of understanding and facilitating change.

## Self as Instrument

In the process of presence, the therapist uses his or her *self as an instrument* to understand the client as a guide in responding. This understanding is a synthesis of the received experience of the client with the therapist's own personal, professional, and intuitive understanding of what has been shared. This inner synthesis informs the therapist in the process in words, feelings, images, or bodily sensations.

One therapist discussed his experience of feeling and responding from his bodily sense of being with the client:

Usually I feel, in those moments of presence, I do have some sense of what Rogers was talking about, as if, the "as if," in which that what the client is experiencing I seem to be experiencing in some way . . . and often it's a bodily, a bodily sensation for me, but I'll also often find that the things that they're trying to formulate that I'll just have words for. And you know, I have no idea, of course, where they come from. But I'm not aware of doing any particular cognitive sort of processing. It just seems to rise out of my experience with them.

Therapists' inward information is experienced in images, visions, intuitions, inner voices, ideas about techniques or interventions, emotions, or bodily sensations and are experienced as corresponding to what is important for the client's process. Therapists experienced that using the self in this way supports responses that are accurate and important for the facilitation of the therapeutic process.

### Increased Spontaneity and Creativity

Therapists remarked that their inner experiences were more creative and spontaneous and had a greater number of possible responses and techniques or approaches available to their awareness. Therapists from different theoretical backgrounds expressed having greater openness to new information and to novel approaches and greater awareness of multiple perspectives when dealing with an issue. One therapist described this aspect of therapeutic presence as "doing things that could be unexpected and unconventional, unplanned."

A therapist interviewed remarked that it is the removal of perceptual limitations and boundaries that allows for more information to be received:

> Well, how it connects to presence is that it's only in the presence that everything becomes possible, that everything expands. So time expands, all the boundaries begin to disintegrate. And so, whatever is there usually, that you can't see because of the restrictions we place on ourselves becomes available.

Although presence allows for more options and creativity in responding, there is a degree of trust—and risk—involved in these novel responses.

### Trust

In the process of presence, therapists trust these spontaneous intuitions even if what arises deviates from prescribed ways of responding to clients or seems different or risky. With experience, the therapist will take more risks and will trust and respond from an intuitive sense. One therapist described a lack of attachment or control that enabled the therapist to intervene in a certain way with a client when in presence. A different therapist discussed feeling greater "creativity and a freedom, a sense of freedom to just let myself go" in presence. He noticed that when he responds in this way it accelerates the client's therapy process.

Trust and risk taking create a feedback loop when therapists risk sharing their intuitive images, insights, and inward experience. Their response moves therapy forward for the client, which allows for more trust to emerge and for taking the risk to share as intuition emerges. This risk taking and deepening of trust further allow truly novel experiences to emerge. In contrast, when not in presence, therapists may deliberate about their insights and responses as well as experience self-doubt about their own inner understanding of images, words, and responses. A therapist interviewed summed up the process of trusting within as follows:

> I always have intuitions, but I don't always trust them. I think in the present mode I don't even stop to think about whether I trust it. I just do

because I just go with it so I guess I do. But I might, when I have intuition in other modes, I might question it.

The rejection of one's intuitive responses feeds the therapist in becoming less present in the session, which can result in a client's feeling unheard and unacknowledged. A client recently told the first author (S. G.) of an experience with a previous therapist in which she kept trying to share the problems that were occurring in her marriage that were deeply disturbing to her. Her therapist kept walking her through a series of steps involving challenging cognitions, which had some relevance to what she was sharing but missed the essence of her struggle. She then saw a different therapist, who was from a cognitive–behavioral background but was more present in her approach. Although the second therapist may have been following a protocol, her responses and choice of interventions felt directly relevant to what the client expressed in the moment, and she felt there was flexibility to the protocol based on what was being shared. This client described feeling deeply understood, and she felt that her therapy process accelerated when her therapist had this level of presence, listening, responding, and adaptability.

### Authenticity and Congruence

Being authentic and congruent in one's self in the moment with the client is also a natural manifestation of presence and inwardly attending to one's own flow of experience. The therapist's feelings are available, and he or she is willing to experience them in the relationship with the client if doing so is of therapeutic benefit. Being fully one's self means first being aware of one's own feelings, experience, and intuition, then authentically expressing, verbally and nonverbally, one's authentic self.

Congruence then has two components: (a) the ability to be aware of one's own internal experience or *authenticity* and (b) the willingness to communicate to the other person what is going on within or *transparency* (Lietaer, 1993). Both are aspects of therapeutic presence, and both are reflected in therapists' discussions. Authenticity is discussed here as part of the internal awareness component of therapeutic presence. Transparency is discussed in the next section of this chapter, Extending and Contact. Authenticity reflects the aspect of being human with the other person. Although this sense of realness or authenticity in the session is of benefit for the therapist because he or she is more real inside, it is realness with sensitivity to the client and the impact that the authenticity may have on the client, as highlighted in the following excerpt:

> I do think it helps them to be safer and open up and disclose more but I
> think it is sort of a reciprocity of authenticity. But it is delicate because if I
> am too, you know, sitting there all fully present like that it is too scary or

too weird. So then it would have the opposite effect of leading them to close up, so it has to be met. So I don't think it is a good idea to meet somebody in a fully present state, like it is important to be social at first and sort of respect the normal ways of connecting.

This therapist highlighted a view of presence and authenticity that includes levels of intensity (see Chapter 7 for a discussion of levels of presence). In this vein, it is important for the therapist to be in tune with the client's level of openness and readiness to receive the therapist's authenticity and for therapists to attend inwardly to assess whether this is therapeutically appropriate. For example, if one's authentic experience includes distraction or absorption in one's own issues, it is more valuable to use authentic awareness to bring one's attention back to the moment.

### Returning to the Present Moment

An essential aspect of presence for the therapist is being aware when he or she is not present and using that awareness to return to the present moment. When such wandering occurs, important opportunities to understand and to respond to the client can be missed. Inwardly attending, however, allows the therapist to be aware of inner distractions in the moment and to bring one's self back into presence.

One of the consulting experts in our study termed the process of returning to the present moment *self-conscious presence* or *the struggle to be present*. She described an example of grappling with a difficult emotion:

> It's more like I noticed the struggle, and then depending on how the struggle resolved itself I would be present or not. If I didn't resolve the struggle, then I wasn't able to be fully present. If I resolved it on the side of cutting myself off from some of my own emotional experience, even that which I thought was relevant to the current interaction, then I was much less present. And if I resolved it on the side of "Oh well, I'll take my chances," then I was more fully present and some of what I would be present with is a sense of fear and perhaps a bit of dread of potential embarrassment or disruption.

Therapists' inward reflection on what is being experienced can also aid in working with countertransference. One therapist described a deep emotion emerging as a client was speaking of something that affected her. She took a moment to connect to her affective state, discovered that it was her own difficulties that were causing her to be struck, and hence made a conscious choice to temporarily put aside what was occurring for the duration of the session (we discuss presence and countertransference in Chapter 8). Hence, an awareness of one's own countertransference can help one to return to the moment, with a commitment to later exploring or resolving whatever issues emerged, either in supervision or with a therapist.

Being able to attend skillfully to their own experience holds numerous benefits for therapists, such as recognizing the source of distraction; accessing intuition and bodily resonances of the client's experience; and guiding the therapist in responding to the client authentically, appropriately, and effectively. For the process of presence to keep deepening, therapists' receptivity and inward attending need to flow naturally through extending one's self and being in deep contact with the client, a process we call *extending and contact*.

## EXTENDING AND CONTACT

The third subcategory of the process of presence involves extending one's self to the client and meeting and contacting the client in a very immediate and human way. *Extending* is the act of expanding one's boundaries to include the other and offering one's internal self, images, intuition, insights, understanding, or personal experience, depending on what is immediately relevant to the client's in-the-moment healing process. *Contact* involves directly encountering the essence of the client with the essence of one's self, whether in shared silence or in verbal expression. This process also involves sensitivity to the field that is created between and from the meeting of these two unique beings.

In therapeutic presence, the therapist is engaging in the complex process of attending to all aspects of the moment, including maintaining awareness of the client's in-the-moment experience and of the relationship between client and therapist, while extending one's self outward and having direct and immediate contact with the client. This section elaborates on all aspects of extending and contact, which include being accessible, meeting the client deeply and fully, being transparent and congruent, and responding intuitively.

### Being Accessible

Therapists offer their whole selves professionally, personally, and experientially to their clients and attend to the essence of their clients from the essence of themselves. One therapist interviewed discussed the experience of being accessible in one's humanness:

> This is who I really am. This is how I really feel about you or see you in the moment and that we're connected as two human beings. So that I'm not, I'm still a therapist, I'm still a professional but, in as much as it's possible for me, as far as it's possible for me in that moment, I'm being another human being with you.

In therapeutic presence, the therapist's humanness is accessible to the client, which includes offering one's whole self to the client in a direct and unmediated way. This is in stark contrast to maintaining a detached and objective stance; rather, it is having appropriate boundaries but still being subjectively connected in an I–Thou encounter.

PAUSE MOMENT. We invite you now to pause and consider the experience of being accessible:

- What do you notice about the qualities of being physically present with someone and being psychologically and spiritually present or open?
- Practice being with someone in your life and not saying a word. Allow your mind to wander, feeling yourself physically there but mentally somewhere else.
- Notice how that feels in yourself. Notice also how the other is or is not affected by your physical presence yet distant state.
- Now practice being in silence with someone, yet being in direct contact with that person.
- Allow for eye contact, practice having your attention be with yourself and the other, attuning to what is occurring in the relationship between.
- Notice how that feels in yourself. Notice also how the other is or is not affected by your full presence being in contact with them, even in silence.

## Meeting

When therapists put aside their distinction or separation from the client and instead allow their humanness to be accessible to the client, there is a greater opportunity for a true meeting to occur between them. According to Buber (1965, as cited in Heard, 1993), when the therapist and client engage in a genuine *meeting*, a new reality is created between them. It is in this new reality, this larger state of connection that goes beyond each individual, that true healing occurs. The therapists interviewed interpreted this notion by describing the experience as "sharing space" with the client, a sense of joining with the other and a dissolving of spatial boundaries.

In meeting, therapists described feeling that they have greater access to the client's inner world and a sensitivity to the client's experiences, including emotions, dreams, memories, and reflections. A therapist interviewed described his experience of sharing space with the client:

> It's more like presence, where I am operating in the space with the client. We sort of share the space. That things come into that space from my

own consciousness, my own awareness, then they move through that space . . . and there are times where I cannot get in that space.

Therapists also identified feeling a sense of "synergy" with the client and a rhythm and tempo in the interaction as they meet in this shared "sacred space." There is a balanced interaction or connection between the two, which includes the therapist not overwhelming or dominating the client and not feeling overwhelmed or dominated by the client. Although therapists described feeling a sense of merging with the client in the meeting, they also maintained a sense of separateness. In the presence process, the therapist oscillates between the dominance of feeling merged with the client and connection with and attention to one's own self and experience.

## Transparency and Congruence

When extending one's self to the client, the therapist may share his or her authentic self or genuine experience as it is clinically relevant. Transparency is the outer expression of authenticity (Lietaer, 1993). Transparency is not predicted but occurs at moments when the therapist is in contact with the client and with his or her own experience and feels it is right or appropriate to express him- or herself in service of the client. Sharing in this way, as with all aspects of expression and process in presence, is guided by both what is alive in the moment and what may facilitate the client's healing process.

A therapist interviewed described his experience of transparency in presence:

> Present as a person, this is present. Most of these experiences have to do with me self-disclosing something to the person so that I am present as a person with them. Rather than being present empathically as a listener or understander, I am present as myself and sharing my own experience of how they, of how I feel emotionally about what they are talking about or about them as a person.

Another therapist described his experience of transparency and presence:

> There are these moments where I feel present in the sense of my own person, with the person. So I might disclose my reaction to them . . . the client's been describing deep emotional pain or suffering in her life and I might say, "I feel like you don't deserve the pain that you have gone through." So I'll share a reaction, my own personal reaction to the person, to the client's life or situation that they are in.

Authentically sharing in this way can initiate a powerful healing process for the client in hearing the therapist's honest and genuine feelings. However, this sharing needs to be in direct response to the client's in-the-moment experience and not infused with the therapist's agenda.

## Intuitive Responding

The process of accessing and trusting one's own *intuition* is in some ways a microcosm or mirror of the entire process of presence. The therapist receptively takes in the experience of the client and then attends inwardly to his or her bodily experience of what has been received. The therapist's inward experience in the moment of the client is synthesized with his or her bodily knowledge of past learning and theory, and an undirected, unmediated, and intuitive response in the form of words, images, or sensations arises. Therapists trust this internal response with little deliberation and respond to the client from this internal, in-the-moment, experience. The therapist is on the edge of each moment, and he or she responds from the immediate internal experience and understanding of what is occurring and what is important and necessary in the therapy process. One therapist reflected on his experience of this process:

> Psychotherapy was an immensely difficult task in some way because it seemed to be driven by listening to my brain and it became an easier task for me when I started just listening to what my experience said to me. Sort of this multiple voices notion and so that I could be informed by what the theory said, but I could also listen to this more intuitive bodily felt [experience]. And that in actuality, the more I learned cognitively, the more this part of me became. I've also had this experience when I've been doing bodily stuff that if I could learn a new technique or something that it becomes then a part of my intuitive experience. Sort of mediated by a different process.

Therapeutic presence does not imply an absence of learning theory, technique, or technical approaches to psychotherapy. In the process of presence, the therapist does not decide prior to the session which approach or step he or she will use, but instead lets go of theories and conceptualizations as conscious guides and instead allows the response or intervention to emerge from the deeply felt experience of the moment with the client. In therapeutic presence, the therapist trusts and responds from these inner resonances.


## CONCLUSION

The process of therapeutic presence overall has been described as involving a receptivity to the client's in-the-moment experience, inwardly attending to how that experience resonates in the therapist's body, and extending and making contact with the client as a person and from his or her experiential sense of the moment. Chapter 6 describes the therapist's in-body experience of being in therapeutic presence.

# 6

# THE EXPERIENCE OF
# THERAPEUTIC PRESENCE

The way to experience nowness is to realize that this very moment, this
very point in your life, is always *the* occasion.

—Trungpa (1984, p. 71)

The experience of presence is the third major category of the model of
therapeutic presence and involves qualities of the state of *being* fully present.
The value of understanding the experience is that therapists can sense what
areas they may need to develop to heighten their sense of presence. Four
subcategories of the experience of presence emerged from the qualitative
inquiry (Geller & Greenberg, 2002). The first reflects therapists' sense of being
*grounded*, which includes feeling centered, steady, and integrated inside one's
own body and self. Second, the therapist is fully *immersed* in the experience of
the moment with the client. The third subcategory involves a sense of spaciousness, or an *expansion* of awareness and sensation while being tuned into the
many nuances that exist in any given moment with the client, within the self,
and within the relationship. The fourth is the intention for presence to be *with
and for the client's* healing process. These different aspects and their components
in the experience of presence are presented in this chapter.

A distinction between presence and therapeutic presence can made.
Therapeutic presence comprises the four subcategories, whereas presence can
exist in life without one of these aspects. For example, immersion and expansion can be experienced during a sunset; these aspects can be experienced in

art, dance, love making, or meditation, but may or may not include being grounded. In fact, presence in these situations can include a loss of the experience of self. However, with therapeutic presence the therapist does feel a sense of grounding and centeredness, being in contact with oneself, and providing a secure ground for the other. Furthermore, when we hold the intention of *being with and for the client* in service of their healing process, being present is taken into a therapeutic realm. Nonetheless, the experience of presence in everyday life can help to cultivate therapeutic presence.

PAUSE MOMENT. We invite you to return to your own personal understanding of presence so that your conceptual knowledge can blend with your own inward experience:

- Take a moment to pause, breathe, and go inward.
- Reflect on a time when you felt completely present, such as when watching a sunset or a powerful view in nature or seeing a puppy or a baby. What did you feel in your body?
- Reflect on a time when you were with a friend in distress and you felt very present and helpful to him or her. What were the qualities of that experience? Did you experience a sense of calm or being grounded? What allowed you to access that calm in the face of distress?
- Reflect on a time that you were fully present with a client, when you felt open and intuitively in sync with what the client was experiencing and your responses emerged easily and seemed right for the other. What did you feel during that experience? What allowed you to feel that way? How was it beneficial to the client?
- Jot down some of the qualities that you experienced when you were present.

We will provide further detail about some key qualities of therapeutic presence and invite you to check these against your inward experience with being fully in the moment.


## GROUNDING

The first major subcategory of the experience of presence that emerged in our research is *grounding*, which reflects a sense of inner steadiness and centeredness. Although therapists described being immersed in the pain and suffering of the other, they equally feel grounded, centered, and in contact with one's healthy and integrated self.

Grounding is a concept that is not well defined in the psychotherapy literature, yet therapists typically understand what it means to be grounded.

Grounding has been defined in the leadership literature as including "rooting ourselves in something" (Cunningham, 1992). This includes grounding in the physical (how they present themselves), spiritual (having a theory or living according to the guidance of spiritual or religious practice), professional (operating by principles rooted in a professional education and theory), and locational (being consistent in one's location). A translation of grounding to psychotherapy would include being in alignment in body and mind, with a solid and upright standing, sitting, or walking position, which may include a strong and aligned posture; with openness and solidity in one's facial expression and physical appearance (physical); with a personal spiritual or religious practice that helps guide ethical and personal choices (spiritual); with a good background education and working knowledge about therapy, change, and human nature (professional); and with a good and consistent working space for both the therapist and clients to feel comfortable and safe (locational).

### Presence Practice: Tree Meditation

The following is a commonly used grounding exercise that can be powerful for therapists and for clients. The first author (S. G.) once offered this exercise to a student who was experiencing unremitting anxiety and was about to leave school to avoid giving a presentation. A 5-minute walk through this exercise not only allowed her to complete the presentation (she also suffered from presentation anxiety) but also to obtain a sense of calm and achievement that she had not known before. Use of the following exercise or a variation of it can help to access a state of being grounded:

- Take a moment to pause, drop your eyes, and connect to your breath.
- As you inhale, imagine clean, fresh air filling your whole body. As you exhale, imagine stress and tension dropping away through the soles of your feet and hands.
- Now invite your awareness to the soles of your feet, particularly at the spot where the soles of the feet meet the ground.
- Visualize roots growing from underneath your feet (or base of spinal cord if sitting). Visualize the roots burrowing deeper into the ground, going beneath the floor, through the concrete below, through layers of soil and bedrock, pushing deeply into the earth.
- Imagine the water deep in the earth, and as your visualize your roots reaching the water, imagine drawing the cool fresh water and sustenance from the earth.
- Continue inhaling nutrients while releasing stress and toxins through the exhale.

An expansion on this meditation would be the following:

- Continue this visualization, maintaining an image of roots growing from the soles of your feet or base of your spine.
- Bring awareness to the body, imagining your legs and body as the trunk of the tree.
- Visualize your arms and head as the branches of the tree, knowing that while they sway and move in the wind, there remains a solidity and unwavering grounding in the feet and their connection deep into the earth.
- Allow yourself to rest in that sense of grounding, while we describe further aspects of grounding.

## Centered, Steady, and Whole

Grounding—feeling centered, steady, and whole, even while experiencing a range of difficult emotions—can result in *equanimity;* that is, amid the pain or challenge of difficult emotions or experiences there is a sense of calm. A participant in our research described her experience of remaining centered:

> It is being aware of your experience and not being taken by it . . . being aware, "Oh, that's what's going on" . . . on all levels, I mean you can even physically experience some sensation. But being very aware that this is just a surface experience, surface sensation . . . having much greater, much more profound awareness of silence, of steadiness, of centeredness, of just being.

There is a subtle difference between being too distant and removed from the experience of the moment and being overly involved and inside the client's emotional state, feeling vulnerable, shaky, and a loss of a separate self. The therapist stretches his or her boundaries to include the client while separating his or her own feelings, sensations, and experience:

> It's like being, feeling so steady so the client can go through all that and you are really aware of that terrible suffering and the details of the suffering, but you feel so steady that it does not touch you.

Being centered as an aspect of therapeutic presence implies an ability to experience a healthy sense of self and personal integration of body, mind, and heart, while taking in or experiencing the depth of what is occurring around us.

Centered, steady, and whole have subjective and objective elements in play simultaneously. Clark (1979) suggested that we need to be open and detached first to experience the fullness of the other. We propose that both can happen simultaneously; however, starting from a grounded, whole, and centered sense of self is helpful in allowing therapists to fully open to the depth of the experience of the client without being overwhelmed.

Approaching present moment experiences with centeredness allows individuals to discern between their painful experience and negative mental states and the awareness that the pain and negativity are not the totality of the person (Siegel, 2007). To be able to deeply connect yet discern separation from another's painful experience, one must first develop this discernment within by attending to one's inner state and one's own painful experiences with compassion and inner peacefulness. Siegel (2007) defined *discernment* as a type of disidentification from the activity of the mind, as a witness, or a deeper place of awareness where one can see suffering and difficult mental states from a place of calm and trust. Discernment also deepens therapists' ability and wisdom to interact with their clients' pain and suffering with compassion and understanding.

Being centered, much like being grounded, is focused in the body. It means inhabiting our body fully and completely and allowing it to be the foundation for alignment between the body itself, the heart (feelings), and the mind (cognitions). Training in psychotherapy is typically a mental training, with some schools of thought allowing for focusing and attunement on the level of emotions. In any case, some simple and more intricate body-based practices can help one to align internally or, at least, provide a basis for what centering can feel like. A skillful means for returning back to one's center again and again can provide an ease in session when one needs to realign in the face of emotional turbulence, countertransference triggers, or distraction. In this way, returning to center, through a bodily practice or awareness, can be an entry point for therapists to return to presence.

### Presence Practice: Core Body Centering

This exercise is adapted from Silsbee (2008), who recommended beginning in a standing posture; however, after greater mastery, this practice can be adapted, and one can begin centering while sitting on one's own or with a client. Learning to center can occur through three dimensions of the body: length, width, and depth (Silsbee, 2008). Remember, centering is an internal state, and accessing presence through the body in this way is more about aligning ourselves internally rather than a specific body workout or postural adjustment.

- Length: With both feet firmly planted on the ground, become aware of your posture and align your body in relation to gravity so that you feel effortlessly supported. Place your feet slightly apart, knees unlocked, and pelvis rocked forward slightly to straighten the spine. Sense the bottoms of your feet, where the soles rest firmly against the ground. Relax your shoulders, letting them gently drop. Hold your eyes open, letting your gaze be soft and your peripheral vision be available to you. Allow your jaw to relax. Imagine that the top of your head is connected to the sky as if it were held by a string. Allow your attention to drop to the center of gravity in your body, two inches below your navel.

- Width: Gently rock your weight from right to left. Find the neutral balanced position in the center of the width of your body. Be aware of the equal weighting on each of your feet as well as the width of your body and the space you take up. A helpful image is to imagine walking in a room, knowing that you fully belong, feeling an expansion in your chest that gives you a sense of taking up space.

- Depth: Allow your awareness to be with the front and back of your body, aligning yourself in this way. A gentle rocking back and forth, from heel and toe, can help to find a balance point. We are used to focusing on what is in front; however, allow yourself to also sense the space behind your body. Become aware of the weight and mass behind your body, as if you had a giant tail extending out from the back along the ground. Allow yourself to be supported by both the front and back of your body, allowing your belly to soften and open. Allow yourself to sense your center, that point or area that aligns you from top to bottom, side to side, and front to back.

This centering exercise can be done daily, spending a few minutes on each step. Eventually, through practice, you will develop a greater ability to shift and return to an internal centered place throughout the day.

### Inclusion

Inclusion is an extension of centered, steady, and whole, with an emphasis on maintaining a sense of one's own personal existence while entering the client's world. We discussed this in Chapter 5 as part of receptivity, but it is also an aspect of grounding, where the ability to feel whole and centered inside allows the therapist to receive the depth of the client's experience without getting lost or disconnected from his or her self.

Staying in contact with one's self in inclusion is distinguished from traditional descriptions of empathy, which focus on feeling the experience of the other *as if* it were your own (Rogers, 1957). Buber (1988) called inclusion a bold swinging of one's whole being into the life of the other. Buber (quoted in Rotenstreich, 1967) noted that "in order to be able to go out to the other you must have the starting place . . . you must be with yourself" (p. 127).

### Trust and Ease

Therapists described a sense of basic trust in one's self, in the client, and in the process when in presence. There is a sense of deep trust in all that is occurring. A therapist explained it:

> I think in this mode, in the more present mode, I won't control what I say. I think I mean I have more trust somehow in myself in that mode. Like I am really connected to the client and it just feels okay to say whatever I say. I don't question it.

Even when difficult emotions emerge (for client or therapist), there is an inherent trust that the movement of therapy is toward the positive or healing direction for the client. Even though there is often an unknown or ambiguity in what will emerge or how to proceed, the therapist maintains a sense of trust in the process and in the unknown.

Trust within one's self to remain centered and steady and trust in a larger domain are aspects of grounding. Therapists described being in touch with the unknown and accessing a sense of trust and connection that goes beyond an everyday state of consciousness. This can suggest a mystical or spiritual dimension to presence that Rogers (1980) suggested near the end of his life. The experience of accessing intuition cannot be preplanned; rather, aligning oneself with a sense of grounding and openness to the moment can allow therapists to trust what does emerge, even when it does not make sense.

## IMMERSION

The second major category of therapeutic presence, immersion, involves being intimately engaged in the client's and therapist's in-the-moment experience. Therapists experience an intimacy with the moment, and all their attention is on being with the client in this therapeutic encounter. Their bodily sense is one of high absorption, and they feel as if nothing else exists in the moment except the encounter with this other human being. From the grounded place we discussed in the previous section, the therapist is able to immerse fully and deeply into the experience of the other. Aspects of immersion are described next.

## Absorption

Expert therapists interviewed described a sense of absorption with the client and the therapy process. One of the consulting experts described what the therapy process may look like if she were observed while being fully absorbed in and engaged with a client during a session:

> You would see probably two people who are showing signs of being deeply engaged in a conversation that would be hard to interrupt. You would see a show of feelings on people's faces. I probably wouldn't be sitting back, my body would be more erect and more alert, and the auditory tone of the conversation would have intensity to it most likely. The auditory rhythms back and forth would have a dance quality to them.

An aspect of absorption is a lack of distraction by anything "outside the range of interaction with my patient" while experiencing presence. The therapist's awareness is fully engaged—emotionally, cognitively, intellectually, and bodily. For example, one therapist noted that in presence he feels "intensely involved at multiple levels. Some of which are cognitive, intellectual, and such. Some of which are emotional, bodily."

### Presence Exercise: Absorption

This exercise offers possibilities for experiencing the absorption quality of presence. Read the directions for each part and then do the exercise itself.

- Sit in front of something that really touches you. It could be an object or item of great meaning, a window view, a picture of a loved one, or a sculpture or other work of art.
- Really look at the object, view, or picture in front of you. Notice its intricate details.
- Now allow yourself to take in a small detail of that picture or item, whatever stands out to you. Notice it with great interest and curiosity.
- Now close your eyes and visualize that image. Hold it in your mind's eye, paying attention to visual detail as well as any visceral sensations that emerge in response to that image.
- Now slowly open your eyes and look again at the object or image as if it were the first time you saw it. Allow yourself to be fully aware of what you notice, what you see, what you feel, with interest and curiosity, as you look at this view or item with new and fresh eyes.

You can do variations of the exercise by choosing a body part (e.g., hand) or tasting food (e.g., a raisin) and allowing yourself to be aware as you slow yourself down enough to just see, feel, and sense.

## Experiencing Deeply With Nonattachment

*Experiencing deeply with nonattachment* reflects the changing nature of experience rather than our tendency to attach onto and grasp an experience or thought. Nonattachment reflects the ability to be with an experience that is being expressed or encountered and then to let it go. This can be especially challenging as therapists attach onto a thought they have about the client's experience and hold on to wanting to share it. What is relevant in the moment, this moment, may be irrelevant in the next moment. Hence, achieving the ability to let go, moment to moment, opening freshly again to each new moment, can be especially challenging.

Nonattachment also refers to an absence of control over what will be experienced within one's self or by the client and a willingness to enter into the unknown with the other. One of the therapists elaborated:

> So I am sitting in a place of awareness with no attachment to what might occur here. So much like I would do if I was meditating. I wouldn't be meditating going, "No, I don't want to think about that" or "I hope anger doesn't come up." Whatever is emerging, is emerging. And being present with that, without attachment.

The therapist must learn to let go so that he or she does not embody the client's experience or pain. Another challenge regarding nonattachment deals with not attaching to a particular outcome for the client. Therapists need to accept the rhythm, pace, and path that the client chooses to get to the client's desired outcome. At the same time, the therapist needs to let go of what he or she thinks is important for the client to change or experience, or even the idea that change should occur, and trust the client's innate wisdom as to what change means to him or her. This allows the therapist to care for the other and to be involved in a therapeutic endeavor to bring about a change for that person without worrying or taking on the emotional burden for the client to change. One therapist described this aspect of nonattachment as "being professionally responsible but not emotionally responsible" for the client. Another therapist described his understanding that presence means letting go of responsibility for a particular outcome:

> And I just had the sense that I wasn't, one of my issues was my being responsible for their changing. It suddenly occurred to me in, again, ways that don't make cognitive sense to me. I wasn't responsible for making

these clients, all these clients change. I was only responsible for what I brought into therapy and that was very freeing for me. It allowed me to be a lot more present for my clients. Because I was clearly attached to when to make sure, that they turned out okay. And the frame to change eventually became that I went to being, that my intention was to help them to create a healing process. Which is better, which is different than turning out okay.

The therapist is therefore able to provide the client with the opportunity to heal, if that is what the person desires, with the understanding and acceptance that what that person needs for healing must come from that person. A therapist described how he came to understand this point:

I was working in the hospital with people who were dying of various things and I became aware one day that I couldn't keep them from dying. That healing wasn't about whether they lived or not, healing was about something that happened inside of them. And in the same sort of way I couldn't be responsible for what healing really meant for a person. I became aware that healing was something different than either one of us necessarily assumed that it was and it was my task to, at some level, to bring what I could to help them be open to that healing process inside of them.

Letting go of this attachment to "curing" someone is a significant release for the therapist and in fact can allow him or her to be more fully attuned to being in a healing relationship with the client. Being fully present without attachment also allows a larger perspective to emerge for both therapist and client and opens the door to new possibilities for change to emerge.

### Present-Centered

An essential part of the therapist's experience of immersion is the ability to focus on what is occurring in the present, to be present-centered. A therapist interviewed reflected on this: "Presence means present, I was going to say, of course, it always means being in the present, and we haven't sort of talked about the nowness element of presence." Another therapist described this experience in presence as "like not future, not past." While in presence, all that exists in one's experiential world is the moment; there is an absence of thinking of the past or the future because the most important experience for the therapist when in session with the client is being with the client in the encounter in that moment:

In presence there's again, there's no judgment, there's just what is in the moment. There is nothing else, nowhere else to be. This is it. This is the moment. And so connecting with this other human being is all there is. Because that is what we are doing.

This does not mean ignoring the past or the future but rather allowing them to emerge in resonance with what is experienced in the moment.

## Aware, Alert, and Focused

Therapists claimed that when in presence, they are intensely focused, aware, and alert in their involvement with the client and the therapy session. As one therapist stated:

> I'm really focused. I am not distracted. I am not in my interpretative head or in my daydreaming head. I am not so aware of "Am I tired?" "Am I bored?" "Am I happy?" "Am I comfortable or not comfortable?" I am not focused on anything other than what is happening in the process.

Another therapist illustrated how nonpresence, in contrast, includes this sense of distraction:

> I know when I am not present with a client that things come into my mind that get in the way of my hearing them. I'm distracted or I'm not entirely listening to them. So I know what that is, that's unpleasant. I don't like that.

Greater attention to detail is a corresponding quality in presence noted by therapists. As one therapist observed, "I'm much more aware of what the client is saying. The associated affect, the associated cognitions, the subtleties of it, the taste of it, the smell of it." A therapist described his experience of being focused and not distracted:

> I think for me the major characteristic is, is not having anything else in mind so that I don't have any other thoughts or feelings in mind so that I'm just fully in the room, nothing else really exists. So I mean the room itself doesn't really exist. So somehow I am just in contact with the other person and attending to whatever might be going on there, you know, and in the moment.

We know that this full-focused attention cannot always be sustained, yet it is equally important to be aware when one is not present. Awareness of distraction is a good indicator that can call attention back to the present. This awareness can be developed through awareness training.

## Presence Practice: Calling Our Attention to the Moment

The following is a simple yet profound awareness exercise that can enhance focus as well as train ourselves to bring our attention back when it wanders. Ideally this should be practiced on a daily basis, starting 5 minutes at a time and increasing to longer periods (e.g., 20 or 30 minutes) to deepen practice.

- Close your eyes, attune to your breath. Find a place in the body where you experience breathing the most, perhaps in your belly or chest.
- Pay attention to the rise and fall of your belly or chest, as it moves with the breath.
- When your mind wanders, as it will, notice the wandering, name it using one word (e.g., thinking, planning, worrying) and then invite your attention back to the breath.
- Just as in training a puppy, when you invite the puppy to sit it runs off; and you again invite the puppy to return and sit, and you do this again and again. In this way, we can train our attention to return to the moment, by inviting it back again and again.
- Practice paying attention to your breath when you notice your mind go off, trying not to get involved in the story of what you are thinking about, but instead name it with one word (e.g., thinking, planning, worrying) and continue to invite attention back to the breath.

Through the development of greater immersion and an ability to maintain a sense of grounding in the body, we can open to a larger sense of expansion in feeling, awareness, and sensation.

## EXPANSION

A sense of inner expansion, both on a bodily level and on the level of consciousness, accompanies presence. Therapists interviewed described a sense of spaciousness and even joy that is the backdrop to all felt experience. There is immersion in the details of the suffering accompanied by a larger sense of flow and energy and calm.

Therapists described an expansion of consciousness wherein the details of expression and experience are more vivid and acute than usual. Thoughts and emotions of self and other are sensed on a subtle level where the quality and experience are palpable and kinesthetically alive. Awareness of self and other's experiencing is likened to hearing a pin drop in silence or seeing a feather float to the ground.

Theorists who have incorporated an Eastern framework have recognized an expansion of awareness as key to accessing wisdom and multiple avenues from which to approach the client. Chung (1990) described an expansion of awareness as going beyond the self or ego. This facilitates a superior state of concentration and focus that stems from direct contact with the true nature of self. Going beyond or transcending the self is possible only after first accessing a healthy and mature sense of self (Geller, 2003). Then the dissolution of the ego can be a positive spiritual state rather than a destructive or psychologically harmful state. The more skilled the therapist becomes at expanding awareness, the more clearly the therapist can see the client's experience and reality, and hence greater possibilities in responding open up.

### Presence Practice: Expanding Beyond the Boundaries

The following exercise will help you to expand beyond your boundaries:

- Settle yourself into a seated or standing position. Allow yourself to attune to your breath.
- As you breathe, become aware of expanding your diaphragm as you inhale and releasing deeply as you exhale.
- Open your eyes slightly and allow your attention to be with your physical body.
- Pick a body part that is visible and allow your awareness to be with that (e.g., hand, finger, ankle). Notice the details of that part of your body.
- Now shift your awareness slightly to notice what is just around your body, perhaps seeing the different colors and shapes of whatever is within a two-foot radius.
- Allow your breath to expand into the space just around your body.
- Now invite your attention to expand, noticing a larger image, such as the room or area where you are right now. Notice what is present in that space. Allow your breath to be attuned as you become aware of what you are feeling and the look and details of all that is around you.
- Allow your awareness to expand even further. Perhaps go even further to the space around the building. Keep expanding your awareness, including other parts of the town or city where you, to an awareness of the country, to the rest of the world. Include in your expanded awareness a sense of the water bodies (e.g., lakes, oceans) and mountains of the continent you are on.
- Keep expanding awareness outward, even going beyond the earth's atmosphere toward the sky, constellations, the sun, and the moon.
- Allow your breath to expand in synchrony with your awareness of space all around you as if in a vast ocean of awareness.
- Imagine extending your awareness downward toward the earth's core to the center of gravity. Allow yourself to imagine

a connection to an even subtler level of universal wisdom or collective unconscious or an actualizing tendency.

- Allow your awareness to vacillate between your own body and the space around you, above you, and below you. Become aware of the contact place between yourself and other sentient beings, including animals and people from all across the world.
- Rest in that deeper sense of expansion and connection.
- When you are ready, slowly bring your awareness back to the body, back to the breath.
- Feel your feet on the ground as you integrate that experience, returning to the breath.

Spend a few minutes integrating that experience and reflecting on what an expansive quality means to you. When have you experienced this quality in your life? How would accessing this state be beneficial to you as a therapist? We now explore additional aspects of expansion.

### Timelessness

In presence, there is a sense that the movement of time does not exist, a sense of timelessness. Instead, time and spatial boundaries seem to drop away and the experience is one of merging with one's self, with the other, and with a larger field of energy. One therapist expressed this quality of presence as

> the transcended awareness, in that the experience becomes one that's much larger than thought. So it becomes a somatic experience. It transcends temporal boundaries, spatial boundaries, so that the feeling of being with this other person is a feeling of being in a timeless place.

Therapists' descriptions focus on their being unaware of the passage of time or of the space around them while engaging with the client. One therapist described this sensation as an "eternality" that is an essential and irreducible aspect of presence. She explained that "timelessness is a quality that you can't have if you are . . . self-consciously thinking."

Another therapist described "forgetting time and space." Complete engagement in an activity that relates to this loss of awareness of time and spatial boundaries is akin to the flow experience described by Csikszentmihalyi (1990). The lack of time awareness was noted by a therapist interviewed as varying in degree, relative to the degree of presence:

> And of course time, that's another part of it because I don't experience time particularly. There could be other times where I am looking at my watch thinking "Well, 30 seconds has gone by and that's it." You know I'm looking at my watch, looking at my watch, looking at the time. Other

times, 15 minutes gone, without any sense of time moving. No time perception at all.

While timelessness is a part of the presence experience, in the state of nonpresence, such as when you engage in frequent time checking, you have an opportunity to pause and gently invite awareness and attention back to presence.

## Energized and Flowing

As we discussed in the Introduction, being in therapeutic presence facilitates a healthier and more alive state for the therapist and for the therapy process. Therapists noticed a feeling of energy and flow, a sense of inner vitality that accompanied presence:

> There is an aliveness and it is very contactful. So there is high excitement and it comes actually right from my genitals right up . . . I mean it is a very full-flowing feeling, right, and it's very interpersonal. I mean they are all characterized by "nothing else is going on." Everything is just whatever is in the moment.

This sense of vitality is described as heightened energy with a vibrancy felt in the body while one's breath feels open and easy, an experience of calm alertness. The therapist quoted above described a feeling akin to sexual energy—not toward the client or any particular object but a heightened energy that is a part of his bodily sense. Another therapist interviewed discussed a similar feeling of warmth or heat in his body while in presence. A third therapist noted that her breath felt slow and deep during presence, while at the same time she felt heightened energy:

> There is kind of a relaxation quality to being present where there is sort of an openness and things are flowing through me rather than me trying to do anything so it is a spontaneity quality. I think I am sort of aware of feeling just very open so there is a flowingness to it and I don't know if that could be observed but I think the sort of flowing quality is very important. I mean, I guess that would go along with the feeling part or the sensation part. So everything flows and there is a real flow experience.

This sense of energy and flow is partially how presence sustains energy and prevents burnout.

## Presence Exercise: Holding the Suffering With the Love

The following practice is adapted from work by Rick Hanson (2009):

- Bring to your awareness a positive experience. Perhaps it is an experience where you felt strong, whole, happy, or a larger sense of love and belonging.

- Allow yourself to connect with the bodily feelings of being whole, happy, and at peace.
- Now bring to your attention a negative or painful experience.
- Allow yourself to be aware of the love, strength, and wholeness and the pain and suffering. Notice how you can hold both of love and pain in your awareness.
- Allow the love and strength to hold the pain and suffering, and notice what it feels like.

The sense of energy and flow that accompanies presence allows the therapist to fully be with the pain and suffering of the client, while feeling a deep sense of calm, trust, and spaciousness.

### Spaciousness

An aspect of expansion is a feeling of spaciousness within the body of the therapist as well as beyond the boundaries of the therapist's self or body. The feeling of spaciousness within oneself is described as a bodily sense of openness or expansion:

> I have a sense of openness, clearing . . . it's not a hold, but a clear space. There is room for the client. Those are all metaphors. What does it feel like in my body? Like an easing, like a letting go, like letting a breath out, all that.

In the preparation for presence, we presented the process of clearing a space as an active part of preparing for and inviting in the experience of presence. However, once presence is manifest, inner spaciousness becomes the essence of the experience itself, which, in turn, helps to maintain and deepen the experience of presence.

The second dimension of spaciousness refers to the feeling of connection to something larger, which reflects a spiritual domain. This spacious quality is suggested in Freud's "oceanic feeling," which he originally described as the sense of boundlessness and oneness felt between the ego and the outside world. Buber (1958) described this sense of spaciousness and connection as being a part of a larger existence. He noted that it was suspending judgment and being with the now in the moment that allowed space for the numinous and spiritual dimension to emerge (Hycner, 1993).

### Enhanced Awareness of Sensation and Perception

A heightening of sensation and perception also accompanies this expansion quality of therapeutic presence and reflects when feelings, bodily sensations, and intuitions are experienced with greater depth and palpability than is typical. One therapist interviewed shared how this experience, for him, involves a heightened visual perception:

> I mean I am just visually highly aware . . . it's like I can see a speck of dust floating down between us. I mean I am very there, right. In the feeling state, I don't think I am so visually, there is not such visual acuity . . . I wouldn't see something coming between us because my focus is sort of very focused usually on the person and on their face, right? But I would see their eyes, anything twitching, I mean I'd see things, I'd see their skin and so on. So there's a visual acuity that goes with it.

In addition, the therapist's own thoughts and feelings and the imagery that is stirred by what the client presents are experienced with greater subtlety and sharpness than during nonpresence states:

> And so perceptually the patient is vivid for me. The sound of their voice is vivid, the imagery that is created by what they are saying is vivid, their affective tone is vivid for me. Sometimes it is not clear to me who is feeling what. In certain moments it doesn't matter who is feeling what, it is just in the room.

## Enhanced Quality of Thought and Emotional Experiencing

Similarly, there is an enhanced quality of thinking and emotional experiencing when in presence, whereby thoughts and emotions are highly detailed and reflective of what is necessary and helpful to the client. As described by one therapist:

> My senses are more alive. My cognitive sense, my thinking, my emotional, my awareness of the body, and all those kind of stuff. I am more sensitive, in connection to the client. It's resonance kind of sensing.

The therapist's thoughts are clearer, sharper, and focused on the client or on what is most immediate. A therapist talked about an absence of reflection or deliberation, enabling him to focus on what is emerging and relevant to the experience of the moment:

> I certainly have thoughts while this is happening, but the thoughts will be very much about what is going on. It will be my understanding of it, what is happening for the client. "It's fear, I can see the fear," and even that, I don't think I do a lot of that. There is not all of that self-reflection. What I mean about metacognition is thinking about my thinking. Analyzing, interpreting, figuring out, deciding, weighing alternatives. I do that sometimes as a therapist but a lot of times I don't do that when I am here.

While we have described presence as including grounding and immersion as well as this sense of expansion, they are not the whole experience of presence. Most important, therapeutic presence is guided by the intention to be in service of the client's healing process.

## BEING WITH AND FOR THE CLIENT

Therapists are not just present for the sake of being in the moment but present *with and for the client* in that person's healing process. Therapists' actions and expressions are in the service of helping this other person. Being with and for the client includes the experience of seeing the inner nobility and the inner wisdom and wholeness that lie deep within the client as well as the pain and disconnection he or she may be experiencing. It is being able to be with clients with full acceptance and care, taking in the depth of their experience, while they uncover layers of their pain and suffering. It is to have the capacity to stand grounded while they cry and bleed, or roll up in a ball, or put up a wall, while still seeing the true inner beauty and wisdom in the other. It is meeting all the layers of the other person, completely and fully in the moment, from a place of spacious acceptance and a steady ground, and offering acceptance and care and compassion.

It is natural for us to shield ourselves in the face of suffering. Our instinct is to put up barriers, even subtle ones, to really meeting the client. We can hide behind the shield of our professional name or the clipboard or perhaps behind our own egos or inner wounds. Therapeutic presence demands that therapists engage in deep inner work and mastery to put down that inner shield and really allow the other in, without judgment, blame, or distance. Being fully with and for the client, and facing the intensity and waves of clients' pain or defense, demands an inner steadiness and commitment to being and showing up fully. Being steady does not mean being detached, but rather steady and deeply connected to the other from a compassionate, caring, and loving place.

The capacity for compassion for another human being demands self-compassion; to develop compassion for others requires the initial work of self-compassion. Our ability to be fully there with another is limited by our ability to be fully there with our own self and our own experience with acceptance and presence.

### Presence Practice: Cultivating Self-Compassion

The following exercise, adapted by Brach (2003), helps cultivate self-compassion based on forgiveness:

- Take a moment to pause, breathe, and go inward.
- Allow yourself to become aware of a situation or a relationship for which you hold anger, resentment, or blame. It could be a current ongoing situation or a past unresolved situation.
- Allow yourself to become aware of what is underneath that anger—explore your more primary emotions such as vulnerability, hurt, or shame. Feel the dimensions of those emotions in your emotional and physical bodies.
- Offer self-compassion to those primary feelings in you. Through words or inner gestures, try being compassionate, accepting, and deeply loving to your inner vulnerability or pain.
- Be aware of whether there is a struggle within you and offer that struggle compassion, care, and love.

Through the experience of self-compassion, we can generate a greater capacity for staying present and compassionate toward others' pain. Being truly present for another in the psychotherapy encounter begins with holding the intention for our presence to be with and for client's healing.

### Intention for Client's Healing

While the intention for the client's healing occurs before stepping in with a client, it can also be returned to within one's self throughout the session. This intention is described in the following:

> I think I have an intention to be connected, I have an intention to be involved in their healing process. I have an intention to be nonjudgmental, to be present with them, to facilitate whatever process I know how to facilitate. I think I bring an intention into it. It's more clear to me when it doesn't arise.

This therapist also expressed confusion between his intention to be there with a client and the interference of being consciously aware of holding that intention when in presence:

> I go in with who I am and the intention to be involved in something that is a healing process for them. And that sometimes, in my awareness that I have right now, intention is helpful in my presence, with them, that there is something that occurs when I am with them that facilitates things moving and happening and their deepening their self and sometimes my intention gets in the way. I haven't really quite figured this out.

This confusion between the therapist's intention being helpful and not helpful was clarified later in the interview as differentiating the intention to be in a healing process from the intention of facilitating a particular outcome. The intention for healing does not mean knowing what the client needs or what a particular outcome should be. Rather, being with the client in his or her pain and suffering with the intention for healing allows for what that person needs to emerge from within that person's core, in his or her own unique way, rhythm, and style.

The experience of presence allows therapists to attend to and embrace the wholeness of the client, to really experience and know the client's true nature, which is whole and pure. Recognizing the inner wholeness of a client enables the therapist's responses in presence to focus on honoring and uncovering the wisdom in each person. This is described by a therapist who noted presence as being "more selfless. You're more selfless in that process. Less of the curiosity for your own curiosity needs . . . closer to the ideal of 100% of the stuff of therapy being oriented to the patient's goals." Another therapist referred to the intensity of his experience as "other focus":

> I am not focused on anything other than what is happening in the process. What has the client talked about, how is the client coming across, what is going on for the client. It is really very much an "other focus." And I guess to some degree the relationship, but it kind of feels I am more really connected to the client.

With this "other focus" in therapists' presence, there is often a natural emergence of respect, awe, and compassion.

## Awe, Wonder, Warmth, Compassion, and Love

When the therapist's intention is being with and for the client, he or she may experience feelings of awe, wonder, warmth, compassion, and love. The therapists interviewed used terms such as "compassion," "caring," "profound respect," "awe," and "admiration" to describe their feelings toward the client when in presence. A therapist interviewed described this feeling:

> Just awe of, I mean a wonder, struck, I mean they are so wonderful. I mean I am sitting there and saying thank you God for showing me another wonderful person. So often you have that experience of being grateful to be shown wonders of another being. And I think that is really why it all works. It doesn't have to be expressed verbally, but if you really feel that another person is so wonderful, you truly, truly experience it, somehow that person picks it up at some subtle level and starts to feel wonderful.

Seeing the wonder and beauty in the client offers the client the opportunity to begin internalizing that sense of inner acceptance and love.

**Presence Exercise: Seeing the Inner Nobility**

This exercise will help you see the inner nobility of other people:

- Begin by pausing, going inward, and paying attention to your breath.
- Allow your attention to pull your mind and body together by bringing your attention to the physical body and breathing deeply into your core. By opening up the diaphragm through breathing, visualization, and focus, we are in fact opening up our core.
- Now allow the faces and images of different people you know to appear in your mind's eye. Some people imagine a screen inside to help this process, either in the diaphragm or between the eyes. See each person as he or she passes, nodding slightly as you witness and truly see the wholeness and nobility in him or her.
- Begin by seeing someone you love, a family member or friend. Allow yourself to nod in reverence of their pure nature and inner nobility.
- Now allow the image of a person with whom you share a difficult relationship to emerge. Imagine seeing that person in the screen in your mind's eye or in the center of your body. Nod slightly, acknowledging and sensing the pure wisdom and nobility in that person.
- Imagine a client with whom you struggle or feel some level of judgment or distance, notice and nod to that person's inner wholeness and nobility.
- Now imagine yourself at the center of that screen or image. Nod gently, honoring the pure wisdom and nobility within.

Take a moment to pause and see the feelings that arise and, perhaps, the struggle that emerges to see that inner wholeness and nobility, particularly in the face of someone you have difficulty with. Notice the barriers to that acknowledgment. What do you need in order to go beyond those obstacles to really seeing the wholeness in that person?

The sense of compassion, respect, and positive regard toward the client occurs in therapeutic presence because the therapist is in an open, accepting, and nonjudgmental state. For example, one therapist related that in presence, "internally I am experiencing profound respect, incredible compassion, and a willingness, openness to whatever is coming up." It is this warmth, admiration, awe, and respect toward the client that in part allows the client to feel safe and supported in his or her inner work.

## Absence of Ego Involvement or Self-Consciousness

Therapists discussed having a lack of self-conscious awareness or ego involvement in oneself as a therapist, professional, or any other label that would interfere with being wholly there in the moment with the client:

> I think what would be the absence of certain things that would indicate presence, is the absence of, in more general terms, what we'll call an ego, a sense of the self. It's very obvious when you start to do psychotherapy. I recall, "Why did they come to me? I mean such a big problem they could go to that person, they are so much better." So it's thinking about one's own capacity, lack of it, or even thinking "I'm so great." It's also the "I." This is an indication that there is less awareness of the self in presence.

As this therapist indicated, the awareness of ego involvement or self in a judgmental or ruminative way is an indication that one is not in presence:

> The times in which I feel less present are when I start to become more aware of myself . . . more aware of connecting back into, wondering "What's going on?" "Why aren't we, we don't seem to be in sync with each other," I don't seem to be able to connect to where the person is. I don't seem to be open to the person . . . is there some part of me that is disconnecting.

The awareness of self can be an opportunity to return to presence or perhaps reflect on a deeper level one's countertransference responses that may be causing a level of self-consciousness. This requires a high level of self-reflection on the part of the therapist.

Therapeutic presence also includes an absence of rumination about self-concerns such as pain, fatigue, or physical appearance, as one therapist related:

> . . . and really the intensity of my lack of self-awareness. My lack of my body because for me when I am not present I am aware of "my shoulder's sore or my neck isn't, I feel like stretching or I am not comfortable or my tush is sore," "I don't know what is going on here." "I don't know how to help this person," "Why is this person coming to see me?" "I don't think I should be a therapist," all this kind of other, these distracting kind of things.

Awareness of self-concerns, doubts, or other self-focused thoughts or feelings that are not relevant for the client's process is an indication that the therapist is not in presence. It may also reflect a disconnection within the therapist and hence an opportunity to return to the moment:

> Sometimes those things happen because something a client says races off something that is unfinished within myself, for instance. And I sort of

regroup myself and do whatever I do with that thing, and move back into presence with a client.

The qualities of therapeutic presence, such as lack of concern with the self or intention for healing, optimize the therapy process and offer an opportunity for deepening a connection with the client.

## CONCLUSION

The in-body experience of presence is not any one of the aforementioned qualities in isolation. Rather, it is a combination of being grounded, immersed, spacious, and with and for the other that makes up the whole experience of being fully in the moment with a client. Understanding the larger categories as well as the details of the in-body experience of therapeutic presence can help therapists to begin to recognize what aspects of therapeutic presence may need to be cultivated. For example, practice and the ability to generate an awareness of being grounded and centered can allow therapists to shift slightly in session when they need to reground themselves. Practice in bringing one's attention back to the moment can help therapists to easily recognize distraction when they are with a client, understand the source (i.e., countertransference), and bring their own attention back swiftly.

The next few chapters build on the model presented in Chapters 4 through 6 by providing alternative views and perspectives on therapeutic presence and include seeing presence in levels, exploring the challenges to therapeutic presence, and examining the neurobiological aspects of therapeutic presence.

# III

## ADDITIONAL
## PERSPECTIVES ON
## THERAPEUTIC PRESENCE

# 7

# LEVELS OF THERAPEUTIC PRESENCE

Stillness, insight, and wisdom arise only when we can settle into being complete in this moment, without having to seek or hold on to or reject anything.

—Jon Kabat-Zinn (1994, p. 54)

In describing the experience of therapeutic presence in Chapter 6, we explored the intensity of experience in those profound presence moments within the therapist. To arrive at the optimal depth of presence, therapists often have to go through a path of deepening in themselves and in relationship with the client. Once contact is made within one's self, therapists' presence can move outward toward the client and deepen at different levels of relational contact and sharing.

In this chapter, we present an applied view with respect to becoming present before a session and toward deepening into presence when in session with a client. We first provide a four-step sequence to help therapists in preparing to become present prior to a session. We then apply a five-level model to relating with therapeutic presence in session, which includes moving further into relational presence through a deepening in contact with the client and the presence process. While being present may start at the surface contact with the client, this state unfolds to a deepening of presence that allows for greater psychological and, perhaps, spiritual contact within the relationship. To set the foundation for viewing levels of therapeutic presence, we first discuss presence as a continuum.

# PRESENCE AS A CONTINUUM

Although we have spoken about presence as a state of being and relational stance, we do not view presence as a concrete state that one either has or does not have throughout the course of a therapy session. For example, one therapist in our qualitative study stated:

> I think it is degrees also; it is not am I present or not. It's [the] degree to which I am there. I would say that it is almost an intensity continuum in terms of the presence . . . the intensity of my connection, the intensity of my focus, the intensity of my concentration and empathy, and really the intensity of my lack of self-awareness.

The opportunity to be in the varying intensities of presence is there all the time, although as therapists we are not always aware of this within ourselves. One therapist noted:

> I think presence is there all the time, it's just realizing it or experiencing it to different degrees. I think it is a sensitivity that grows within the person, more than a skill. It's a sensitivity to something that is there.

In this perspective, presence is a state that we can experience at more or less different degrees of intensity as we open to a greater sensitivity and relatedness with the other.

# LEVELS OF THERAPEUTIC PRESENCE IN PREVIOUS MODELS

There are various depths or levels of presence; for example, a greeting at the door would be a lighter version of presence than a profound interpersonal experience with the client, which would reflect a relational depth of presence. We are inspired by the nursing literature here in reexamining presence in levels.

Gilje (1993) provided a model of presence that describes the deepening in the experience of presence itself as nurses go from managing patients' rooms without making much contact or bringing much awareness of the person into their activities to making emotional or psychological contact during an exchange with their patients. As they deepened into the connection, a larger sense of transpersonal presence revealed itself. Nurses described transpersonal presence as going beyond the immediate connection with the patient to a larger sense of spirituality or vitality with all of life. Gilje (1993) described these three levels of presence as intrapersonal, interpersonal, and transpersonal presence.

Osterman and Schwartz-Barcott (1996) extended that perspective to describe four levels of presence for nurses: physical presence (e.g., reading a book in the room with a patient); partial presence (physical presence plus focus on a task relevant to patient; e.g., reading to the patient or changing an IV); full presence (partial presence plus attending and listening to the patient); and transcendent presence (beyond the two individuals and into the spiritual realm; i.e., having a mutual experience of "oneness"), in which both people experience peacefulness, calm, positive change, and transformation. Furthermore, the authors argued that full nursing presence is anchored in reality but that transcendent presence is devoid of boundaries and limitations and has the potential to transcend reality itself. In this fourth level, the nurse recognizes a sense of oneness between the self and the patient.

Integrating the perspective of levels of presence from the nursing field with the current model of therapeutic presence creates a view of presence that deepens as contact is made in a psychotherapeutic context. In this vein, presence can be viewed as a top-down process that occurs in two stages: prior to the session itself and in session with the client. An exploration of levels of therapeutic presence in psychotherapy provides an understanding of the different degrees of presence that unfold as therapists deepen into the moment within and with their client.

## A FOUR-STEP SEQUENCE TO BECOMING PRESENT PRIOR TO THE SESSION

Therapists can prepare for and deepen presence before the client walks through the door by

1. arriving,
2. preparing the ground,
3. touching ground with self, and
4. preliminary contact with the client (notes, etc.).

*Arriving* in the present moment means inviting or intending your whole being to be present as well as preparing the physical space to welcome the client. The former includes bringing yourself into the room, taking care of any physical needs (washroom, hunger, thirst, clothing for warmth, or air conditioning), and arriving in your body and mind as well as physically being in the room. The latter includes turning off telephones, adjusting temperature, removing clutter, and closing computers and any other devices that may act as distractions.

*Grounding in the body* means making contact with a steadiness in one's self. This could be done through a few moments of feeling one's feet on the ground in a standing position or perhaps one of the centering techniques we presented in Chapter 6. It could also include taking a few breaths to calm your nervous system and to enhance equanimity within. A gentle body scan could also support grounding: scanning your awareness through your body, starting from the toes up through each body part, and allowing the awareness of each body part to support a gentle release and softening of any tension. Being in contact and fully in your own self and center can help to prepare to open to the depth of whatever the client brings in, without attachment or feeling overwhelmed or shut down. Grounding in the body also helps to create contact with your own self and sensations so that attending inwardly and using the self as a sensor of what the other is experiencing flows naturally and easily.

*Clearing a space* means putting aside any personal issues or preconceptions the therapist is experiencing. This can occur through consciously visualizing putting one's issues or needs on a shelf, knowing that you can return to them at another time. Clearing a space can also involve letting go of tension in the body and mind as well as creating a greater sense of spaciousness in one's self through deep breathing or expanding one's awareness to the space in and around the body. Clearing a space, along with grounding, can help to support a state of nonreactivity and prepare an open, receptive place to take in whatever experience or emotion the client brings into the session.

*Preliminary contact with the client* could include looking at notes from the previous session or just imagining or visualizing the client on a physical, emotional, and energetic level and preparing to meet this unique other before he or she walks in the door. This does not mean creating plans or preparing what to speak about in session. Instead, it means connecting with a sense of the person before meeting him or her, perhaps by recalling a past conceptualization of the person that can be triggered in consciousness and let go of when this person is actually met. Preliminary contact can create an awareness of prior experience with this individual (or if the client is new, a recall of a phone contact you may have had) so that it is accessible in session if something emerges in the moment that is relevant. After this preparation process, there is a readiness to walk to the door and greet this other unique being, with a focus on the present, opening and connecting with the other.

The path to becoming present prior to the session allows for presence to begin with the other moments before actually meeting him or her so that the therapist is ready and accessible to the client. This process does not need to be long—it can take just 5 minutes—but what it gives back in terms of the ability to be present with the other is tremendous. These gentle pauses allow for presence to emerge more easily.

## FIVE LEVELS OF DEEPENING INTO PRESENCE IN SESSION

Drawing on the Osterman and Schwartz-Barcott (1996) model of presence, we present a model of five levels of presence contact that occurs from the moment of meeting the client, which begins from opening the door to this unique person in this unique moment:

1. physical presence (light presence)
   a. contact with other—light presence (superficial or small talk)
   b. settling into the room/chairs
   c. awareness of own body (present moment awareness, contact with chair)
2. psychological presence (partial presence)
   a. hearing the story, checking in
   b. listening, attending, attunement, caring, openness, and interest
3. emotional presence (presence with and for the other)
   a. understanding, compassion, acceptance, empathy, unconditional positive regard
   b. responding or providing intervention or empathic response in resonance to what the client is sharing
4. transpersonal presence (presence with spirit)
   a. body as a vessel
   b. contact with deeper connection between therapist and client
   c. contact with deeper intuition
   d. contact with spirituality (vitality, enhanced sensation, and perception)
5. relational therapeutic presence (all the levels)
   a. vacillating (dancing) between what is needed in the moment of deep contact with self, with the client, and with a deeper spirituality and intuition
   b. being fully with and for the other yet filled with energy, vitality, and a spiritual transcendence.

When we greet a client at the door, welcoming the other in through direct physical contact and exchange of hellos, we enter into the first level of in-session presence, which we call *physical presence* or *light presence*. Physical presence refers to the moment of initial contact with the client. It is not a time to go deep into issues but rather to check-in with a hello and greeting. It includes the initial welcoming of the client into the therapy space and may include general talk about the weather, traveling to the session, and so on. This is an important part of the process of arriving and being present with each other in that there is a human warmth and contact that lets the client know you are happy to see him or her, you are interested in his or her day-to-day life, and that you are two human beings in contact with each other. Physical or light presence includes settling into a comfortable sitting position and just generally settling into the room together. This physical or light presence can also include therapists' awareness of their physical body by being aware of the body on the chair and feeling that contact place as another invitation to show up, be present, and to have a general awareness of one's own sensory tool, the body.

The next level of presence is *psychological presence* or *partial presence*, which includes beginning to check-in and hear the content of the client's experience. Checking in with the client includes hearing the client's initial story about what has been going on for them during the week or perhaps what focus they have for this session. As therapists invite themselves to show up for the client, they begin to listen and attend to clients' sharing of their experience with caring, openness, interest, and acceptance. This is the beginning stage of the therapists' presence: allowing for an attunement to what the client is bringing into this particular session.

A third level involves being *emotionally present* to the client, or *present with and for the other*. This deepening into presence on an emotional level occurs as the therapist begins to experience an emotional resonance with and empathy for the client. The therapist begins to gather a level of understanding, acceptance, and compassion for the client's concerns and may offer an empathic response that reflects that understanding. The therapists' responses as they deepen into emotional presence, with and for the client, emerge in direct resonance with what the client is sharing. The therapist is simultaneously listening and absorbing the content and nonverbal gestures or processes that the client is experiencing and looking within his or her own sensory body for information on what the client may be experiencing. Listening, understanding, and responding are held with the intent to be with and for the client.

A fourth level that may emerge in the therapist as the session unfolds and the relationship deepens in the moment is a *transpersonal presence* or *presence with spirit* or presence with something larger. Although therapists can, with practice, enter into the session with a sense of this larger presence, they also gather this larger sense of spaciousness and transcendence from being in physical, psychological, and emotional contact with their client.

In transpersonal presence, therapists recognize their body as a vessel for healing that is taking in the depth of experience of the client yet is connected to a larger state of energy or support. The contact between the therapist and the client is felt on a deeper level by the therapist, where there is a palpable presence between the two people. Therapists also experience greater contact and access to their own intuition as they take in the depth of experience of the other and access their own inner wisdom, professional knowledge, or appropriate response technique, which stem from this resonance with the other and with a larger felt sense of energy. As the deepening between therapist and client occurs, the therapist feels in contact with a larger sense of spirituality as well as a high-level sense of vitality and an enhanced sensory and perceptual experience in direct relationship with the client. Transpersonal presence can emerge in special presence moments or through deep intersubjective sharing (Stern, 2004).

The fifth and final level of therapeutic presence is when all of these levels are integrated and occurring simultaneously, which reflects a *relational therapeutic presence*. Relational presence involves holding all of the levels simultaneously and vacillating among what is emerging and poignant in the moment, which may include contact with self (i.e., checking in inwardly with what is being experienced), deep contact with the client (i.e., felt experience of being with and for the other, attuned deeply to the other's present moment experience), and contact with a deeper sense of intuition, spirituality, or a transcendental force. This relational presence includes being fully with the other yet filled with energy, vitality, and a spiritual transcendence as emerging from the direct present-centered relationship with the client. It is this profound relational presence that allows for the emergence of flow, riding the waves of the unknown, yet trusting in the process and in the therapist's own intuition and responses when they emerge from that place of deep connection. In relational presence there exists great opportunity for deep healing to emerge from the level of multiple present moment connections (with self, other, and transcendence or spirit) and from the quality of what unfolds in the depth of the relationships between these connections.

The emergence of healing in therapeutic relational presence reflects Rogers's (1980) experience, quoted in full in Chapter 1, where he spoke of being close to his "inner intuitive self" and "transcendental core" and the moments that "our relationship transcends itself and becomes a part of something larger. Profound growth and healing and energy are present" (p. 129).

## CONCLUSION

We propose that therapeutic presence can occur at multiple levels and can be experienced in different depths and at different moments, depending on where the client is and what he or she needs to stay in contact. Some clients need more time in physical presence to settle into the session and the encounter in a deeper way. Other clients have greater comfort with their own experience and with the relational encounter, so physical presence is only a momentary experience as they prefer a deeper emotional opening and encounter early in the session. Our ability as therapists to tune in to the multiple levels of therapeutic presence, as well as to where the client is and needs to be to stay in contact, serves as the ultimate guide in the unfolding of the therapeutic encounter.

While the dance of present-moment awareness and deepening into relational therapeutic presence with clients is healthy and desirable, there are challenges to becoming and being in presence with clients, both within the therapist and with particular clients, which we explore in Chapter 8. The recognition of these challenges in the present moment is essential to deepening in the therapeutic relationship. As Stern (2004) noted, all moments of present moment experiences, when recognized and given attention, are moments of kairos, or a moment of opportunity in the moment, in which we can act or respond in a way that could change the course of one's destiny, either for the next moment or for a lifetime.

# 8

## CHALLENGES TO THERAPEUTIC PRESENCE

If you think you're enlightened go spend a week with your family.
— Ram Dass

To optimize the moments of *kairos* (opportunity) in the therapy relationship, in ourselves, and with our clients, therapists must be aware of and work through the potential barriers to relational therapeutic presence. A level of intimacy with the moment is needed for therapists to go deeper through the levels of therapeutic presence, which can be scary and make one feel vulnerable. In particular, it can be more challenging to rely on one's self and the deepest strata of one's being to facilitate a response or choose a technique in resonance with what is most poignant for the client in the moment than to rely on a therapy plan or a particular technique. The challenges to engaging intimately in the moment in a psychotherapeutic encounter can arise from within the therapist (*internal* barriers) or from the client, the relationship, or other demands (*external* barriers). Although it is helpful to conceptually categorize challenges as internal or external, even those that emerge externally (e.g., the client's anger) are ultimately internal challenges to the therapist to be aware of and work through.

The challenges we examine in this chapter include internal ones such as countertransference, trust in the process, and personal barriers (stress, lack of self-care, appropriate use of energy) as well as external factors such as working with challenging clients (e.g., clients with dual diagnoses or receiving end-of-life care, trauma survivors). However, first we invite you to pause briefly to uncover your own personal obstacles to being present with a client.

PAUSE MOMENT. Stop and notice any obstacles to presence:

- Take a moment to pause from reading and turn your attention inward. Close your eyes, soften your gaze in front of you, or jot down some notes.
- Focus briefly on your breath and allow yourself to bring your awareness to your bodily experience of breathing.
- What are you first aware of as you pause? Notice the busyness of your mind, judgments, or discomfort in your body that may prevent you from feeling centered or still. Notice any rushed feeling, as in wanting to get to the next page, the next moment, or the next task. Notice it without judgment, keeping awareness on your breath without following the thoughts about what you are experiencing, allowing each breath to take you back to the moment.
- Now reflect about the difficulties in being present with a client. What kinds of obstacles emerge in session with a client that hijack your focus or attention? Notice what they are. Then let them go.
- How do you know when you are not present with a client; what are the clues? How do you bring yourself back to the moment in session? What is one way you can work on noticing your barrier to being present and bringing your attention back in session?

## INTERNAL CHALLENGES TO THERAPEUTIC PRESENCE

In this section, we explore some of the internal challenges that therapists can face as they open up to the contact that therapeutic presence entails. Being fully in the moment with a client requires having a level of self-awareness and inner health and integration. Presence is not just a passive state but an active engagement with one's whole being, which demands a level of engagement with the other that requires that we take care of ourselves on a personal and professional level. Even so, we are human beings, and the challenges that can arise for us include countertransference, tolerance of uncertainty, the role of stress, and appropriate use of energy.

### Countertransference

*Countertransference* is defined as "the therapist's internal or external reactions that are shaped by the therapist's past or present emotional conflicts and vulnerabilities" (Gelso & Hayes, 2007, p. 25). Although the notion of countertransference may have originated in the psychoanalytic tradition, the possibility of countertransferential reactions, or feelings in the therapist in relation to clients, can occur in any therapeutic modality. Note the perspective of Gelso and Hayes (2007):

> Countertransference is universal in psychotherapy . . . by virtue of their humanity, all psychotherapists, no matter how experienced or emotionally healthy, do have unresolved conflicts and vulnerabilities, and that the relational intimacy and emotional demands of psychotherapy tend to exploit these conflicts and vulnerabilities, bringing them into play in the therapeutic work. (p. 133)

We believe that countertransference reactions, such as therapists' emotional reactivity, are highly possible in present-centered work because therapists are open and in direct emotional, physical, cognitive, spiritual, and relational contact with their clients as well as present in these domains within their selves. In the presence process, the therapist is using the self as a sensor or an indicator. Therapists are taking in the depth of the client's experience and accessing and attending to their own internal experience as a key indicator in understanding and responding or offering an intervention from moment to moment. We also believe that being aware of one's self and the other, in the way that therapeutic presence evokes, allows therapists to recognize countertransference reactions when they do emerge and either work with them internally to let them go and not act them out or use them in a positive therapeutic manner to reflect what the client is experiencing or may be evoking in the other.

No matter how great the intention to clear and manage the therapist's own issues outside of session, therapists are human beings, and even resolved issues could rise to the surface in session. However, the level of self-insight, self-awareness, and commitment to one's own growth that cultivating therapeutic presence demands, such as attending to one's own inner experience, serves both as protection from countertransference and as an antidote to countertransference reactions. Furthermore, the cultivation and experience of presence can help therapists to quickly distinguish intense countertransference reactions from intense emotional reactions that may be therapeutically useful.

Self-awareness and a continuous attending to one's internal world are keys to recognizing and managing countertransference reactions. Gelso and Hayes (2007) described self-insight as a necessary precondition to connecting the therapist's experience with the experience of the client. To use the self as a sensing instrument, "therapists must be able to see themselves, to understand their fluctuating needs and preferences and shortcomings and longings" (Gelso & Hayes, 2007, p. 108).

VanWagoner, Gelso, Hayes, and Diemer (1991) compared therapists who were perceived as excellent by their peers with general therapists. They found that master therapists were viewed as having greater self-insight, empathic ability, anxiety management, and self-integration. Interestingly, these qualities, which are a part of mastery, are also aspects of therapeutic presence, such as self-insight, self-integration (grounded and centered), attunement to the other, and ability to manage anxiety. These skills are central to mastery, as therapists who are perceived as excellent are better able to notice and manage countertransference reactions before they become problematic or manifest in therapy and potentially impede the client's process. Hence, the practice of presence can also protect against countertransference reactions.

In addition, therapists' insight, self-awareness, self-care, and psychological health as well as their training and professional experience, which are all a part of cultivating presence, will support the therapist in effectively using his or her own receptive openness to understand and facilitate the client's therapeutic process toward healing. In fact, openness to one's own feelings has been associated with less countertransference behavior (Robbins & Jolkovski, 1987). It is often the therapists who have lost touch with what they are feeling or are unaware of their own experience in the moment who do not notice what is interfering with their ability to help or be there with their client.

To get out of the way of our client's therapy, we need to get our own unresolved issues out of the way. Yet even when it is not possible or we are taken by surprise by a feeling (e.g., a sense of incompetence or frustration or anger), we need to develop agility in recognizing the source of that feeling and moving our awareness back into the moment and back to an open yet grounded place.

The following clinical vignette demonstrates how the therapist's self-awareness helped her to recognize her own sense of detachment and countertransference response and recoup her attention when she was struggling in session with a client:

> Jane was discussing the loss of her son through an illness encountered when he was 8 years old. She was discussing the "deep hole" in her chest from the hurt and pain she felt at her son's death. She expressed feeling overwhelmed by having to cope with everyday tasks, as she could barely "face each day." As she spoke, I found myself cognitively responding to her pain by reassuring her, while my attention felt like it was moving further and further out of the room. I noticed my clipboard, which I rarely use, in my hand with my pen writing furtively. At that moment I recognized that the clipboard was almost acting like a shield to the overwhelming pain she was experiencing. I brought my attention to my present moment disconnection and became aware that underneath the emotional distance I felt to Jane was a feeling of deep sadness and fear of loss. I realized that I had

created a blockade to that pain. I also felt overwhelmed with the notion that I could not take away or lessen her pain in any way. With that awareness of my resistance to being present, for fear of being overwhelmed by sadness and incompetence, I noted and invited my attention back to presence. I became aware of this vulnerability in me, and imagined putting these fears on a shelf, with an intention to return to these at a later time. I was then able to take a breath and invite my attention back to a sense of grounded presence, where I could feel once again my own inner stability yet open to a sense of support and the vastness of pain felt by Jane.

In this example, the therapist noted her nonpresent behavior of furiously writing and her distraction. She was able to quickly attend to her detachment and underlying pain and fear, notice and regulate her emotions, note these as something she needs to attend to at a later time, and return her attention to the moment. The inner dialogue and returning attention to the moment can be brief if therapists are skilled in their own self-awareness and ability to understand their emotional experience.

Practice in presence and self-awareness can also help therapists to discern the source of a countertransference reaction and to work with it effectively. For example, the therapist who is experienced in self-recognition may feel sleepy in session and discern that it is not fatigue per se but a sense of disconnect with himself or herself or with the client and hence bring their attention back to the moment. Another possibility for the source of that fatigue is the therapist's resonance with the client's disconnect from his or her own experience. Hence, it is a good opportunity to reflect this back, which would invite the client back to his or her own experience.

Therapists can also use the presence practice of in-the-moment bodily awareness to attain ease in recognizing the underlying needs that the countertransference reactions, in the form of a lack of presence, could be indicating. For example, anxiousness may reflect a need for a break or a need for stretching or exercise. Tiredness may be physical fatigue or may result from a lack of direction or connection in the session. Boredom may mean that the therapist is burnt out or perhaps that the client is avoiding and speaking about his or her surface experience. Becoming more aware of and attuned with one's own bodily sensations can maximize the intention to be fully and optimally present in the room with the client. This self-attunement can also provide a map for inviting and returning one's own awareness back to the moment.

### Tolerating Uncertainty and Trusting the Process

One key aspect in preparing for therapeutic presence is to bracket theories, preconceptions, and therapy planning. Bracketing allows our receptive attunement to the uniqueness of the moment to guide the therapy process and allows the right technique or direction to emerge from this level of openness. However, opening to the moment means opening to the unknown and having periods in session that may feel entirely uncertain.

Therapists' discomfort with uncertainty can lead them to respond in a way that is out of sync with the client. In relational therapies, this may leave the client feeling not heard or accepted and hence shut down. With manual-based therapy, such as cognitive–behavioral therapy, this may result in speeding through required steps without attuning to where the client is in the moment and hence having less therapeutic impact. Therapists face a similar challenge with silence. Tolerating the discomfort of silence or of the unknown is integral to a good therapy process, as it is through uncertainty that one can allow for the emergence of material or responses that could be important and relevant for the client. Silence can also allow the client to work internally with what has been offered through the therapist's response or intervention, and the therapist's discomfort with this and filling the silence could actually impede the client's healing and learning processes. To be able to trust in the unknown takes practice and the knowledge that tolerating discomfort can leave space for the emergence of poignant therapeutic material.

The challenge of trusting in the unknown occurs often near the beginning of a session, when the client begins to delve into his or her experience but what he or she is feeling or what might be needed is still unclear. Whether therapists are practicing from a relational or manual-based therapy perspective, there needs to be time for clients to develop comfort and safety in the relationship and hence bring their issues into full awareness. Therapists' anxiety at this beginning stage can force a rushed sequence of interventions before their clients have had time to build trust or before the relationship has had time to develop. In particular, new students may lean on technique as a way of managing this anxiety and as a result minimize the therapeutic efficacy that they could bring to the therapeutic encounter because their interventions are not attuned with the client. Even with manual-based therapies, for optimal efficacy the therapist needs to adapt what he or she is doing in relationship to where the client is at the moment, which in certain moments requires a level of being with and tolerating space and the unknown. It can be likened to an artist staring at a blank page. It is often the blank page that can be most intimidating and make even the most talented of artists cower. Yet it is through the artistic process that the artist learns to wait patiently for emerging material, to tolerate the unknown, so that what needs to take form or the actual technique that should be used can emerge in resonance with the moment.

It is the same in present-centered psychotherapy, in which we need to learn to be still and to listen, and perhaps even to tolerate the anxiety about not knowing how to help this person who is suffering, so that we can really listen to the other and to our deepest self and respond or intervene in resonance with the client in the moment. It takes a level of psychological resilience as well as understanding and trust that something healing can happen by being deeply present with clients in their suffering. From this unknown transition space, true healing can occur, as the therapist does not try to rush forward into an intervention or to fix the pain of the other. Rather, the responses and techniques that emerge from pausing in presence with the other turn out to be most facilitative for the client's healing.

To manage anxiety about the unknown, therapists need to develop trust in the process, that by staying fully present in the moment and in the discomfort of the unknown, what is revealed will allow for their responses or interventions to be in the direction of healing. This comes through experience with relational therapeutic presence. However, there are some specific tools to manage that discomfort, such as returning to a focus on the breath, doing full abdominal breathing, or silently reminding yourself to stay in the present, to trust in the process, to trust in being in the moment. The therapist can also have an internal dialogue with himself or herself, including self-soothing or a gentle reminder to have trust or open fully.

## Stress and Multiple Roles

We are in an era in which we are bombarded by demands on our attention, time, and emotional energy. Computers, faxes, cell phones, landlines, BlackBerries, e-mails, tweets, Facebook, and other technology-based communications demand responses with an immediacy that was not expected even a decade ago. In addition, the multiple roles that many therapists play in their daily lives in the current reality carry their attention out of the moment and away from their own experience. The multiple demands in therapists' lives and attention are stressful and can make the challenge of being fully present even greater than it is. The era of traditional roles is gone, and on one level this means a wonderful gain in equality and diversity in relationships and career choices, but on another level this has resulted in increased expectations and demands to fulfill multiple roles.

The first author (S. G.) conducted a stress-reduction workshop for health care workers, with the intent of facilitating an understanding of the stress in their lives as well as ways of increasing presence in the workplace. She asked participants to name the different roles that predominate in their day-to-day lives. She was struck by the many roles each person described: health care practitioner, parent, caregiver for aging parents, supervisor, manager, professor, coworker, friend of someone with a terminal illness, caregiver for in ill sibling, driver for children, single parent, and so on. This is just a small list of what was expressed in this circle of 15 people. When asked to describe the time they spent just pausing, being still, or doing something they love for themselves, one woman recalled the last time, which was 2 or so years ago, she went on a walk in a park alone and felt refreshed . . . for that day! It is no wonder that the benefits from these rare and precious self-nourishing moments so quickly disappear.

The process of presence, or deepening into each moment, involves daily time for preparing one's own self to be in the moment. We can aspire to be present and live a life in which we daily make a commitment to caring, compassion, presence, learning, and practice. However, demands are made on us constantly by technology, by environmental stresses, and most profoundly by our multiple roles and the split attention that is created by a busy and stressful life. The subtle (and not-so-subtle) demands on our attention and time need to be countered by an awareness of the effects of stress and by managing stress and cultivating in-the-moment attention.

To allow for presence, we need to work to open to moment-to-moment awareness in our own selves, in our personal relationships, and in our relationship with what is true inside of us. To access that inner steadiness we have to commit to riding through our own inner terrain with greater ease and assurance, while being a part of a something larger, whether it be a sense of community or through spirituality. This can begin with a simple awareness of the multiple roles we hold as therapists in the 21st century.

PAUSE MOMENT. Take a moment to increase your awareness of the multiple roles you play:

- Pause, gently lowering your eyes and attending to your breath.
- Reflect on the multiple roles you play or the demands you face in your life. How many different people are you responsible for (at work or at home, your children, parents, siblings, friends, supervisees, administrative staff, colleagues, and of course your clients)? Take a count of the people who need your regular attention.
- Reflect on how much time or what percentage of your day or week is spent in fulfilling those responsibilities as well as in meeting general daily demands (e.g., answering e-mails, phone calls, taking care of the house).
- Now note how much time or what percentage of your day or week goes to fulfilling your own needs or self-nourishment.
- Notice the gap between the amount of time spent in giving to others and in attending to yourself.
- Take a quiet moment to reflect on how that gap could be reduced; that is, in what ways can you commit a little more time

to your own self-care and personal growth or to the care of those around you?

By becoming aware of the obstacles and stress in our lives, we can turn our attention to clearing space regularly for presence in life and with clients.

## Misunderstood Energy

In moments of heightened connection that can occur at deep levels of relational presence, therapists can experience sexual feelings, not toward clients or toward anyone in particular but as a heightened sense of energy throughout the body. A master therapist interviewed in our qualitative study (Geller, 2001; see Chapter 2, this volume) described the energy experienced from presence:

> There is an aliveness and it is very contactful . . . there is high excitement and it comes actually right from my genitals right up. I mean it is a very full, flowing feeling, right, and it's very interpersonal. I mean they are all characterized by nothing else is going on. Everything is just whatever is in the moment.

This energy can be scary, threatening, or misplaced when it is not understood. The first author (S. G.) recalls when feeling a surge of energy in relation to a moment of relational contact and presence. She found it confusing and knew that she also had no physical attraction to this person. She had to sit with that feeling, curious about both it and her trepidation around it. In speaking to her supervisor at the time, she discovered that part of it emerged from the flow of being fully in the moment with this open and vulnerable human being and an openness within that ensued. The confusing part was that by closing down this feeling, she knew would have closed down to the client. Yet to be open to it fully felt inappropriate and wrong. Over time she experienced many other flow experiences in moments of relational therapeutic presence and realized it is not just emotional or sensory, it is energetic.

Energy is discussed more often in Eastern traditions or in relation to somatic practices such as yoga, qigong, or tai chi. In tantric practices, it is understood that energy is a life force that can travel throughout the spine and the body. Energy can be called sexual when it is directed toward another human being in a genital-based way. However, therapists who are not familiar or comfortable with these energy concepts could either shut their feelings down, and therefore shut down presence, or direct their feelings inappropriately toward the client.

Therapists must have an understanding of energy from different perspectives, as well as a healthy relationship with themselves and their professional ethics, to avoid misusing or becoming distracted by this feeling when it emerges. It is also important to understand the relational dimensions of therapeutic presence and that it is guided by an intention of being with and for the client, in service of the other's healing. Being aware of this intent is essential for therapists to avoid misuse, becoming confused, or shutting down.

While we are distinguishing this energy from a countertransference feeling of attraction to a client, when misunderstood, this energy can lead to countertransference reactions. The few therapists who have not taken the steps to understand what is occurring, whether it be a heightened energy that accompanies presence or a countertransference attraction, develop personal and intimate relationships with their clients. Some are good therapists from a clinical perspective, yet they crossed a personal boundary and then terminated therapy too soon, after engaging in sexual and intimate relationships with their clients. It is not just completely misguided, highly inappropriate, and an ethical violation, but also an easy line to cross if one is not aware of the powerful feelings that can accompany relational connection and how to have appropriate and clear intentions or to access supervision.

Personal practices with energy work, such as qiqong, tai chi, or other somatic practices, could help in gaining comfort with the experience and the appropriate use of energy. Supervision is also important when the energetic responses emerge and become confusing or create the danger of an ethical violation. The self-awareness that is essential in cultivating presence as well as the awareness that therapeutic presence is about being in service of the client's healing can help therapists to stay open and behave in ethical and appropriate ways.

## EXTERNAL CHALLENGES TO THERAPEUTIC PRESENCE

There are certain patients, whether because of their personality styles or their diagnoses or their overwhelming pain, who can be more challenging for therapists to be open to and present with. Examples include an angry or defensive client (especially if fear of confrontation or anger is part of the therapist's core issue) or a client diagnosed with borderline personality disorder who may suffer significant inner pain and suicidal ideation or may use the relationship to manipulate for his or her needs. Certain clients can also hook therapists into reactivity more than others. Other examples of challenging clients could include those in tremendous inner or outer pain, such as clients facing dying and death. Therapists can feel overwhelmed in these situations because they cannot fix the client and can at most bear witness to the client's pain. The challenge in these moments is not only in staying receptive, open, and present but also in not being so open and enmeshed that we lose ourselves. A related challenge in these moments is to not create distance or manipulate the client into shutting down or closing up without becoming aware of the driving force behind that distancing or feeling of enmeshment.

Witnessing a client in unbearably deep pain or grief is a challenge for many therapists, as the pull to fix the pain can be strong, which is often a self-protective response to witnessing pain or grief. The ultimate acceptance that being present provides may be healing for many clients, and it is the most challenging of clients that can benefit the most. In fact, this level of presence can be a lot more challenging, and perhaps emotionally draining, than being half present or partially focused. Some examples of presence with challenging clients are explored next.

## Personality Disorders

Dual diagnoses are common, and such clients can be challenging for many therapists. For example, in working with someone who has sought therapy for depression but who also displays narcissistic tendencies, cultivating a present attitude and working with one's self are helpful in not feeling as if you are drowning in an ocean of protective reaction. On the one hand, narcissism is a disorder based on a lack of love; on the other hand, narcissism is expressed through arrogance, anger, and selfishness. This can create difficulties in the responses of therapists, who can sometimes experience the shame that narcissists create or a reactive and aversive response in the face of arrogant selfishness. In the face of such ingrained behavior, therapists can find themselves feeling angry, defensive, and hopeless.

Narcissism stems in part from parents' inability to attune to their children at a time when the child needed that for self-development, and therapists' attunement is essential in the healing. The tricky balance for the therapist is between being aware of and nonreactive to the outward expression of arrogance or the demands these clients make to have their greatness reflected and attuning to the deeper shame or sadness underlying these behaviors yet are highly protected by the client.

While the technique that therapists use with personality disorders such as narcissism is valuable, whether it be emotional regulation, increasing interpersonal skills, self-soothing practices, enhancing empathy, or cognitive–behavioral techniques, what is most valuable is how the therapist is in the room with the client. The technique does not matter if the client is not met with a warm, accepting, open, and grounded presence in the therapist. On the flip side, although people with narcissism need the presence and compassion of the therapist, they are not enough. For example, only when the narcissistic mirror is challenged can people with narcissism start to heal. However, to know how and when to challenge these clients is highly dependent on the therapist's inner steadiness, compassion, and attunement to the client in the moment, as the client can initially react to the therapist. Hence, there is a greater need for the therapist to remain open, connected, and grounded yet nonreactive for his or her approach to be effective.

An example of the acceptance that is necessary to facilitate technique emerges from dialectical behavior therapy, a behavioral approach developed by Linehan for patients with borderline personality disorder. With clients with borderline personality disorder, the internal or affective world of the therapist is vital in providing the basic acceptance that is needed to make the behavioral techniques effective. Linehan (1993a) provided an interesting commentary that speaks to the challenge and necessity of present moment acceptance:

> In relationship acceptance the therapist recognizes, accepts, and validates both the patient and himself or herself as a therapist with this patient as well as the quality of the patient–therapist relationship. Each is accepted *as it is* in the current moment; this includes an explicit acceptance of the stage of therapeutic progress or lack thereof. Relationship acceptance, like all other acceptance strategies, cannot be approached as a technique for change—acceptance in order to get past a particular point. Relationship acceptance requires many things, but most importantly it requires a willingness to enter into a situation and a life filled with pain, to suffer along with the patient, and to refrain from manipulating the moment to stop the pain. Many therapists are not prepared for the pain they will encounter in treating borderline patients, or for the professional risks, personal doubts, and traumatic moments they will encounter. The old saying "if you cannot stand the heat, don't go into the kitchen" is nowhere more true than in working with suicidal and borderline patients. (pp. 515–516)

A therapist who is skilled at acceptance and presence has the ability to be with the deep pain and to provide support from within where the client is at. Furthermore, the skilled presence therapist can recognize the source of the anger or manipulation that could be directed at him or her and not react to or ignore the anger or manipulation.

Gabbard (2001) noted that in working with a patient with borderline personality disorder, the therapist can be placed in the role of "bad object," with anger being directed toward him or her as a projection of the patient's abusive parent. An optimal state in the therapist is a state of being even, in the "middle ground," experiencing some of that anger inside but maintaining a capacity for empathy and helping the other. Gelso and Hayes (2007) supported Gabbard in rejecting the traditional psychoanalytical model of being nonreactive when pulled by a patient's rage by creating an objective distance from the client, as this can anger the client further and deepen the client's experience of rejection. Similarly, if the therapist is overinvolved in the dynamic of blame and defensiveness and reacts angrily or distances himself or herself, it can overwhelm and damage the therapeutic relationship. This optimal state that Gabbard (2001) described reflects the experience of therapeutic presence, the state of being deeply connected, in the moment, authentic, in connection with self, yet expansive in holding both the emotional authenticity and the intention for healing with and for the patient.

The therapeutic process with people with personality disorders is often long and difficult. Although presence allows for deeper attunement, nonreactivity, and inner steadiness, it is sometimes hard for therapists to sustain these states during the long therapeutic process. In addition, allowing a sense of closeness and interpersonal connection with someone with narcissism or borderline personality disorder can at times create within the therapist a state of shakiness and lack of confidence in his or her own self. The challenge here is for therapists to discern their experience of lack of confidence and not knowing how to help from an inner interpersonal reaction to the client that can be clinically useful.

The therapist's own personal practice becomes essential in enabling him or her to remain open yet hold steady when faced with a client's potential aversive reactions. A colleague recently discussed how she felt more drained of energy in relation to her patients with personality disorder when she became more present with them, instead of just partially attentive, which is how she previously practiced. She realized that the demands of being open and connected in some ways were greater and required balancing her schedule and life practices so that she had healthy ways to take care of herself (e.g., time between sessions, debriefing, and mindful walking) to release any residual tension. Maintaining this inner state of openness, grounding, and nonreactivity, a state that is essential in working with personality disorders, takes a great deal of inner commitment on the part of the therapist. Presence is a significant underlying state that can help people with personality disorders, yet cultivation and commitment are essential in sustaining it.

## Dying and Death

Being with someone who is dying, or with someone facing a terminal illness, is one of the greatest challenges for therapists as nothing can be done to fix or relieve this reality for the other. As therapists we like to see relief, we like to feel we can help someone navigate through intolerable feelings or situations into a new life with peace and wholeness. Yet that is not the case when facing persons who are dying. We cannot help them to live a healthier life; at most we can help them to accept their terminal situation and come to peace with any unfinished business in their lives or to live their final days with acceptance of the reality of their life and their transition to death.

The most powerful therapeutic stance we can take with people who are facing death is to be fully present with them, in their fear, their pain, and their suffering. They need to be listened to and heard, as many people are fearful of talking about death and so avoid the topic with the dying person. This level of presence in end-of-life care demands that the therapist open up fully to the other and the other's pain, and likely to his or her own reality of dying and death, and move through the painful suffering and loss that may be experienced without shutting down or feeling overwhelmed. This requires facing fear and the barriers to opening to generate a level of inner resiliency, and it requires skill in being open yet grounded and emotionally stable.

The compassionate care movement has brought attention to the importance and value of presence in end-of-life care (Halifax, 2009). This runs counter to our Western orientation, which involves fear and avoidance of death and any discussion of dying. We cannot avoid our own fear of death when we work with people who are dying. Facing a life-threatening illness calls us to a place inside that is raw, vulnerable, and real, and if we avoid dealing with that reality then we avoid life, and we avoid offering our pure presence to the client who is facing death.

Roshi Bernie Glassman, as discussed in Halifax (2009), teaches three tenets of compassionate care for the dying as helpful when being with someone facing death. The first tenet, *not knowing*, reflects giving up fixed ideas of ourselves or others and opening to the spontaneity of the beginner's mind. The second tenet, *bearing witness*, reflects being present with the suffering and joy in the world, without judgment and without attachment to outcome. The third tenet, *compassionate action*, reflects a commitment to free others and ourselves from suffering.

Frank Ostaseski, founder of the Zen Hospice Project in San Francisco and the Metta Institute in Sausalito, California, developed five precepts of service as companions on the journey of accompanying the dying (Ostaseski, n.d.). He described these as bottomless practices that can be continually explored and deepened and have to be lived and communicated through action.

- *The first precept: Welcome everything. Push away nothing.* In welcoming everything, we may not like what is arising, but it is not our work to approve or disapprove, but just to listen deeply. This is a journey of continuous discovery; we have no idea how it will turn out, and it takes courage and flexibility.
- *The second precept: Bring your whole self to the experience.* In the process of healing others and ourselves, we open to both our joy

and our fear. It is not our expertise, but rather the exploration of our own suffering that enables us to be of real assistance. This precept reflects the importance of the exploration of our own inner life in enabling us to be empathic and respond compassionately to the other person.

- *The third precept: Don't wait.* This precept calls for patience and an honoring of present-moment experience, rather than waiting for death. When we wait for the moment of death, we miss so many moments of living. This allows for the awareness of the precarious nature of this life to reveal what is most important, that calls us to enter fully.

- *The fourth precept: Find a place of rest in the middle of things.* Rest is often something people look forward to that arrives when we are at the end of the day or going on holiday. We imagine that we can only find rest by changing the conditions of our life. But it is possible to discover rest right in the middle of chaos and difficult emotions. This rest reflects the experience of presence, which is always accessible to us and emerges from bringing our full attention, without distraction, to this moment.

- *The fifth precept: Cultivate don't-know mind.* This describes cultivating an open and receptive mind that is not limited by agendas, roles, or expectations. From this open receptivity we allow the situation itself and the relationship with the other, in the moment, to inform our actions. This aspect of presence involves listening openly to the other, as well as listening to our own inner voice, sensing and trusting our intuition. We learn to see, feel, and look with fresh eyes.

Glassman's three tenets and Ostaseski's five precepts reflect the whole experience of therapeutic presence, from the need to be receptive and open to the unknown and to others to be fully present and nonjudgmental to what is being expressed or experienced without attachment to outcome, to the need to be present with and for the client with the intention to be with the other in a way that is healing. This offering of presence and compassion requires therapists to look deeply at their own attitudes and fears in relation to illness and death as well as to recognize the cultural and family attitudes that they may have internalized, and to open fully to the multiple dimensions of the experience of dying and death. To face and move through their own potential fear of death and to have or strengthen a level of inner resiliency and stability require deep inner work on the part of therapists, so they can offer the gift of being present and bearing witness to the client's suffering, without shutting down, holding back, or becoming overwhelmed.

## Trauma

Riding the waves of uncertainty is acutely challenging when the client is expressing or reexperiencing trauma. In particular, learning the details of rape or abuse in a client's childhood or seeing and hearing the effect of a sexual or physical violation on a child or adolescent is heartbreaking. Yet the reality is equally hopeful because that person has made it to the therapist's office. There is nothing more profoundly healing than offering a traumatized child, adolescent, or adult your complete self, with the capacity not only to hear and feel but also to stay steady and hold that pain.

The presence of the therapist allows the trauma survivor to feel understood and supported, as trauma survivors often feel alone in their suffering and believe that no one can understand what they may be experiencing. A trauma survivor could feel that even the therapist, not having experienced the trauma that he or she went through, is outside of the wall that the survivor has created for protection and survival. Hence, therapists' presence may include an acknowledgment of the truth of not having the shared experience of trauma, but a willingness to be there, to listen, and to take in the experience with openness, compassion, and a capacity for understanding.

The risks are complex for a therapist who has not experienced the trauma of the survivor (or survivors, as it could be a community trauma or disaster) and is trying to be as present as possible. The resonance with feeling the tragic experience can create in the therapist either an urge to rescue and protect the client from further distress or a deep emotional upset or horror in knowing too much about what the survivor has experienced (Lanyado, 2004). Exposure to the details of the trauma may create an internal defense to protect one's self from the effects of witnessing the horrific through the verbal account of the event. Even the most present and skilled therapists are not immune to this response in the face of trauma. Hence the agility to recognize this state for what it is (a mirror response or defensive reaction) and to work with it through inner recognition, and perhaps a calming of one's own anxiety, is central to remaining or returning to being fully present with the client.

Nothing is more potentially challenging to the strata of one's being than to witness the sheer expression of pain associated with trauma. Furthermore, there is an occupational hazard of becoming overwhelmed, depressed, defensive, and burnt out in the face of trying to help people process or cope with trauma (Lanyado, 2004). However, if therapists begin to feel overwhelmed and lose hope in the face of trauma, they are more inclined to attempt to fix, distance themselves from, or overidentify with the client's experience, which can result in a failure in the ability to be present and helpful, and the client will be at risk of not feeling safe and likely shutting down. In working with trauma, it is essential that "therapists ensure that they do not consciously overwork and that they do make sure that their leisure time really replenishes their emotional reserve" (Lanyado, 2004, p. 13).

Working with trauma survivors, and the constant witnessing and fully being there with some of the horrific experiences clients retell and reexperience, can create a shutting down or vicarious traumatization in therapists if they are not taking care of their needs and finding a release for that which is carried in their own emotional bodies after session. Here the danger of not being present as a way to self-protect is higher. This is where peer supervision, self-care, and time after session or the workday are imperative. Some therapists find it helpful to talk to a colleague, meditate, play music, engage in artistic or creative activities, walk or exercise, or have some time at the end of the day to decompress by walking home from the office or going to a park or somewhere else calm. Cultivating and sustaining a nonreactive yet open state, which is essential in working with challenging clients, is equally important for therapists in training as well as expert therapists.

## CONCLUSION

Although the potential for healing with therapeutic presence is great, the challenges are equally great. Being fully open and engaged with the client brings internal challenges such as countertransference reactions and managing busyness, multiple roles, and stress, as well as external challenges such as meeting or being with difficult clients or clients experiencing great pain, trauma, or loss. This speaks to the increased requirement for therapists to take care of their own internal worlds and mental health, cultivate and maintain self-awareness, as well as leave time during the day and between sessions to release and be connected to their own needs for self-care and relation to release emotional residue and to minimize compassion fatigue.

Next we look at the neurobiological correlates of presence and how shifting one's own biology in the direction of calm and openness can help to cultivate presence and work through the challenges that accompany presence.

# 9

# NEUROBIOLOGY OF
# THERAPEUTIC PRESENCE

You have the power in the present moment to change limiting beliefs and consciously plant the seeds for the future of your choosing. As you change your mind, you change your experience.

—Serge Kahili King

Although the focus of this book has been on the experiential aspects of therapeutic presence, this chapter provides an additional lens through which we can view presence. By understanding what presence entails from a neurophysiologic perspective, we can specify which practices promote greater experiencing of presence. We can also use specific practices to cultivate presence to build the neural structure that reflects the experience of presence. With long-term practice, we can potentially change our neural structure so that presence becomes more of a characteristic or trait rather than just a momentary experience.

There is an exciting field of research in which neuroscience and psychology overlap to provide a neurobiological understanding of what occurs when we experience certain states. Initial studies looked at metabolic changes as well as electroencephalogram (EEG) patterns to identify changes in physiology and brain activity. For example, physiological studies have suggested that a focus on the breath elicits a relaxation response as suggested by decreased physical arousal (heart rate, breath rate, and skin conductance rate; Delmonte, 1984; Wallace, Benson, & Wilson, 1971). The use of EEG has allowed scientists to note different dynamic patterns and different types of brain activity that may occur during practices such as meditation or relaxation (Lazar, 2005). For example, Benson, Beary, and Carol (1974) showed that the relaxation response was similar when induced by Transcendental Meditation practice or by other autogenic training (e.g., yoga, hypnosis) and included slow alpha wave activity as well as decreased theta waves.

These early mechanisms to measure brain and physiological activity were followed by the recent development of two neuroimaging techniques, functional magnetic resonance imaging (fMRI) and positron emission tomography (PET), which together have allowed scientists to study and identify activity occurring inside the brain and in specific regions in relation to tasks and feeling states (Lazar, 2005; Lutz, Dunne, & Davidson, 2007). For example, meditation may show a pattern similar to rest or relaxation in brain wave activity; however, studies that combine EEG with fMRI and PET scans clearly demonstrate that the meditative state is different from rest, relaxation, or sleep (Lazar et al., 2000). Although many believe we are in the infancy stage of understanding the complexity of the brain, the potential is significant for understanding specific brain mechanisms and neurological processes that relate to activities that enhance presence and overall wellness.

Scientists are showing that the mind, experience, and the brain routinely change each other. Practices that are directed toward heightening a particular part of neurological functioning can enhance the cultivation of certain desired qualities, such as the qualities of therapeutic presence. For example, research is showing that practicing a form of breath awareness or meditation adds billions of synaptic connections and thus a measurable thickening of brain tissue in the regions that deal with attention and sensory awareness (Lazar et al., 2005). Furthermore, practices that generate a sense of acceptance and calm can increase serotonin, the neurotransmitter that regulates mood and sleep (Hanson & Mendius, 2009). Practices that generate positive mood states, such as gratitude practices, can stimulate dopamine reward circuits and encourage surges of norepinephrine (which alert and brighten the mind; Hanson, 2009). Hence, understanding the potential neurological and biological systems that are enhanced with the experience of therapeutic presence can provide a doorway to and validate engaging in practices that foster aspects of therapeutic presence, such as attention, calm, alertness, spaciousness, and being grounded and centered.

In this chapter, we present physiological and neurological correlates of presence by relating what is known from current research to our understanding of therapeutic presence. We start with a description of neuroplasticity. We then explore presence in relation to the prefrontal cortex and follow with an examination of aspects of presence and the physiological and neurological underpinnings.

# NEUROPLASTICITY

To paraphrase psychologist Hebb (1949), neurons that fire together, wire together. That is, any two neurons or groups of neurons that are repeatedly activated simultaneously will, over time, develop synaptic connections with each other so that activation in one facilitates activation in the other. The ability of the brain to change and adapt as a result of experience is known as *neuroplasticity*. An implication of neuroplasticity is that momentary *states* of presence can become enduring *traits* if cultivated and practiced with regularity; that is, the repetition of experience can result in a change in brain structure. Current research shows that although negative experiences are stored immediately and are rapidly available for recall, positive experiences are typically registered through standard memory systems and need to be held in consciousness for 10 to 20 seconds for them to sink in (Hanson & Mendius, 2010). When we allow ourselves to rest in experiences of calm, centeredness, acceptance, immersion, and equanimity, we are increasing the possibility that these experiences will become "neurological imprints" and will be readily accessible for recall, for example, when we are in session with clients.

The concept of neuroplasticity is a profound breakthrough from neuroscience and teaches us that our experiences have direct effects on our brain and that our brain changes in relationship to every experience that we have. Experience can therefore change our neurological structures in enduring ways.

Some relevant examples of neuroplasticity in relation to qualities of therapeutic presence are emerging. For example, when people practiced mindful meditation, a practice that helps to cultivate present-centered attention, they showed an increased thickness of the middle frontal area, bilaterally, and of the insula, particularly on the right side of the brain (Lazar et al., 2005). Other researchers have found an increased coordination of neural firing, especially in both sides of the prefrontal areas of the brain, when practicing compassion (Lutz, Greischar, Rawlings, Ricard, & Davidson, 2004). Although research is still emerging in this area, preliminary studies involving brain functioning reveal that paying attention to the present moment with openness and acceptance changes the structure of the brain (Cahn & Polich, 2006).

Several authors have proposed that the mind can be used in an intentional way to change your brain, which can benefit your whole being and all of those you interact with (Begley, 2007; Doidge, 2007; Hanson & Mendius, 2009). This suggests that through experience, for example, in the cultivation of the experience of presence, associated neurological structures can be changed and strengthened. So each time we experience presence, in our personal life or professional life, neurological imprinting and increased cellular activity are associated with that experience. The neurological strengthening of the parts of the brain that are associated with presence then allows that experience to be more accessible and familiar. This supports our experiential observation that presence becomes more accessible with practice.

## Prefrontal Cortex

Overall aspects of therapeutic presence appear to be focused around activity of the prefrontal cortex. Siegel (2007) described nine functions associated with activity of the middle areas of the prefrontal cortex, all of which reflect aspects of the presence experience:

- *Body regulation:* Involves the activation and inhibition of the autonomic nervous system based on what is needed to bring homeostasis to the body.
- *Attuned communication:* Involves input from another person's mind and experience as it coordinates with one's own mental and experiential processes, which involves a resonance process with the prefrontal areas.
- *Emotional balance:* Middle prefrontal regions monitor and inhibit limbic firing with high levels of bidirectional flow, enhancing emotional life but not so much that it becomes chaotic.
- *Response flexibility:* The capacity to pause before responding or taking action. The middle prefrontal regions work in conjunction with the side areas to allow for this flexibility in responding.
- *Empathy:* Limbic and bodily changes are initiated as we perceive another's experience. Next, the middle prefrontal regions use interoception to integrate these bodily and subcortical states into the prefrontal region by way of the insula. Bodily and mental states are interpreted as reflections of what the other person might be going through.
- *Insight or self-knowing awareness:* The middle prefrontal cortex has input and output fibers to many areas, including past emotional experience and how it relates to current experiencing.
- *Fear modulation:* May occur through release of gamma-aminobutyric acid onto the lower limbic areas that mediate fear. Although fear may be learned through the limbic system, the unlearning of fear may be possible through growth of the middle prefrontal fibers that modulate fear.
- *Intuition:* The body's wisdom is a neural mechanism by which we process deep knowing via our body's parallel distributive processing system that surrounds the viscera. This input is registered in the middle prefrontal cortex and then influences our reasoning and response.

- *Morality:* Studies suggest that activity in the middle prefrontal cortex is involved in the mediation of morality. This involves taking in the whole picture and imagining what is best for the whole and not for just one's self. Moral thinking is impaired when the middle prefrontal region is damaged.

The ability to balance one's bodily and emotional states, attune to ourselves and others, respond with flexibility on the basis of what is presented in the moment, empathize, access insight and intuition, manage or moderate our fear, and respond (morally) in a way that is with and for the client and not driven by self-interest are reflections of therapeutic presence and suggest involvement of the middle prefrontal cortex in the experience of therapeutic presence.

The relationship between the prefrontal cortex and presence is also reflected in a measure of "presence" in virtual reality research. In particular, virtual presence, or "the feeling of being there" in a virtual experience that is subjectively experienced as being a real experience, indicates that the presence experience is modulated by the dorsolateral prefrontal cortex (dlPFC) (Beeli, Casutt, Baumgartner, & Jancke, 2008).

## Practicing Presence Leads to Sustained Presence

If we engage in activities or efforts to cultivate and allow for the emergence of the experience of presence, then an eventual strengthening of related brain structures (i.e., middle prefrontal regions) can occur, and eventually this presence state of awareness can be accessed without effort. Initially, this intentional presence practice activates the side of the prefrontal regions that are involved with working memory. However, ongoing commitment and practice may induce the neuroplastic changes that lead presence to become more of a personal trait, which is characterized by an ability to effortlessly access a state of presence, and without involving activity in the side prefrontal regions (Siegel, 2007).

As noted previously, the term *neuroplasticity* is used when neural connections change in response to experience (Siegel, 2007). Findings from mindfulness studies indicate that paying attention in the moment with openness and nonjudgment, a way of paying attention that cultivates presence, promotes structural changes in the brain (Lazar et al., 2005). Furthermore, Davidson (2004) found that approaching emotional experience with an accepting in-the-moment attitude as opposed to avoiding emotionally laden experience results in a left anterior shift, which results in greater ability to regulate one's emotions.

Davidson and Lutz (2008) found that long-term meditators showed greater activation in brain regions associated with monitoring (in the dlPFC) and engaging attention (visual cortex) than did novice meditators.

Furthermore, structural changes reflected an inverted U-shaped curve, meaning that long-term meditators (19,000 hr of practice) had increased activity in these regions compared with novices. The long-term meditators who were deemed expert meditators and had a longer practice (44,000 hr of practice compared with 19,000 hr) showed less activation in those areas and reflected the general research on skill acquisition. In particular, the authors suggested that this latter finding supports the idea that after extensive practice of meditation, minimal effort is necessary to sustain attention (Davidson & Lutz, 2008). This suggests that presence practice can potentially lead to greater access and sustenance of aspects of the presence experience.

## Being Calm, Centered, and Alert: Balancing the Autonomic Nervous System

When we are fully present, there is an activation of the central circuits of the nervous system and the parasympathetic nervous system (PNS), a component of the autonomic nervous system (ANS; Hanson & Mendius, 2009). The PNS is responsible for the fundamental maintenance of the bodily functions, which include breathing, heartbeat, digestion, rest, and sleep. Activation of the PNS is the normal, steady, resting state of the brain and body and includes a quieting of mind and body and a sense of tranquility, and it complements the fight–flight response in the sympathetic nervous system (SNS). Activation of the SNS is a change in the baseline of equilibrium of the PNS to respond to a threat or an opportunity (Hanson & Mendius, 2009).

The PNS and the SNS work together to maintain a sense of calm alertness, which is the core experience of therapeutic presence. It is possible that through practice the circuits of the calming PNS become more sensitized to creating a reduction in stress reactivity and increase in balance and equanimity (Hanson & Mendius, 2009). A mild activation in the SNS reflects a sense of awakening and alertness. Hence, activation of the PNS and a mild arousal of the SNS create an optimal state for presence to emerge.

Any practice that can reduce stress and physiological arousal, such as diaphragmatic breathing, relaxation practice, yoga, rest, grounding or centering exercises, can elicit the relaxation response, which represents a decrease in measures of physical arousal (skin conductance, heart rate, and breathing rate; Lazar, 2005). The exact neurological mechanisms by which this change may happen differ depending on the activity; however, this type of stress reduction can activate the PNS and through repeated practice help to sustain and provide easy access to a calm and centered place. A practice that heightens alertness (rather than a state of alarm) can activate the SNS. Every time the ANS is calmed by stimulating the PNS, one is leaning the body and mind toward greater calm and well-being.

Balancing the ANS on a regular basis can also help therapists to develop qualities of presence such as grounding, centeredness, and equanimity. These qualities can increase a person's ability to experience painful or difficult events with less reactivity (Lazar, 2005). Furthermore, with sustained practice a person could acquire a greater ability to feel the depth of the other's experience, and even one's own resonant pain, and let go of any painful feelings. For example, Goleman and Schwartz (1976) found that people who practiced meditation, a technique that helps generate relaxation and concentration, had even a slightly larger increase in skin conductance response than controls but then returned to baseline more quickly than people who did not have a sustained practice. This illuminates the possibility that through repeated practice of calming the PNS and enhancing an alert focus of the SNS, the therapist can develop the capacity needed to engage and resonate with the client's painful experience and yet return to a state of calm and equilibrium quickly.

### Presence Exercise: Nudging Toward Calm Alertness

A simple practice that can heighten the PNS as well as mildly alert the SNS is highlighted in Hanson and Mendius (2009), *The Practical Neuroscience of Buddha's Brain: Happiness, Love, and Wisdom:*

> Take five breaths, inhaling and exhaling a little more fully than usual. This is both energizing and relaxing, activating first the sympathetic system and then the parasympathetic one, back and forth, in a gentle rhythm. That combination of aliveness and centeredness is the essence of the peak performance zone recognized by athletes, businesspeople, artists, lovers, and meditators. It's the essence of the SNS and PNS . . . working in harmony together. Happiness, love, and wisdom aren't furthered by shutting down the SNS, but rather by keeping the autonomic nervous system as a whole in an optimal state of balance:
> - Mainly parasympathetic arousal for a baseline of ease and calm
> - Mild SNS activation for vitality, attention and alertness (pp. 59–60)

The practice that Hanson and Mendius (2009) described helps to cultivate presence, particularly this alive, calm, and centered place that is heightened by taking a few full breaths. The ANS helps to regulate every other system and our conscious actions and experience have the greatest direct influence over the ANS than other body systems (Hanson & Mendius, 2009). Thus, stimulating the parasympathetic aspect of the ANS and balancing with a slight activation in the SNS can help to activate the presence experience and promote heightened attention and alertness while remaining calm and relaxed.

## Perceiving the Whole: Right Hemispheric Stimulation

The expansive awareness of presence is related to right hemispheric stimulation or the ability to experience the whole of a situation. Consciousness in and of itself has been defined as the capacity to differentiate as well as to integrate information. At a high level, consciousness demands that we be aware of the whole of a situation but adapt to new information as it is presented. This relates to the capacity in presence to allow one's sensory and cognitive awareness to move moment to moment through experience and to integrate information and experience as they are presented. Taking experience in, integrating it, and letting it go in any conscious capacity reflect the process of presence.

By being in an open, receptive state we are in an optimal position to take in the whole of what is being expressed and experienced by the client in the moment, which then becomes integrated in the therapist's consciousness. This information (as well as our prior learning and experience of therapy, life, and the client) becomes part of the therapist's conscious experience and ultimately guides responding, as it is based on both the integration of material and what is presented or expressed by the client in the moment. Equally important is not holding onto the details of what is being experienced but rather taking it in, allowing for a sense of integration, and then letting it go, all the while being in contact with one's own experience and with the client.

When we focus on the body, as we do in practices of grounding or body-centered practices of coming into the moment, we are inviting a functional shift away from language and conceptual facts (left hemispheric functioning) toward the nonverbal imagery and somatic sensations of the right hemisphere (Siegel, 2007). Through body-centered practices, such as body scan, tai chi, or yoga, we can intentionally support the shift from a more conceptual left-brain dominance to inviting in the spaciousness and holistic perspective that can accompany right-brain functioning.

### Neuronal Integration

Neuroscience research suggests that when one is in the alert, calm, and expansive state of presence, neuronal integration occurs and reflects this experience. This begins with the intention for presence and relates to the sense of being aware of one's self as well as of others, in a calm, accepting, attuned, and nonreactive way. The particular aspects of presence that reflect aspects of the brain and hence reflect neural integration are described below.

## Intention for Presence: Frontal Lobe, Orienting, and Priming

As noted in Chapter 4, having an intention for presence is helpful in allowing for presence to be experienced in session. From a neurological perspective, intentions engage the frontal lobe and create an integrated state of priming, which is a gearing up of our neural system to be in the mode that we are intending (e.g., to be present; Hanson & Mendius, 2009; Siegel, 2007). This neural priming for presence helps to prepare therapists to receive, sense, focus, and behave in a way that is therapeutically present. When we set an intention to be present, we are directing our attention and our body toward the presence state itself, which allows the neuronal correlates of presence to activate.

Siegel (2007) proposed that the intention to be open likely primes the areas of the brain that reflect openness, interoception (sensing inwardly), and receptivity. Siegel (2007) noted that "intentional states integrate the whole neural state in the moment" (p. 178). When an intention comes to fruition, the inner experience of this coming together of intention into a unified aim (e.g., intention for presence turning into the actual experience of presence) reflects a neural coherence (Hanson & Mendius, 2009). Repeated activation of intention and the experience of presence can result in structural changes in the brain toward neural integration.

Taking a few moments to set intention and cultivate presence just prior to a session can stimulate an entire physioneurological process in the body and brain. In these few moments before seeing a client, setting the intention will likely engage some of the neurological underpinnings of the presence experience itself. The parasympathetic wing of the ANS is stimulated by pausing and being still, inviting a greater sense of calm. A mild activation of the sympathetic wing may commence by focusing your attention on your intention for presence. Your muscles may relax a little, and the softening of your facial muscles may begin to mirror and heighten the experience of presence in your body. Just as creating the facial muscles of an emotion can enhance that emotion (Niedenthal, 2007), reproducing softer, more open facial muscles can enhance the experience of presence. You will likely activate the limbic system if you are able to focus on the good feeling associated with presence, making it possible to be increasingly drawn to this state in the future. Also, you can add the power of cortical language (Hanson & Mendius, 2009) by commenting in sync with your breath ("letting go of busyness, coming into the moment"). A sense of neural integration can begin to occur, particularly if you begin to feel yourself becoming more present with respect to your intention. Hence, a few moments of setting intention and arriving into the present can support the physiological and neurological experience of presence.

## Receptivity and Neural Integration

Receptivity, a key aspect of therapeutic presence, means creating a space inside to be open to whatever arises in the therapeutic encounter. Although the particular brain state that is associated with receptivity is unknown, Siegel (2007) proposed an overall brain state of "neural integration" connecting body, brain stem, limbic regions, and cortex that reflects what may be occurring in this receptive state. Being open and allowing in this way means letting go of what we think should or might occur and moving from a premonitory reactive state to one of becoming open and receptive.

Receptivity needs to include a component of self-observation and self-regulation, which are directly associated with activation of the middle prefrontal areas, that is, the medial prefrontal and anterior cingulated cortex (ACC; Beitman, Viamontes, Soth, & Nitler, 2006; Decety & Chaminade, 2003). Siegel (2007) proposed that it is self-attunement that creates a neural state of integration, which then forms the basis for this receptive awareness. Being aware of one's self and one's emotions, having an ability to self-regulate to put aside what is pulling attention, and creating an open receptive state inside may reflect neuronal integration. The state of interoception (sensing our internal word) is largely reflected in the ACC (Hanson & Mendius, 2009). Hence, attention to fostering this neural integration is essential in allowing a receptive state to emerge more easily.

## Inward Attending and Emotional Regulation

To be present, the therapist needs to be attuned to the self, which promotes neural integration (Hanson & Mendius, 2009; Siegel, 2007). What, then, is the benefit of neural integration? The notion is that neural integration supports coordination and balance in the functioning of the brain (Siegel, 2007). This allows for greater balance in systems such as the ANS, which supports the presence state of calm alertness. Hence, the integration of positive brain functioning, internal attunement, and attunement or connection with others supports an overall state of presence and a deepening of relationship with the client.

Inward attending also allows for greater ability to regulate one's emotions. The ACC, which is part of the limbic system, has been identified as a key player in the regulation of emotions. Regulating emotions and general self-regulation (i.e., body regulation) are helpful not only in cultivating a state of present-focused otherness but also in sustaining this state of presence when therapists may be triggered by difficult emotions in their own life or in the therapy encounter.

Research indicates that increased focus on strengthening brain circuitry is related to improvement in emotional regulation, leads to a greater ability to regulate emotional arousal, and lessens the time needed to recover from an aroused and difficult emotional state (Rueda, Posner, & Rothbart, 2005). Overall, the specific areas associated with regulation are part of the middle prefrontal regions, and the development of these areas appears crucial for emotional and attentional in-the-moment focus and functioning (Siegel, 2007).

Davidson (2000) demonstrated the effects of present-moment or mindfulness practices on emotional regulation and has explained this relationship in terms of affective style. *Affective style* "refers to consistent individual differences in emotional reactivity and regulation" (Davidson, 2000, p. 1196). Affective style in resilient individuals refers both to the capacity to regulate negative emotions and a decrease in the duration of negative affect when it does arise. Nonreactivity is central to resilience and, according to Davidson, is centrally focused on the relationship between the prefrontal cortex and the amygdala. Affective style is not fixed as had been typically thought, but rather can be viewed as a skill that can be learned through experience and is highly teachable.

Research in psychology and neuroscience has shown that people who use words to describe their internal states (including their emotions and perceptions) are more flexible and capable of regulating their emotions in an adaptive way (Oshsner, Bunge, Gross, & Gabrieli, 2002). Researchers have noted in brain scans that labeling intense emotions that are generated through seeing a picture keeps limbic firing more in balance than observing an intensely emotional experience but not naming it (Hariri, Bookheimer, & Maziotta, 2000). Furthermore, the ability to put words to emotions represents a state of integration between the activity of the left hemisphere (language) and the right hemisphere (balance of the arousal of the limbic amygdala; Siegel, 2007). This supports the notion that being with our experience, and naming it or labeling it, activates a neurobiological process that then helps to calm or regulate the intensity of the experience. Hence, being with, sensing, and naming internally therapists' intense emotional arousal, either in session or in life, can help to generate greater emotional regulation and hence support the ability to be present and open to whatever is being experienced without being overwhelmed.

## ATTENTION AND WITNESSING WHAT IS MOST POIGNANT: THE ACC, THE LIMBIC SYSTEM, AND THE PREFRONTAL CORTEX

At this stage in research, there is no definitive evidence of the neurological underpinnings of the kind of attention that is cultivated through presence practice. Most research on attention is focused on tasks that are active, such as attending to a stimulus or flexibly altering attention when a stimulus is changed (Siegel, 2007). Attention associated with presence is of a different quality and reflects more of a receptive, open, and immersed attention as well as a meta-awareness of experience. The research suggests that attentional networks can be modified with practice. For example, a pilot study showed that mindful awareness training could significantly improve the executive functioning of attention in adults and adolescents with genetically vulnerable forms of attention-deficit/hyperactivity disorder (Zylowska et al., 2007). Participants reported both an improvement in well-being and an increased capacity to focus attention, which suggests that attention is a teachable skill.

With respect to particular forms of attention, it is well-accepted that there are three types: alerting, orienting, and executive attention. *Alerting* involves sustained attention, vigilance, and alertness, which reflects a readying of our minds to be open to whatever arises, the open and receptive position of presence. Imaging studies suggest that the frontal and parietal regions, especially on the right side of the brain, are key to sustaining this alertness (Siegel, 2007). *Orienting* reflects the capacity to select certain information from a variety of options, such as when we pay attention with presence to that which is most poignant. Although most of the research on orienting has centered on visual attention, it is limited in terms of a full understanding of the attention of presence. Nonetheless, areas of the brain specific to the stimuli tend to be those that are activated, such as the superior parietal cortex in voluntary shifts of attention (Siegel, 2007).

*Executive attention* has different features, which include selective, supervisory, and focused attention. Brain imaging studies have implied that the ACC is central to executive attention (Hanson & Mendius, 2009). The ACC is also involved in distributing attentional focus and in regulating emotional arousal (Siegel, 2007). Research on mindfulness meditation reveals that there is involvement of the ACC when participants experience an associated stability and calmness both on the level of the body and attention (Cahn & Polich, 2006). Hence, activities or practices that require focused attention on the breath or an object can stimulate the neuronal regions that can mediate neuroplastic changes in the brain and can then help to sustain focused attention.

## PRESENCE AS BASIS FOR EMPATHY: MIRROR NEURONS, ADAPTIVE OSCILLATORS, AND THE INSULA

There is evidence to show that the ability to attune to one's own internal state, or inwardly attending in presence language, is the basis for attuning to and understanding the other (Siegel, 2007). Although attuning to others facilitates a similar mirror process in ourselves, attending and attuning to this internal felt sense of the other in the self allow therapists to access their own bodily understanding to reflect back to the client.

The attunement and deep understanding of the other as based in the self, which therapeutic presence allows for, can be partially understood by mirror neurons, adaptive oscillators, and other similar processes that neuroscience has yet to reveal. The discovery of mirror neurons has been critical in understanding the neurobiological mechanisms involved in reading other's people's emotions and states of mind, resonating with another, experiencing what someone else is experiencing, and basically empathizing with another and establishing intersubjective contact (Stern, 2004). Mirror neurons sit beside motor neurons and fire in a person who is doing nothing except watching another person behave or feel. That is how therapists' experience the client *as if* they were in the other's experience, neurologically acting and feeling as if they were the other person. The therapist gets a sense from the inside out of what the other person is going through. Hence, attending and attuning inwardly to the therapist's own sensory experience, a key aspect of presence, can provide the foundation for understanding and attuning to others.

Hence, when the therapist is present, receptive, and deeply engaged in the moment with a client, he or she is taking in the experience not only on a felt level but also on a neurobiological level, which allows him or her to access a personal and bodily centered sensing of what the other is experiencing. This intersubjective neuronal sharing is experienced as a deep connection, knowing, and intuitive sensing of the other's experience. The emotional resonance that is felt by therapist and client when they share a moment in presence is said to be a functional outcome of attunement (Siegel, 2007). Therapists are using their sensory awareness to take in the client's experience, and the mirror neurons perceive these sensations by way of the insula and limbic (emotional) and bodily states to match a level of what is experienced in the client. The therapist draws on these bodily and limbic shifts through the process of interoception, an inward perception of the therapist's experience of the other. In this way the therapist senses in his or her own body, a part of the process of presence, what is occurring in the emotional and physical body of the client. Hence, for attunement and empathy to occur, the therapist needs to first be open to the other and present with his or her own internal state in order to sense the felt experience of the other.

The other neuronal correlate, adaptive oscillators, could explain the experience of knowing the other through direct engagement in the moment with him or her. To take in and resonate with another human being, one needs to be in sync with that person. Like a dance between partners who move in temporal coordination, there is a participation in the other's experience (Stern, 2004). Adaptive oscillators act like clocks in the body, which can be reset over and over so that their rate of firing is adjusted to match the rate of firing of the incoming stimuli. In clinical terms, when the therapist is open and in sync with the client, there is a shared reality (or intersubjective consciousness) that is reflected in the adapting of the therapist's neural firing so it is in sync with the client's neural firing, which further deepens the sense of synchronicity and deep knowing of the other. When two people are in synchronicity, they are participating in an aspect of each other's experience and living partially from each other's inner world (Stern, 2004).

## NEUROCEPTION OF SAFETY: THERAPIST'S PRESENCE AND CLIENT'S SENSE OF SAFETY

We have proposed that the therapist's receptive presence sends a message to the client that he or she is going to be felt and understood in a safe environment and that receptive presence has a neurological correlate. When the client feels felt by the therapist, he or she not only feels aligned with the therapist but also the brain likely establishes a state of "neuroception" of safety (Porges, 1998, 2009). Porges (1998, 2009) proposed that the nervous system evaluates the state of safety or threat and activates the brain stem's vagal and ANS to respond to a sense of open receptivity with safety or to a closed state with threat. If the client senses threat, then the nervous system either goes into a state of fight–flight with activation of the SNS or freezes with the PNS creating a state of collapse. When approached with the open, receptive state of presence, attunement is possible between the therapist and client and a sense of safety is created, which follows with a biological response of softening of facial muscles, relaxation in vocal tone, and a perceptual openness to the therapist (Siegel, 2007). Porges (1998) noted that with the neuroception of safety there is a possible release of the hormone oxytocin, which we propose supports the client in becoming softer and more open. This release of oxytocin contributes to the creation of a loving relationship between the therapist and client.

## CONCLUSION

Experience imprints the brain with lasting and enduring effects. Hence, our present-moment experiences are cumulative, and they matter for both the experience in and of itself and the lasting residues it leaves, which become woven into our neurophysiology and can therefore enhance both neurologically and psychologically the ability to access presence. Hence, when we generate the experience of presence we are strengthening neural substrates that allow for presence to emerge, in ourselves and in our clients.

Although there is a whole field opening up in neurobiology, which is in its beginning stages, we need to balance this understanding without getting too simplistic or reductionist. We know that the experience of therapeutic presence is much more than our nervous system reflects; we know that it is multifaceted and includes experiential, cognitive, spiritual, and physical components. What neuroscience does give us, however, is growing evidence that cultivating presence can lead to neuronal changes that allow for a more ongoing familiarity and accessibility of the experience of presence.

# IV

## THE CULTIVATION OF THERAPEUTIC PRESENCE

# 10

## BUDDHIST MINDFULNESS: A WAY OF ENHANCING THERAPEUTIC PRESENCE

The most precious gift we can offer others is our presence. When our mindfulness embraces those we love, they will bloom like flowers.
—Thich Nhat Hanh (2007, p. 20)

Mindfulness is a profound way of cultivating present-moment attention and hence can be a way of facilitating therapeutic presence. The Buddhist and mindfulness perspectives recognize that at the core of who we are is deep potential for wisdom and wholeness. Unlike humanistic approaches that see the self as a process that is evolving or actualizing through life experiences, the Buddhist approach sees our core as already actualized. Through the dropping away of identity, needs, hunger for attention, longing, greed, and desire, our innate wisdom is illuminated. Mindfulness practices focus on quieting the mind and facing and resolving our core grasping to our needs and hungers. Like the ocean of mind, when the waves of hunger, grasping, and aversion settle, the presence and innate wisdom at the depth of being can emerge.

In this chapter, we explicate mindfulness as one way that therapeutic presence can be facilitated. We look at the cultivation of presence with mindfulness through the *four noble truths* in Buddhism: Life is suffering; causes of suffering; cessation of suffering; and the path to the cessation of suffering. We explore the benefits of mindfulness in the cultivation of presence as well as present a clinical vignette as to how mindful awareness can help in session. We also look at some of the research, including the neurobiological studies of mindfulness, that indicates an enhancement of qualities of presence through mindfulness practice. Although mindfulness practices continue to broaden and diversify and are important for developing presence, we also discuss additional individual and relational practices that can be used to enhance one's sense of therapeutic and relational presence.

## WHAT IS MINDFULNESS?

Mindfulness is based in Buddhist philosophy and has been adopted in Western approaches as a therapeutic aid as well as to help in the development of present-moment awareness. Although references to mindfulness have recently exploded in the literature (Bien, 2006; Cole & Ladas-Gaskin, 2007; Germer, 2005; Germer, Siegel, & Fulton, 2005; Hick, 2008; Linehan, 1993a, 1993b; Mace, 2008; McKay, Brantley, & Wood, 2007; Shapiro & Carlson, 2009), it is sometimes a broadly based term that can lose meaning in its general usage. A general definition of mindfulness is a way of paying attention to the present moment, on purpose and without judgment (Kabat-Zinn, 1990, 2005). A similar basic description or definition of mindfulness includes moment-to-moment awareness of present experience with acceptance (Germer, 2005).

Mindfulness involves "clear seeing yet with undiminished compassion" (Salzberg, 1999, p. 7). Mindfulness involves a willingness to come close to our pain and discomfort without judgment, striving, manipulation, or pretense (Salzberg, 1999; Santorelli, 1999; Welwood, 1996). Mindfulness with ourselves and our experience parallels humanistic approaches to being with and accepting clients' experience—but it is mainly focused on the self rather than the other. It is a way of being genuinely with our own experience, with empathy, unconditional positive regard, and acceptance. Therapists' personal practice of mindfulness can help to cultivate qualities of acceptance, empathy, compassion, and presence within one's self and, by extension, ultimately within the client.

Mindfulness is based on the Pali term *satipatthana*, with *sati* generally meaning "attention" or "awareness" and *patthana* meaning "keeping present" (Germer, 2005; Thera, 1973). The teachings of satipatthana are among the oldest of Buddhist teachings, outlining specific meditation techniques for cultivating present awareness or mindfulness (Deatherage, 1975). To be completely mindful is to be aware of the full range of experiences that exist in the present moment (Marlatt & Kristeller, 1999).

Mindfulness was operationalized for research purposes as having five facets: (a) nonreactivity to inner experience, (b) observing/noticing/attending to sensations/perceptions/thoughts/feelings, (c) acting with awareness/ (non)automatic pilot/concentration/nondistraction, (d) describing/labeling with words, and (e) nonjudging of experience (Baer, 2006). These dimensions represent distinct facets of mindfulness, with some overlap but a lot of independence.

Dimidjian and Linehan (2003), working within a dialectical behavioral therapy (DBT) framework, also developed an operational definition of mindfulness as having three qualities and three associated activities. The three qualities are (a) observing, (b) describing, and (c) participating. The associated activities are (a) nonjudgmentally, with acceptance, allowing; (b) labeling, describing, and noting; and (c) doing these effectively. Bishop et al. (2004) operationalized mindfulness as having two components: metacognitive skills and orientation to the present moment.

Mindfulness practice helps one develop an open and accepting relationship with one's own present-moment experience. Mindfulness is a skill that helps one to be less reactive to what is occurring in the moment, such as to one's own pain and suffering (Germer, 2005). The main idea behind mindfulness is that if we have less reactivity to our experience, whether it be positive, negative, or neutral, our suffering will be reduced. Hence, mindfulness is a set of skills that allows practice in cultivating presence.

## DISTINCTION BETWEEN MINDFULNESS AND THERAPEUTIC PRESENCE

As discussed in the Introduction to this volume, therapeutic presence and mindfulness are distinct in two important ways. First, mindfulness is a *technique* that can help to cultivate the *experience* of presence. In this vein, mindfulness is a method that allows an opening and being with one's emerging experience in a nonjudgmental and accepting way, whereas presence is the state achieved through mindfulness practice. Second, mindfulness is primarily presented in the literature as an approach within an individual (i.e., within the therapist or more so as a skill for clients to develop) to work with his or her internal world, whereas therapeutic presence is a relational therapeutic stance that includes the therapist's present-centered sensory attention in direct relationship to the client's in-the-moment experience.

The term *mindfulness* is sometimes used interchangeably with *presence* in the literature; however, this is a confusion of terms. For example, mindfulness has been noted to be an "embodied state of being" (Hick, 2008). We view mindfulness as a practice or a set of skills that supports the cultivation and maintenance of the experience of therapeutic presence. This view is supported by Hanson (2007), who distinguished mindfulness as the practice of clear nonjudgmental awareness of your inner and outer world from presence, which is "the stability of mindfulness, the degree to which you are grounded in awareness itself" (p. 1).

Shapiro and Carlson (2009) attempted to clarify the confusion surrounding the term *mindfulness* by distinguishing between mindfulness as a process (mindful practice) and an outcome (mindful awareness). They defined *mindful practice* as "the systematic practice of intentionally attending in an open, caring, and discerning way, which involves both knowing and shaping the mind" and *mindful awareness* as "an abiding presence or awareness, a deep knowing that manifests itself as freedom of mind" (Shapiro & Carlson, 2009, p. 4). Although mindful awareness reflects more of the presence experience we have been describing, it has not been fully studied or explicated as therapeutic presence has, so it is difficult to compare them. One important difference is that therapeutic presence is a relational experience of being fully in the moment that is bodily, sensory, and interpersonal, whereas mindful awareness is within the self, a mind-based present-moment awareness.

Mindfulness helps the therapist to be open, accepting, and present with one's self in order to be fully open, accepting, and present with others. Mindfulness for therapists can also help them attune their awareness to their own responsive emotional experiences, professional wisdom, and deeper intuition that emerges through their in-the-moment connection with their clients. Mindfulness also helps to develop the capacity to observe and be with experience without getting overwhelmed. An expansion of self and a sense of luminosity or spaciousness are consequences of mindfulness (Epstein, 1995; Salzberg, 1999; Welwood, 2000). The quality of expansion combined with grounding allows one to view and feel experiences with clarity and impartiality, without getting caught in the details of the suffering.

## THE FOUR NOBLE TRUTHS: MINDFULNESS AND THE CULTIVATION OF THERAPEUTIC PRESENCE

The basic teachings of Buddhist philosophy include an understanding of the roots of suffering as well as a way to eliminate suffering. These teachings are called the *four noble truths* and are described next in relationship to therapy. When we understand the four noble truths as a way to reduce suffering by removing barriers to presence and opening to present-moment awareness, then we can see how mindfulness can help to cultivate therapeutic presence.

### First Noble Truth: Life Is Suffering

The Buddha taught that suffering is inevitable. When he left the shelter of his father's kingdom, Siddhartha Gautama (Buddha) was said to be shocked by the reality of aging, illness, and death. The Buddha recognized that people spend much of their lives in pain, stress, and confusion. In short, the first noble truth is based on an acceptance of the fact that life is suffering.

Many therapists enter into the practice of psychotherapy from a childhood or life filled with wounds and challenges. Seeking freedom from this pain through helping others can further deepen one's difficulties through an overidentification as a helper or healer. In particular, our own wounds that have not been worked with or healed become the greatest barrier to effectively helping others find intra- and interpersonal freedom. A recognition of the natural suffering that is tied to human living is a necessary step in proceeding through an understanding of the four noble truths.

A quick assessment of our own daily lives and the lives around us provides a clear indication of this fact: We see and experience great stress. The multiple roles we take on as therapists, supervisors, educators, researchers, parents, sons or daughters, friends, teachers, and so on are a mere beginning to the stresses we carry. There are minor stresses, such as traffic and computer breakdowns, and there are much greater stresses that we deal with in our daily lives, such as the loss of a loved one, illness, financial burdens, and relationship breakdowns. Advertisements are created to remind us of what we are missing, and shopping for clothes, homes, new products, music, alcohol, and so on helps to distract us from our pain and misery. In fact 60% to 90% of all physician visits result from stress-related disorders (Cummings & VandenBos, 1981).

Whereas human suffering is not new, a whole other level of suffering derives from our developed yet complex emotional worlds, which is reflected as interpersonal suffering (Kramer, 2007). Sickness and death from cancer, high rates of divorce, and stormy emotional worlds that are sometimes hard to control are just a few examples of interpersonal suffering. A particular form of suffering that we see too frequently is deep loneliness; because we live in a time of a breakdown of families and communities, the loss of an intimate other or sense of belonging causes some people great suffering. Our work as therapists, in individual offices and separated from a larger community of support, can also evoke this sense of loneliness. Often it is our deep fear of death and emptiness that is at the root of this sense of isolation (Yalom, 2008).

Social and environmental suffering is also of great concern as we witness the depletion of our planetary resources and see that global climate change may be contributing to tsunamis, earthquakes, and flooding that cause the destruction of entire communities. The reality is that multiple levels of suffering—physical, interpersonal, and social—coexist in our personal lives and in society by virtue of the mere fact that we are human (Kramer, 2007).

The first noble truth in Buddhism calls us to look directly at the suffering that we experience, on both a personal and a societal level. We are shaped to avoid this direct witnessing through the distraction of our busyness or fear that we are being too pessimistic. However, ignoring the fact of our suffering and how we contribute to it is not helpful and, in fact, feeds the continuity of our suffering. The Buddha taught that the distraction from and ignorance of this reality cause further suffering. An alternative view is to slow down enough to enhance the capacity to observe suffering and to observe how our emotional reactivity and drive for busyness and distraction contribute to the source of suffering and create barriers to intimacy. From direct witnessing, we have more opportunity to create different choices to alter some of our internal and life reactivity and busyness that are creating barriers to presence and living a whole and contented life.

## Second Noble Truth: Causes of Suffering

The second noble truth is based in an understanding of that which causes deep suffering, which, according to the Buddhist perspective, is a consequence of attachment to a particular state or feeling, sense of identity, longing, greed, or desire. Suffering also emerges from viewing experiences, thoughts, and sensations as fixed and static. Suffering from a Buddhist perspective is also based in desire. Whenever there is a gap between one's natural experience in the moment and what one wants to have happen, suffering is inevitable.

The second noble truth, causes of suffering, can be translated to therapists as both attachment and aversion in relationships with our clients, others in our lives, and ourselves. With clients, attachment to a particular outcome for the client, such as healing, means leaving this relationship or having a particular experience that can cause greater suffering in the therapeutic relationship. Therapists' imposition of their own need to help as well as their interpretation of what helping means, blocks clients from discovering within their own experience what their pain is and what is necessary or helpful for them to lead a fuller or easier life. As therapists, we often think we know what others need, not just our clients but our friends, family, and loved ones, and this can cause both a shutting down from the other and between self and other. Furthermore, our own discomfort with the deep pain that our clients may experience can cause deeper suffering as we are inclined to fix rather than to learn how to meet or be with a client where he or she is.

## Third Noble Truth: Cessation of Suffering

The third noble truth reflects what is necessary for the cessation of suffering. According to Buddhist philosophy, true freedom comes from viewing the transient nature of experience, and relating to our pain and distress, and joy and happiness, with an attitude of nonattachment, compassion, loving-kindness, and acceptance. The perspective here is that if we can accept life and experience as they are, without wanting them to be different, the cessation of suffering is possible. This is not to say that pain is not a part of the human experience but that the suffering that arises from reacting to pain (or pleasure) with aversion or grasping can be eliminated through practice.

The Buddha spoke of the gradual eradication of suffering rather than an abrupt shedding of its causes (Kramer, 2007). In this regard, the gradual relinquishing of our attachment as therapists, or to "healing" the client, is directly related to our letting go of our own self-identity as healers. The fading of this attachment means a letting go of our own need to feel good and worthwhile through the helping of others. This requires going deep into our own core beliefs that we are not worthy or that we need the acknowledgment of others to feel good and worthy in ourselves.

Interpersonal Buddhism recognizes the relinquishing of the three hungers—for pleasure, for being, and for nonbeing—as an opportunity to allow our innate presence to be emancipated (Kramer, 2007). Each of these hungers has an associated fear. The desire for pleasure is accompanied by the fear of pain. When we sit with clients in their pain and suffering, our resonance with pain emerges, and it is through the fear of feeling this pain that we can shut down our ability to be present with clients. The hunger for being is accompanied by the fear of invisibility. The therapist's own need to be seen and recognized as powerful and helpful can provide an obstacle to the ability to put one's self aside and be there fully and completely for the client. This can also take shape in offering interventions or techniques that are not emerging from the present experience of the client, as it may reflect a more subtle need in the therapist to show competence or feel he or she is making a difference. Finally, the hunger for nonbeing, or escape, is shadowed by a fear of intimacy and engagement. The closeness that therapeutic presence can demand can be frightening for therapists, particularly if they do not have a sense of inner stability and groundedness. The terror of losing who we are can prevent us from opening with pure receptivity to the client. Kramer (2007) described the root of all of these fears of losing the self as the "terror of emptiness, the concern that this self—personal or social—will die in a cold nothingness" (p. 57).

It is the fading of this attachment to pleasure, being, and nonbeing that allows for a natural opening to a receptive presence. When therapists resolve the attachment to being and pleasure, such as being the healer for their client and being recognized for that role, and gently resolve the fear of nothingness, new ways of relating, based on presence, can emerge. At the core of this fading of the fear of invisibility is a fading of the fear of emptiness. When we can let go of this hunger for being seen and having our egos enhanced through recognition from the other, then we can become freer from these core fears. When we can let go of the craving for pleasure and acknowledgment and not shrink from engagement with the other, presence, wisdom, and compassion can naturally emerge.

## Fourth Noble Truth: The Path to the Cessation of Suffering

The fourth noble truth focuses on how to eradicate suffering. Over the 2,500 years of Buddhist practice, many different ways have emerged that can lead to the elimination of suffering. We discussed the loosening of hunger, grasping, and aversion and allowing the natural presence state to emerge. The traditional path to the elimination of suffering is expressed in what Buddhists call the *eightfold path*. The eightfold path includes guidelines for living one's life in the moment according to ethical or appropriate principles. They are not sequential; the steps along the path can be practiced simultaneously to support and reinforce each other. The eightfold path as adapted from Germer, Siegel, and Fulton (2005) is the following:

- *Right view* includes awakening or seeing things as they really are, without judgment or pretense.
- *Right intention* includes having an intention in one's action, speech, and behavior that is in the best or highest interest of respect and well-being for one's self and others.
- *Right speech* includes being aware of what one says so that our words and tone reflect being truthful, compassionate, kind, selfless, respectful, and in service of healing rather than harm.
- *Right action* was traditionally used in monastic life to reflect living by ethical precepts, which include not killing, not stealing, not lying, not sexually misbehaving, and not indulging in intoxicants.
- *Right livelihood* was a traditional notion for choosing a profession and livelihood that are in sync with ethical precepts such as avoiding killing, stealing, and harming others.
- *Right effort* reflects an effort to develop a wholesome quality of inner and mental life, which includes the intentional cultivation of mindful states and the deliberate elimination of harmful or mindless states.
- *Right mindfulness* includes following the foundations of mindful practice (mindfulness of body, feelings, mind, and mental objects) so that one is constantly applying careful and even attention to phenomena as they arise.
- *Right concentration* includes intentional practice from time to time, outside of daily activities or awareness, to cultivate mental development and qualities of presence. This includes intentional mindfulness practice such as mindfulness meditation.

The four noble truths, culminating in the eightfold path, have been popularized in the West in the form of mindfulness and have become a clinical treatment or an adjunct for therapeutic change in clients. One of the initial popular attempts by which mindfulness was integrated into the medical system was facilitated by Jon Kabat-Zinn at the University of Massachusetts Medical School. Mindfulness-based stress reduction (MBSR) continues to be offered as a treatment approach for people with chronic pain, depression, anxiety, stress, eating disorders, or addictions.

Beginning with studies based on the MBSR program as well as Zen Buddhism, interest in mindfulness has spread, and the approach has been adopted in psychoanalytic approaches (Epstein, 1995; Safran & Reading, 2008), mindfulness-based cognitive therapy (MBCT; Segal, Williams, & Teasdale, 2002), DBT (Linehan, 1993a, 1993b; McKay, Brantley, & Wood 2007), acceptance and commitment therapy (Hayes, Strosahl, & Wilson, 1999), and humanistic and experiential therapy approaches (Geller, 2003). However, the majority of approaches incorporating mindfulness, including the vast amount of research to date, have focused on clients' use of mindfulness skills in changing negative thoughts or affect as well as in developing acceptance or self-compassion.

## INTERPERSONAL MINDFULNESS

Traditionally, the eightfold path has been interpreted according to personal life and personal practice. Mindfulness has traditionally been an intrapersonal practice that is focused on gaining awareness and accepting one's own internal experience. In relation to therapy, the predominant perspective is that by gaining more awareness, acceptance, and equanimity within one's self, one can be more present and accepting for the client. Although enhancing our internal ability to be focused on the present with compassion and deep understanding is said to eradicate suffering and enhance our ability to be in a state of calm presence, it does not always reach the interpersonal domain (Kramer, 2007).

Recent mindfulness perspectives that incorporate an interpersonal focus recognize that it is valuable to practice mindfulness or present-moment awareness with others, given that much of our life is relationally based (Kramer, 2007). This is particularly true for therapists and would add great value in a training program focused on enhancing relational therapeutic presence.

The first author (S. G.) recalls returning from a 10-day vipassana/mindfulness retreat. She achieved a state of calm exuberance in which she experienced a heightened state of sensitivity to the moment combined with a sense of peace and contentment. It was only hours following her return that the tension with her then partner returned. This has always been a struggle for her following retreats, that is, the calm inner space that she so readily achieved in a retreat became a struggle to maintain with family and loved ones. While both intentional and life practice are helpful in enhancing a state of calm in-the-moment alertness, we are relational beings, and mindfulness practice does not often directly attend to this relational aspect of our lives.

Hence, the cultivation of presence needs to occur through reducing suffering and enhancing present-moment awareness both within one's self and in relation with others. When we are with others, it is harder to hide behind the normal distractions and delusions that we use to muddle through our lives, as our distraction is reflected back through either overinvolvement or distancing. Hence, moments or practices of interpersonal mindfulness can enhance the shared presence that can occur in both the personal life of the therapist and the therapeutic relationship with the client. In this vein, the traditional notion of the eightfold path can be lived and practiced both personally and interpersonally.

D. J. Siegel (2010) coined the term *mindsight*, which embodies the intrapersonal and interpersonal ability to see our own and others' internal world and to shape it in the direction of health. According to Siegel, mindsight is more than internal awareness (insight) and more than awareness of others (empathy). It is a skill, complementary to and enhanced by the skill of mindfulness, that allows a person to focus deeply on the inner world of self and other and to move the inner world toward health and integration. Mindsight has a basis in mindfulness practice, yet it is different because it involves the intention to use or move this inner and other awareness toward overall mental, neuronal, emotional, and relational well-being.

While mindfulness practices continue to broaden and diversify, we offer here a look at different individual and relational practices that can be used to enhance our sense of therapeutic and relational presence. The more therapists practice opening to themselves and with others completely and fully, without attachment or overinvolvement, the more they are cultivating their capacity for therapeutic presence.

## MINDFULNESS PRACTICE FOR THERAPISTS

Although the majority of mindfulness research in the context of therapy has focused on clients' experience with mindfulness, some approaches have begun to recognize the importance of a personal mindfulness practice for therapists that is essentially from a Buddhist perspective. A personal understanding of the benefits of mindfulness and particularly present-moment awareness is central to the Buddhist approach. The Buddha himself would often respond to disciples' questions about meditation and practice with an encouragement to form opinions or reach clarity through direct experience. "Believe nothing, no matter where you read it, or who said it, no matter if I have said it, unless it agrees with your own reason and your own common sense."

This notion of personal experience and acceptance of the self is akin to experiential and humanistic approaches in which the value of cultivating therapists' qualities of empathy, compassion, care, and presence in their approach with clients has long been recognized. For example, Carl Rogers (1951, 1957) founded the person-centered approach on the notion that creating an environment of safety through the therapist's offering of genuine empathy and unconditional acceptance was essential for the development of a therapeutic relationship and for clients' growth. Clients' natural growth tendencies can emerge under conditions of respect, safety, and acceptance.

Experiential models support the notion that therapists need to have an attuned awareness to recognize client markers and make process directives to facilitate clients in resolving difficult issues. The therapist is supported in attending to nonverbal and verbal responses in the client so that the whole of the client's experience can be captured and worked with to facilitate emotional change. Mindfulness facilitates therapists' attunement in that it helps to deepen their in-the-moment listening and sensing skills.

Other approaches have recognized the therapist's present-moment awareness and ability to cultivate compassionate attention as the basis of a good mutual therapeutic relationship. For example, DBT and MBCT therapies emphasize personal mindfulness practice (Linehan, 1993a, 1993b; Segal, Williams, & Teasdale, 2002) and recognize the value of an accepting attitude from the therapist.

Psychoanalytic therapists (Epstein, 1995; Rubin, 1996; Safran, 2003; Safran & Reading, 2008) have recognized the value of a Buddhist perspective and mindful approaches in their clinical model. Safran and Reading (2008) noted how therapeutic metacommunication is a form of "mindfulness in action" for the psychoanalytic therapist. In the past 2 decades, psychoanalytic therapists have changed their perspective from the therapist as a neutral observer to one who is a cocreator or participant in the therapeutic relationship and process. This interpersonal approach focuses on the mutual emotional environment of the therapist and the client as well as the therapist's ability to regulate his or her emotions during therapeutic enactments or difficult moments. From this view, therapists can use mindful approaches as a tool to regulate their emotions and hence model and support clients through surrogacy affect regulation (Safran & Reading, 2008).

In a recent book, *Mindfulness and the Therapeutic Relationship*, edited by Hick and Bien (2008), a number of authors proposed mindfulness as a way in which therapeutic presence can be facilitated and the therapeutic relationship deepened. For example, Gehart and McCollum (2008) present ways mindfulness practice can be brought into the classroom to facilitate students' experience of presence. Gehart and McCollum also proposed three pathways by which meditation can cultivate empathy: reducing stress, increasing self-compassion, and disidentifying with one's own subjective perception.

Other theorists have proposed that mindful practice heightens qualities in the therapist, such as presence, attention, awareness, warmth, and compassion, that can help to deepen the therapeutic relationship (Shapiro & Carlson, 2009). We know that 30% of variance in psychotherapy outcome can be attributed to common factors such as therapist qualities (presence and empathy) and the therapeutic relationship (Lambert & Barley, 2002; Lambert & Simon, 2008). Hence, it is important to understand if and how mindfulness practice contributes to the cultivation of therapeutic presence and subsequently can deepen the therapeutic alliance.

## CLINICAL VIGNETTE

The following clinical vignette demonstrates how particular Buddhist principles, such as working with aversion, and using mindful practices, such as breath awareness and emotional regulation, can help therapists to notice when they are not present, work with their distraction, and bring their attention back to the moment.

Jeremy's grief over the loss of his father had become difficult to handle, especially given that it had not shifted in the months since his father died. His therapist found herself hesitant and averse to the appointment coming up, noticing her fatigue and internal voice saying that she needed a break from clients in general. The therapist noted her aversion and realized that something larger was at play inside herself, particularly the struggle and lack of competency she felt in not effecting a shift in Jeremy's grief and complete loss of motivation. She silently committed to bringing this issue to her peer supervision this week. However, she still had to meet Jeremy that afternoon and was filled with initial dread regarding how she was going to manage this session.

The therapist's awareness of her nonpresent state in the form of aversion occurred even before the session as she anticipated with dread the upcoming session. Having this level of awareness became a positive invitation to both consciously put this issue of incompetence on a shelf (bracketing) with an intention to return to it at a later time. This awareness can also serve as an invitation to bring her internal state into a more present-centered place prior to and during the session.

Given the hesitancy the therapist was experiencing in approaching the session, she decided to take 5 minutes before the session to bring herself into a more open and centered place. She did some gentle stretching and a mindful breathing exercise that allowed her to feel both her feet on the ground and align her breath with her sense of center, imagining her breath going right through the core of her body. The therapist felt more available when she then approached the door to welcome Jeremy in. Even just a few minutes to breathe, feel her feet on the ground, and align her breathing helped this therapist to be in a more open and present-centered place when meeting the client.

As the session began, Jeremy spoke in his usual way about his lack of motivation, his deep sadness, and his sluggishness. The therapist began to experience that open and centered place she felt start to slip away, and a voice in her head taunted her on her inability to help him. The therapist again noted that voice and the discouragement it made her feel, and set an intention to return to it later. She quickly focused on her body and brought her awareness to her feet on the ground and her sense of center. As she invited her attention back into the moment, she really saw Jeremy in a way she had not before. She noticed this 40-year-old executive with the posture of a little boy. He was gentle, curled into the chair with his head slightly bowed. The therapist also noticed him wringing his hands as the therapist looked into his eyes. As Jeremy spoke further about his sadness and loss, the therapist saw the depth of his despair and the word "incapable" flashed in her mind. She reflected to him the deep despair she saw in his eyes and queried his feeling of being incapable in response to his loss. His eyes began to well up, and he looked at her in a way she had not seen before, with such deep sadness yet relief. He quieted for a moment and then spoke about the loss of not only his dad but also the only person that really believed in him. He spoke of the taunting he had experienced by his sisters and even his mother growing up, and that his dad would always quietly support him and tell him how great he was. In fact, the only reason he has the job now as an executive of a successful advertising agency was because his dad coached him before the interview and helped him to feel confident in himself. His tears flowed as he explored his fear that he would be incapable of succeeding without the presence of his father.

The awareness of this overwhelming and distant reaction the therapist had allowed her to pause briefly, regulate her feelings, and find her center as an access point to return her attention to the moment. This was possible through prior practice and self-awareness so that she could quickly recognize what she was feeling and realign her body and her attention. This awareness, prior practice, and preparation before session allowed her to refocus herself back to being centered and present, which then allowed the therapist to see and feel more deeply what the client was trying to express. As the therapist trusted the poignancy of the despair, which she recognized in her client as well as an intuitive sense or guide to the feeling of being incapable, she reflected back this awareness, which allowed for a deeper opening and feeling understood by the client. It is important to note that it is not the client's feeling better that helped the therapist to feel more competent, as this reflection actually opened up deeper sadness. Rather it was her ability to stay or return to presence and hence be with the despair without feeling overwhelmed or turning away, so that the client could feel understood and express the layers of grief that he was feeling.

After the session ended, Jeremy commented that although his sadness was not any less, he felt "softer" and more understood. He began to express an understanding of the depth of his loss and was hopeful that he could continue to work and succeed, despite the loss of his dad and his great sadness. This therapist's practice of returning to a sense of grounding and centeredness allowed her to bring her attention and focus fully back into the moment.

## RESEARCH ON MINDFUL PRACTICE
## AND THERAPEUTIC PRESENCE

There are few formal research studies with respect to mindfulness and therapeutic presence. However, in the qualitative study discussed in Chapter 2 (Geller & Greenberg, 2002), more than half of the therapists interviewed discussed daily meditation as an important contribution to the development of therapeutic presence. For example, one therapist stated, "I do know that by far the main thing that correlates with increasing presence for me is regular meditation practice" (Geller, 2001). A personal experience and practice of mindfulness meditation tends to allow therapists to move easily into being fully in the moment with their clients.

McCollum and Gehart (2010) conducted a qualitative study examining the impact that mindfulness meditation had for student therapists in helping them to develop therapeutic presence. Master-level students who participated in a practicum course on the clinical component of training were instructed on mindfulness meditation as part of their class requirements and asked to keep a weekly journal about their experience. A thematic analysis was conducted of the journals kept by 13 students. The themes that emerged included the effects of meditation practice, the ability to be present, balancing being and doing modes in therapy, and the development of acceptance and compassion for themselves and for their clients. Findings suggested that students' mindfulness practice helped them to develop qualities that are reflective of therapeutic presence, such as the ability to attend to both the clients and their own experience and to respond from a confluence of both attentions. Students also reported greater acceptance and compassion toward self and others. Findings also suggested that incorporating mindfulness practices into clinical training can support the development of therapeutic presence.

Further evidence for the cultivation of therapeutic presence through mindfulness has emerged from an exploratory study. Vinca (2009) confirmed a significant relationship between mindfulness and therapists' presence using the Therapeutic Presence Inventory (TPI-T) (Geller et al., 2010) and a version of the TPI-client. Hence, the more mindful therapists found themselves to be, the more present they found themselves to be, as well as the more present their clients viewed them as being. Vinca also found a modest to strong relationship between therapeutic presence and a positive session outcome. Findings also revealed that both therapist and client ratings of therapist presence were positively related to therapist empathy and inversely related to therapist anxiety. Hence, the more present the therapist was from both the perspective of the therapist and client, the less anxiety the therapist had and the more empathic their clients experienced them as being.

May and O'Donovan (2007) explored the relationship between mindfulness, well-being, burnout, and job satisfaction in therapists. Findings indicated that higher levels of present-moment, nonjudgmental, and mindful awareness were associated with cognitive and emotional well-being and satisfaction at work. While they found that actual mindful practice of therapists did not enhance mindful awareness, the authors suggested that mindful awareness, akin to presence, can improve the functioning of therapists and ultimately improve client outcome.

One study examined the integration of mindfulness into a therapy training program (Grepmair et al., 2007). The researchers found that therapists in training who also were taught and practiced Zen Buddhist mindfulness meditation before sessions with clients had a greater effect on clients' outcome than therapists who did not meditate prior to sessions. This is akin to our theory that therapists' preparing for presence results in clients having better outcomes. In particular, clients of therapists in training who practiced meditation showed greater symptom reduction than clients of therapists in training who did not meditate.

Shapiro, Brown, and Biegel (2007) proposed that an MBSR program can help to prepare psychotherapy trainees for the demanding work of being a therapist by developing self-care and the cultivation of mindfulness qualities as well as reducing stress. The authors used a prospective, cohort-controlled design and found that participants in the MBSR program reported significant improvements in positive affect and self-compassion, as well as a reduction in stress, negative affect, rumination, and state and trait anxiety. MBSR is suggested as one way in which therapists can increase self-care and one way in which trainees can train the self to be more aware and to regulate one's own thoughts and emotions. These qualities would help therapists to cultivate therapeutic presence both within their self and ultimately with their clients.

Although these studies provide preliminary evidence of the beneficial effects of mindfulness practice and the cultivation of present-moment awareness on the development of a deeper therapeutic relationships and positive outcomes, additional studies are needed.

# HOW DOES MINDFULNESS ENHANCE
# THERAPEUTIC PRESENCE?

Mindfulness practice can help to cultivate therapists' presence in four important ways. First, it can heighten the sustainability of focused attention that is needed when being present in session with a client. Second, mindfulness practice can enhance self-compassion in the therapist and therefore should lead to greater empathy and compassion with clients. The compassion and acceptance developed in mindfulness practice is viewed as ultimately valuable as the basis of compassion and acceptance toward others (Dalai Lama, 2001). Third, mindfulness can offer a way to reduce stress and enhance well-being and care for the therapist's own self, which allows for both the prevention of burnout and greater ability to stay present and connected with clients. Fourth, mindfulness can help generate greater openness and receptivity as well as grounding in one's self, so the therapist can then experience the depth of relational presence with his or her client without feeling overwhelmed. The qualities of therapeutic presence enhanced through mindfulness can ultimately allow for a greater therapeutic relationship to develop, which we know contributes to a positive therapy outcome (Lambert & Simon, 2008).

The relationship of mindful practice and sustained and focused attention has been well documented (Jha, Krompinger, & Baime, 2007; Morgan & Morgan, 2005; Pagnoni & Cekic, 2007; Valentine & Sweet, 1999). For example, a qualitative study revealed that graduate students felt more able to sustain attention, be present, and be comfortable with silence with their clients after mindfulness training (Schure, Christopher, & Christopher, 2008). Valentine and Sweet (1999) demonstrated that practitioners of both mindfulness and concentrative meditation showed greater focused attentional skills, and that mindfulness practitioners were not as affected by expectancy effects. This latter finding suggests that mindfulness practice can help the therapist not only to sustain focus but to be less distracted by and negatively affected by extraneous stimuli or the emergence of unexpected experience or emotion in the client. The ability to have focused attention as well as to shift attention to different stimuli (clients' words and bodily expression, therapists' own self-experience, bodily resonance and intuition, the therapeutic relationship) is essential for the therapeutic presence process. This was confirmed by Shapiro and Carlson (2009), who noted that "the ability to focus attention and achieve or at least work toward sustained attention and concentration is crucial for truly being present in the therapy encounter" (p. 19).

Mindfulness practice can also help develop compassion. *Compassion* is defined as having empathy and understanding for others as well as having the wish or intent to use that understanding to help others and alleviate their suffering (Shapiro & Carlson, 2009; Vivino, Thompson, Hill, & Ladany,

2009). As we have seen in Buddhist perspectives, compassion begins with compassion for one's self. This notion was supported by a study that analyzed moment-by-moment psychotherapy videotapes and found that therapists who lacked self-compassion (i.e., were more critical of themselves) were also more critical and hostile toward their clients and had poorer therapy outcomes (Henry, Schacht, & Strupp, 1990). A study by Shapiro, Brown, and Biegel (2007) indicated that mindfulness practice helps counselors to develop greater self-compassion, compared with a control group. To develop compassion for one's self or others, therapists need to have a level of attunement (to one's self or others), and mindfulness practice helps to cultivate that attunement (Siegel, 2007).

Mindfulness practice also helps to reduce stress, tension, and anxiety and increase self-care, in part through the development of affect regulation (Schure, Christopher, & Christopher, 2008; Shapiro, Brown, & Biegel, 2007). To be able to sit with the various emotions that arise in us while sitting with a client, and remain present, is important and challenging. Mindfulness practice, particularly the central aspects of observing, naming, and describing, helps us gain a nonreactive relationship with what we are feeling. If we can see the emotions as they are (naming) rather than as a commentary on who we are, then we have more ability to be with our clients, to not take what we hear or feel personally, and to ride the waves with what emerges in the moment.

Mindfulness also helps to develop greater flexibility and open-mindedness, which are essential aspects of presence and openness to whatever the client brings into session. Brown and Ryan (2003) demonstrated that higher levels of mindfulness were associated with greater openness to experience. The ability to open to each moment as it arises allows therapists to not get stuck on preconceived notions and instead to be flexible with whatever arises. D. J. Siegel (2010) provided an acronym to describe the beneficial outcome of mindfulness practice—FACES, which stands for flexible, adaptive, coherent, energized, and stable. He described the state of flow and integration (on the level of the self, the brain, and relationships) that occurs from mindfulness practice and results in the natural manifestation of the qualities that he coins FACES. Hence, mindfulness promotes these qualities, which reflects being in the moment, in flow, open, and energized with an inner steadiness of mind and emotions.

Mindfulness practices also focus on direct engagement with the present moment. It is through a letting go of our grasping of future and past, of desire and fear, that our natural wisdom is activated. Buddhist perspectives are based on practices of mindfulness that directly enhance our present-moment experience and hence release the tension of future and past, of longing and aversion. Through continued practice the body and mind accumulate direct experience with being released from these tensions, and hence presence and wisdom emerge more naturally. It is possible that through the gentle release of desire, aversion, greed, and ignorance and the heightening of present-moment attention, which mindfulness practice supports, natural aspects and qualities of therapeutic presence emerge.

The benefits of mindfulness practice in the cultivation of therapeutic presence include

- increased focus and attention;
- enhanced compassion and acceptance—both within self and with others;
- reduced stress, anxiety, and inner tension and increased self-care;
- greater affect tolerance and emotional regulation;
- increased flexibility and openness with whatever arises;
- greater calm with whatever is being experienced; and
- release of self-identity, needs, hunger for attention, greed, and desire.

## NEUROBIOLOGICAL BENEFITS OF MINDFULNESS PRACTICE

Emerging research from neuroscience on mindfulness approaches reflects the impact of mindfulness practices on positive changes in the brain structure and function. As noted earlier, changes that support the cultivation of presence include increased attentional abilities and working memory, present-centered focus, and affect tolerance. Mindfulness research from a neurobiological perspective has demonstrated that continued mindfulness practice results in cortical thickening (Lazar et al., 2005) and activates parts of the brain, including the anterior insula, the sensory cortex, and the prefrontal cortex. These three areas are involved in paying attention to the breath and to other sensory stimuli, as is typically done during meditation practice (D. J. Siegel, 2010). Furthermore, the prefrontal cortex is responsible for working memory (Siegel, 2007, 2010), which reflects being able to hold information, such as what clients share in therapy sessions.

The cultivation of grounding, centering, and equanimity through mindfulness practice can increase a person's ability to experience painful or difficult events with less reactivity (Lazar, 2005). Hence, with sustained practice, therapists can develop a greater ease and ability to feel the depth of the other's experience, and even one's own resonant pain, and let it go. For example, Goleman and Schwartz (1976) found that people who practiced meditation had a slightly larger increase in skin conductance response than controls but returned to baseline more quickly than people who did not have a sustained practice. This illustrates the possibility that through repeated practice of calming the autonomic nervous system, the therapist can develop the capacity needed to engage and resonate with the client's painful experience and yet quickly return to a state of calm and equilibrium.

Studies such as those by Davidson et al. (2003) have helped to demonstrate that the more experience one has with mindfulness practices, the greater the left-brain activation. Davidson (2004) examined electroencephalogram patterns of various people and confirmed that people who are more distressed, depressed, anxious, and so on tend to exhibit more activity in the right prefrontal cortex than in the left. In contrast, people who are more content and calm tend to exhibit more activity in the left prefrontal cortex than in the right. Davidson and Lutz (2008) noted that Tibetan monks with many years of experience of mindfulness practice had the most dramatic left prefrontal activation in the direction of contentment.

As noted in Chapter 9, changes in the physical structure of the brain are also reflected in studies by Lazar and colleagues, who explored the reversal of the natural thinning of the cerebral cortex that occurs with age. Lazar examined magnetic resonance imaging (MRI) in long-term meditators (D. J. Siegel, 2010). In a particularly interesting study, Lazar et al. (2005) compared people who averaged 6 hr of meditation practice per week over 9 years with age-matched controls. Results showed an enhanced thickness of the cerebral cortex in older adults who engaged in a meditation practice compared with controls, and the degree of thickening was in proportion to the amount of time the person spent meditating over his or her lifetime.

Another study by Lazar as referenced in D. J. Siegel (2010) showed that after 8 weeks of mindfulness practice, measurable changes were found in a part of the brain stem that involves the production of serotonin, a mood-regulating neurotransmitter. The increased density found in the related area of the brain stem, along with an increase in a subjective sense of well-being, was most pronounced for subjects who did the most practice (personal communication as cited in D. J. Siegel, 2010).

Another research study compared the MRIs of 13 Zen meditators with those of 13 control subjects and had participants in both groups perform a sustained attention task (Pagnoni & Cekic, 2007). The group of Zen meditators had less gray matter than the nonmeditators and had greater attentional abilities. Given the role of attention in a therapeutic context, especially the high-level attention that is part of therapeutic relational presence, these findings support the notion that meditation can help to cultivate the attentional qualities that are related to presence.

Mindfulness practice allows us to feel emotions vividly (have contact with the products of the limbic system) but not to feel so compelled to act or react to those emotions (emotional regulation as reflected in the prefrontal cortex; D. J. Siegel, 2010). This allows the therapist to be open and connected to the depth of the client's experience in the moment while being grounded, steady, and centered within one's self, a key part of therapeutic presence.

Neurobiological studies have also revealed that the close paying of attention that is stimulated by mindfulness practice results in two neuronal processes (D. J. Siegel, 2010). First, the neurons that fire during close attention actually reinforce the synaptic connections at the specific location and strengthen the connections to other local synapses as well as create new connections between synapses. Second, part of the brain above the brain stem releases acetylcholine throughout the brain during close attention. The combination of these two processes allows for the upward boosting of neurons that are firing; this will be more likely to activate genes that allow for the production of proteins to allow for greater structural connections to be made. In this vein, close paying of attention, such as that involved in mindfulness practices, increases neuroplasticity in the parts of the brain that reflect greater attention.

Overall, current research suggests that mindfulness practices play a role in cultivating qualities of therapeutic presence; these qualities can become more accessible experientially and permanent neurobiologically and result in the enhancement of neuronal integration. Emotional regulation, calm, openness, receptivity, enhanced attention, and contentment are some of the outcomes of a practice in mindfulness, qualities that reflect the experience of therapeutic presence.

## A DESCRIPTION OF MINDFULNESS PRACTICES FOR CULTIVATING THERAPEUTIC PRESENCE

We provide practical exercises for heightening presence in Chapter 12. However, in the remainder of this chapter, we describe the different mindfulness-based approaches that can be used to heighten present-moment attention, acceptance, overall well-being, and other qualities of therapeutic presence, which can be beneficial both in session and in the personal life of the therapist. Many of these approaches are geared toward enhancing the present-moment awareness of the individual therapist, which in turn helps the therapist to be more present in session with the client. However, the relational quality of presence is sometimes missed in these approaches. We provide both personal/individual and interpersonal mindfulness practices that can serve to enhance therapeutic presence both within self and with others. Formal and informal mindfulness practices include mindfulness meditation, compassion meditation, mindful breathing, mindful movement, mindfulness in everyday life, and mindfulness in relationship with others.

## Mindfulness Meditation

The most popular way of practicing mindfulness is mindfulness meditation. The key principles of mindfulness meditation were outlined by Kabat-Zinn (1990): nonjudgment, patience, beginner's mind, trusting oneself, nonstriving, letting go, and acceptance. These factors are interconnected and are extensions of mindfulness (Killackey, 1998). The Buddhist rationale is that the cultivation of these positive qualities diminishes the strength of negative attitudes, such as anger, grasping, aversion, clinging, and laziness, and forms the basis of a more compassionate and loving heart toward self and others.

Mindfulness meditation is a formal practice of mindfulness and hence, ultimately, a formal practice of presence. In mindfulness meditation, attention is given to what is being experienced in the moment, either in the breath or body, without judgment or interpretation. While the breath is used as an anchor to return attention to when the mind wanders, no effort is made to constrict attention during mindfulness meditation. Instead, attention is expanded to include as many mental, emotional, and physical experiences that arise, as they occur, from a stance of calmness and neutrality, without elaboration, judgment, censorship, interpretation, attachment, or conclusions (Engler, 1986; Kabat-Zinn, 1990; Miller, 1993).

Mindfulness meditation practice involves eliciting a relaxation response through attention to breathing and then observing bodily parts and bodily sensations (body scan technique) and all perceptions, thoughts, emotions, and internal experiences through an open and accepting focus. The goal of mindfulness meditation is ultimately the acceptance of experience and the release of suffering. By not resisting, judging, grasping, or evaluating experience, including bodily pain and general sensations and emotions, a reduction in suffering is possible.

Daily meditation practice can help to release stress and unclutter the mind, to enhance in-the-moment awareness, and to create a sense of grounding. This can allow for the development of the capacity to be with the depth of experience while maintaining a sense of calm and spaciousness, which allows for clear and undiminished seeing and feeling without being overwhelmed or distant. As Kramer, Meleo-Meyer, and Turner (2008) noted: "Teaching therapists and therapist trainees such forms of meditation is almost guaranteed to help them become more self-aware, more accepting and reflective, more available to the client in the present moment, and more able to choose their responses skillfully" (p. 196).

## Compassion Meditation/Tonglen Practice

Another valuable mindfulness practice for therapists is compassion meditation, or Tonglen practice, as based in Tibetan Buddhism (Brach, 2003;

Sogyal Rinpoche, 1992). This involves going through a series of steps of imagining the suffering of another human being or community that is experiencing significant distress and taking in the details of their suffering on the inhale while exhaling out compassion and love. Tonglen practice is a helpful way for therapists to practice taking in the fullness of the suffering of the other, while offering deep compassion, presence, and care. It also helps therapists to cultivate the ability to be with intense and difficult emotions without getting overwhelmed or shutting down by "fixing" or minimizing the client's pain. This quality of awareness is akin to the aspect of presence that involves experiencing deeply without attachment.

## Mindful Breathing

A therapist in the qualitative study on presence (Geller & Greenberg, 2002) described using her breath as a focal cue to bring herself into presence. Focusing on her breath is akin to her meditation practice, the method by which she practices presence in her daily life. She described her awareness of breath as her aid in moving inward into presence:

> Well, the breath is really taking a deep breath with total awareness. So focus on the breath, and that just anchors me. And then I'm in [laugh] in a sense. So I am totally in my body and not out somewhere. I'm in my body but I'm open at that point.

Mindful breathing can be done formally through practice or informally by pausing throughout the day to use the breath as a focal cue to bring awareness back into the moment. In formal or informal practice, the physical sensation of breathing is used as an anchor for present-moment awareness. As the therapist above noted, breathing with awareness in session can help invite one's attention into presence or bring one's attention back when it has wandered.

## Mindful Movement

Mindful movement includes practices directed at moving the body in an intentional and slow way that is aligned with the breath and with the intention of bringing one's awareness into the depth and ground of the body in the moment. This can be especially valuable for therapists in cultivating presence, as therapists tend to have a very sedentary professional life, given the amount of time spent sitting with clients or on the phone or computer. In therapeutic presence, the body is a gateway for therapists to sense what the client is experiencing as well as to access the therapist's own intuition and wisdom in direct responsiveness to the moment with the client. Hence, practice with present-centered movement can help to develop that deep and direct relationship with one's own body and sense of grounding.

Mindful movement and walking meditation emerge from the tradition of Thich Nhat Hanh (2008), a Vietnamese Buddhist monk. Thich Nhat Hanh grew up in a country with exceptional conflict and violence, and he recognized the importance of each person practicing to find peace within themselves. Mindful movement practice involves bringing awareness to simple and repetitive movements of the body. (See examples in *Mindful Movements: Ten Exercises for Well-Being*, Thich Nhat Hanh, 2008.)

In walking meditation, a particular form of movement meditation, the focus is on walking with the intention of cultivating present-moment awareness as well as a sense of compassion. "Mindful walking simply means walking while being aware of each step and of our breath" (Nhat Hanh, 2008, p. 9). While walking at a slow pace, we become aware of the nuance of each step; hence, the body and stepping motion become the anchor for present-moment awareness. Much like meditation, as the mind wanders, we use our awareness of each aspect of the foot touching and lifting from the ground to bring our attention back to the moment, again and again.

Taoist tai chi practice also involves moving in a slow and intentional way. Tai chi involves a series of steps or bodily movements that require one to stay focused on the movements as they are happening in the present moment (Siegel, 2007). One research study has found a relationship between tai chi practice and increased immune functioning (Irwin, 2005, as cited in Siegel, 2007). Moving with awareness in the moment of one's experience of the movement can help therapists to generate a level of bodily present-centered awareness.

Mindful movement techniques can also be found in qigong practice. According to principles of traditional Chinese medicine, qigong is a form of "mind–body" exercise, which exercises both the mind and the body for treating various chronic diseases and promoting health (Tsang, Cheung, & Lak, 2002; Weil, 2003). Qigong is referred to as the art and science of using breathing techniques, gentle movement, and meditation to cleanse, strengthen, and circulate *qi*, which is also known as life energy. Qigong practice leads to better health and vitality and a tranquil state of mind (Tsang et al., 2002). It has been used by health care professionals to prevent healer burnout and to maintain a positive presence (Valente & Marotta, 2005).

## Mindfulness in Everyday Life

Therapeutic presence can also be cultivated through informal mindfulness practices, such as moment-to-moment, nonjudgmental awareness of all aspects of daily life. Mindfulness in daily life would include exercises such as daily awareness practice. This involves choosing one activity that you engage in on a daily basis and practicing being mindful and aware of all aspects of that experience in the moment while engaging in that activity. For example, climbing the stairs in your house can be a marker for stopping, becoming aware in the moment, and practicing noticing each step, what it feels like, the feel of your feet as they touch the ground or lift up, the sensation of the floor as your foot meets the next step.

Everyday mindfulness can also be accommodated to frustrating experiences such as traffic or waiting in line, for example, using a stop sign as a marker or invitation to take a breath and come into the moment. Opportunities for practice arise in much of life; it is just about being intentional about a particular activity. For example, waiting in a slow line can be incredibly frustrating, or it can be an opportunity to practice what it feels like to be waiting, noticing your feet on the ground or the breath, bringing awareness to the discomfort of anticipation without reactivity. These opportunities for intentional practice of presence allow us to pull back from the anticipation of the next moment or the frustration of being held up and to arrive again and again into the now.

Mindfulness techniques can aid in the therapist's ability to be deeply present with a client. They can help cultivate qualities of presence, such as taking in the fullness of the client's experience while maintaining a separate sense of self. Mindfulness practices can also help to cultivate awareness of when a therapist is not present in the session so that he or she can practice out of session to develop the skill to easily move back in the moment and to hold a range of potential discomforts and tensions without reaction, with full awareness. In brief, moments of mindfulness practice also help us to develop a natural ability to pause, breathe, check inside with one's experience, relax, and expand, which provide a basis or practice for cultivating presence.

An example of a mindful practice in everyday life follows. The first author (S. G.) experienced her first 10-day silent meditation retreat in Thailand in the early 1990s. The participants had to choose one chore that they would be responsible for throughout the retreat. They would then have a practice period of 20 minutes to engage in this one chore, silently, day after day; whether it be to scrub the toilet, sweep the leaves, or cut firewood, this daily task was also an opportunity for mindfulness practice. So the first author chose dishwashing. She washed dish after dish, day after day, in silence. Feeling the water on her skin as it splashed onto the top of her hand, she would practice feeling the sensations of warmth or the feel of the soapiness on her skin. She recalls the feel of the dishes and the (eventual) joy it would give her to just be with each sound and feel. She could hear the subtlety of the sound of scraping the food off, the plate immersing in water, placing it down to dry. She would practice feeling each detail of what the plate felt like, dry and wet, what scraping sounded like, clutching, touching, splashing, rinsing, drying. She would try to keep her mind and experience on this one plate. To this day, she still enjoys and invites herself naturally into the moment when she washes the dishes, as it soothes her and allows her to practice presence.

Mindfulness practice is more than just the cognitive act of bringing one's attention to the moment. It is a practice, an exercise, that can aid in bringing a deeper sense of connection with the self, with others, and with one's own intuition and wisdom. The findings of neuroplasticity suggest that through continued practice, the qualities of presence that we are intentionally cultivating become a part of our neural structure and hence more accessible and more easily drawn on when we need them, such as in the therapy encounter with our clients.

## Mindfulness in Relationship With Others

Practicing presence and mindfulness in relationship with others is profoundly important for therapists because it is the relational aspect of presence that is often most challenging in therapists' personal lives and in direct relationship with clients and their sometimes insurmountable pain. In addition, the well-known impact of the therapeutic alliance on therapy outcome suggests the development of interpersonal or relational therapeutic presence, which has been shown to be related to the development of a positive therapeutic alliance, to be both profound and necessary. Two approaches to enhancing relational presence through practicing mindfulness in relationship are comeditation, which has been used primarily with people who are dying, and insight dialogue, a fairly new area reflecting interpersonal mindfulness.

### Comeditation

Comeditation has been referred to as "cross-breathing" and emerged in the Tibetan end-of-life practice called Phowa (Boerstler & Kornfield, 1995; Hunter, 2007). While comeditation has been used primarily with people who are dying (Fasko, Osborne, Hall, Boerstler, & Kornfeld, 1992), we are proposing that a variation of this approach be used in therapy training for the cultivation of relational presence. If done in a therapy training scenario, each partner can have a turn at leading, extending, or tuning into the other and receiving or allowing oneself to just breathe. The harmonizing of the breath in comeditation can allow for the development of a synergistic relationship and deepening of connection, both internally and with another, which can enhance present-moment intimacy. In comeditation, the concentrated presence of one person meets the relaxed presence of another (Hunter, 2007). "Comeditation can be a helpful practice for anyone who feels that Presenting (being fully aware and present to another suffering being) has value and importance" (Hunter, 2007, p. 3).

The notion behind comeditation is to allow one's self to practice being intimately present with the moment, with another person. Given that psychotherapy is a highly intimate process, it is important for therapists to develop a deep comfort with intimacy both as a receiver and a giver and to gain experience and comfort with being present in a shared interpersonal reality.

*Insight Dialogue*

A more recent approach, insight dialogue, acknowledges that the individual practice that is typical of mindfulness is not always relevant to dealing with the multitude of reactions we can encounter in relationship to others (Kramer, 2007; Kramer et al., 2008). When we meditate alone, we can generate peace and awareness within and hence approach relationship issues indirectly. However, when we meditate with someone else or in practice in a group dynamic, such as with insight dialogue, then we can directly encounter our relational suffering and work with it appropriately (Kramer, 2007; Kramer et al., 2008).

Insight dialogue is a form of dialogic meditation and entails a period of silent meditation followed by people pairing off or gathering in a group to reflect on a topic such as change, doubt, or death (Kramer, 2007; Kramer et al., 2008). Participants are invited to pause periodically to gain awareness of habitual stories or automatic reactions in relation to these themes and to being in relationship in an intimate way, and then invite themselves back to the present moment of interpersonal contact. The basic premise or instructions in insight dialogue involve six aspects: pause, relax, open, trust emergence, listen deeply, and speak the truth (Kramer, 2007; Kramer et al., 2008). Each instruction is geared toward calling on different yet complementary qualities, such as mindfulness (pause), tranquility and acceptance (relax), relational availability and spaciousness (open), flexibility and letting go (trust emergence), receptivity and attunement (listen deeply), and integrity and care (speak the truth; Kramer, 2007).

The practices and instructions that are a part of an insight dialogue exercise appear to be a great complement to psychotherapeutic training. Helping trainees to pause and gather awareness of their own self in the moment, as well as their relational triggers, and to work with them directly with acceptance and compassion can aid in the development of their ability to be present with self and others and to acquire relational therapeutic presence by working directly with their interpersonal barriers. Interpersonal meditation, such as in insight dialogue, can offer an excellent adjunct to the training of relational presence as well as managing countertransference reactions that could interfere with being fully present.

## CONCLUSION

Mindfulness comprises a set of skills and practices that can help one to cultivate therapeutic presence. The research in mindfulness supports the notion that present-centered attention and reduced stress and reactivity can develop through practice. More recent interpersonal approaches have recognized that mindfulness in its traditional form needs to expand to include relational qualities. These interpersonal mindfulness approaches can benefit therapists in working through their own relational issues and barriers to intimacy and hence develop the capacity to be relationally present with their clients.

# 11

# EXPERIENTIAL APPROACHES: SOMATIC, EMOTION-FOCUSED, CREATIVE, AND RELATIONAL APPROACHES TO CULTIVATING THERAPEUTIC PRESENCE

If you can see it, hear it, feel it, taste it, touch it, or smell it, you can be present with it. It is of the present moment, and so it brings to you the opportunity to be present with it.

—Jacobson (2007, p. 25)

While mindfulness focuses on the entry point of the mind to cultivate present-moment awareness, experiential approaches offer different avenues to cultivate therapeutic presence, such as through experiencing the body, heart, and creativity, and through relationships. Experiential and humanistic perspectives are based on the understanding that there is an experiential part of the self that gives rise to inner wisdom. When we are in touch with our flow of experiencing, there is a healthy sense of self-integration that can emerge naturally from that inner congruence. The main principle of experiential perspectives is to check what is said or done with one's own felt experiencing and allow what we say or do to emerge from our direct contact with our inner experience and wisdom. Experiencing is seen as full of information, richly detailed, intense, fluid, and having the capacity to differentiate meaning (Watson et al., 1998). Experiencing acts as an internal barometer allowing the symbolization of experience to be checked against a person's actual present-moment experience to determine accuracy.

Experiential ways to cultivate presence are important for therapists in two ways. First, contact with experiencing supports a healthy emotional and mental life and sense of inner integration, which is the foundation for the cultivation of therapeutic presence. Second, contact with therapists' moment-to-moment experiencing allows for the development of and familiarity with their intuition as well as an internal contact place within their self-experience that can inform them about their client's experience in the moment.

From an experiential perspective, four entry points direct our awareness and intention in opening to presence: somatically (through the body), emotionally (through the heart), creatively (through the soul), and relationally (through contact with others). In this chapter, we explore these four entry points in relation to four aspects of the experience of therapeutic presence (grounding, immersion, expansion, and with and for the client). We also present an integrative program based on rhythm and awareness that can help to cultivate therapeutic presence.

## SOMATIC APPROACHES TO CULTIVATING THERAPEUTIC PRESENCE (THE BODY)

Being in touch with the body, knowing what we are feeling and sensing in the moment, is essential to being present. This can particularly help in generating the first quality of therapeutic presence, *grounding*. Listening and sensing to and from the body are the essence of listening with presence. Although therapists may recognize the value of bodily sensing and listening, most have not learned how to listen deeply, or they do know but end up taking on the depth of emotions of the other, which leads to feeling overwhelmed or distanced. We propose that the deepest form of listening is with all of our senses, which includes sensing and taking in what the other is experiencing from a grounded, immersed, and spacious place. This allows us to hear the whole of what the other is experiencing through sensing with our body, which leads to greater empathy and understanding of the other while remaining steady and balanced in one's self.

Despite the importance of this deep sensory bodily oriented listening, the body is often neglected in the academic and clinical world of psychotherapists. We engage our minds in discussions about our experience and about clinical theory. Even in reading this book, albeit about a topic as experiential as presence, we are engaging our cognitive understanding. Furthermore, we mostly work in sedentary positions and remain sedentary in our leisure time, to review our e-mail or perhaps watch a movie. Our society also promotes sedentary tasks, and the physical movement that was central to our ancestors' survival has been eliminated with cars, telephones, take-out food, remote controls, and computers.

The cost of ignoring the body, including the tension, stress, discomfort, and emotions we experience, "is the festering of disease and dysfunction" (Fogel, 2009, p. 8). On a clinical level, the cost of being out of touch with our bodies is the inability to use our bodily sensory states as indicators of our clients' experience or of our own intuition. On a personal level, familiarity with bodily felt experience is directly related to health and wellness as well as neural integration. Psychoimmunology has taught us that stress affects the body and compromises immune functioning and can sit in the body as tension and discomfort (O'Leary, 1990). Furthermore, many new therapists tend to continue the pace of graduate school without a break, maintaining a highly demanding schedule that is supported by overarousal (i.e., heightened sympathetic nervous system) and high adrenalin. Chronic stress can affect emotional health and lead to muscular or gastrointestinal problems, disrupted sleep, unbalanced eating habits, decreased immunity to illness, anxiety, attention deficits, relational difficulties, and performance impairment (Baker, 2002). A lack of somatic awareness can lead to a neglect of the stress in the body until it compromises our health in some way. As therapists and professionals, we know the effects of stress, yet we can lose touch with the body, and when a health condition or unwanted pain or extra pounds show up, we wonder how it developed.

Although this sense of our body experience can be lost through neglect or through societal and technological pulls, it can also be cultivated through exercises that focus on somatic awareness, such as yoga, drumming, movement, and massage. With a deepened sense of somatic and self-awareness, therapists can recognize their optimal level of healthful stress and stimulation and hence regulate their lives to maintain a sense of balance (Valente & Marotta, 2005).

## What Is Embodied Self-Awareness?

*Embodied self-awareness* (also referred to as *somatic awareness*) is the ability to pay attention to ourselves, including our experience, bodily sensations, movements, and inner sensory world, in the present moment (Fogel, 2009). This is contrasted with *conceptual self-awareness*, which is thinking about what we are aware of or "engagement of a thought process of categorizing, planning, reasoning, judging, and evaluating" (Fogel, 2009, p. 11). Conceptual self-awareness is like meta-awareness; it is what we are doing in this conversation right now, in your reading this chapter and in our trying to articulate and understand the essence and value of somatic awareness. Embodied self-awareness is an internal felt sense of what is true, in this moment, in the emotional, physical, and sensory body.

A concept similar to embodied self-awareness or somatic awareness is full body presence. Scurlock-Durana (2010) defined *full body presence* as the "ability to feel all parts of your body with a good flow of healthy energy moving through you. It also includes a connection to your inner and outer resources for health and a good sense of personal boundaries" (p. xii). Full body presence is proposed as a precursor to therapeutic presence in that it allows a grounding and awareness in the body.

Embodied self-awareness or full body presence involves interoception, sensing the body, breath, pain, fatigue, restfulness, emotions, and experience. *Interoception* is the inner sensory capacity of the body both through physiological feedback and the perception of that feedback (Wiens, 2005). Feeling our experience, physiological and emotional, is generally reflected in the anterior insula and anterior cingulate (Hanson & Mendius, 2009; Wiens, 2005).

Gendlin (1978) described this level of embodied experience as existing prior to and beyond language. Language cannot fully capture this state of awareness, as the experience of embodied self-awareness exists in our feeling state. Language that is used to describe this experience is usually evocative in nature, such as that used in poetry, symbols, gestures, art, and personal expression. The direct source of feeling and understanding of our inner terrain comes from the experience itself.

Stern (1985) described a basic sense of self that has the capacity to expand awareness and is at the very core of our psychophysiological being. This embodied self-awareness begins in gestation and is directly related to body schema self-awareness, which is the bodily sense of where one's own body leaves off and the other begins. Therapists' capacity to be fully aware of the other and of the self, both in the sense of unification and in separateness, is reliant on the experience of being in contact with one's bodily felt experience and inner being.

PAUSE MOMENT. We invite you to pause and experience a moment of self-awareness.

- Take a moment to close your eyes.
- Take a few breaths to anchor your awareness in the present moment. Now allow yourself to sense the inner terrain of your physical body.
- What do you notice as you feel your feet, your legs, hands, arms, chest?
- Allow your awareness to soften around each body part, even for a moment, become familiar with what is there without judgment, just noticing. Now become aware of any emotion that may be dominating your feeling space in the moment.
- Notice what the emotion feels like, its quality and intensity, where it is in your body, the accompanying sensations.
- Without judgment or interpretation, allow yourself to explore how you feel from the inside out.

## What Does Somatic Awareness Have to Do With Presence?

The body is one aspect of ourselves that can transport us literally and figuratively from moment to moment. On one level, there is a biological process involved in showing up, such as physically being at the location of our presence encounter, which is dictated and guided by the brain's messaging and synaptic firing. On another level, there is also a bodily sensory process to presence that involves looking into the body as a receptor and source of sensory information on what the client is expressing and experiencing. Silsbee (2008) emphasized the importance of somatic awareness and somatic literacy as a precursor to presence as it allows us to access the wealth of information that is accessible through the body. Hence, somatic awareness is key to cultivating and returning to presence as well as engaging in present-centered encounters with others.

When we sit in a receptive and open place with the client, our bodies pick up information from the client on multiple levels. Therapists can sometimes feel the client's tension as tension in their own stomach (perhaps a milder version). Or perhaps a wave of tension or anxiety in the therapist's chest is in psychological resonance with the client's panic. Therapists' awareness and access to their own bodily and sensory information about the client's experience depend first on the ability to be aware of their own inner experience.

Awareness of our own sensations, as well as the ability to discern between sensations arising from our own body or from our experience of the other, is essential to presence. The quality of being deeply connected and using our self as a sensor depends on these abilities of awareness and discernment. The first author (S. G.) describes a clinical example:

> When I hear my client describing the loss of her husband and I feel a throbbing in my chest, a quick moment and agility of awareness is important. First I bring my awareness to the sensation of throbbing, with nonreactivity, and then I can discern if it is my pain that is being triggered (countertransference) or it is my bodily sensation or mirror of the client's experience (self as sensor or somatic empathy). If I can stay open and in contact, then I can note the sensation and file it away (in the case of countertransference) or use it as a source of reflection and understanding of the client (self as sensor or somatic empathy).

Familiarity with our bodily felt experience (e.g., somatic awareness practice) not only is an essential aspect of presence but is also directly related to self-care, health, and wellness for the therapist as well as neural integration. The neural pathways that allow us to sense the body internally, such as sensations and emotions, are directly related to the neural pathways that regulate body processes that help to maintain physical and emotional balance and health (Fogel, 2009). Emotional and physical health depend on the ability to be aware and monitor body states, as it leads to the activation of neurobiological responses (autonomic, immune, and endocrine responses), embodied self-awareness (symptom monitoring, stress reduction), healthy behaviors (self-care, rest, nutritional eating), and most important, the capacity to be fully alive in the emotional present (Fogel, 2009, p. 22).

Self-awareness has also been noted as an important, if not an essential, aspect for the professional development and self-care of the therapist (Baker, 2002; Orlinsky & Rønnestadt, 2005; Valente & Marotta, 2005). Fostering self-awareness, which includes the essential aspect of somatic awareness, supports personal integration and hence the ability to be present and respond from a range of options, insight, and creative perspectives with clients (Aponte & Winter, 2000; Valente & Marotta, 2005). Hence, bodily self-awareness is essential to the cultivation of presence and to living a healthy life.

## Clinical Vignette

An example of how a therapist receives and attends to her own bodily experience and to an image inspired by being fully present with her client is provided in the following:

> I am sitting listening to my client tell the story of her life and the unavailability of her parents. She speaks first about her father, who was an alcoholic in a lecturing-talking-at-me style, but then for a moment her voice changes to a more internally focused voice, poignant, filled with pauses and her pace slows and her eyes look sad. I feel the sadness as a clenching in my chest, and see an image reflecting her father walking out the door, and feel the poignancy of this relationship. I reflect to her my experience of her sadness and she says: "My father—he was just never—there for me." She cries as she recalls the pain of not having him around. Eventually, she increases her rate of speech and continues to recognize that she has her sisters and friends as support. Resonating and trusting the image of her father and her sadness, and sharing this with her, brought tears to her eyes and opened up her present sense of loneliness.

Sharing this bodily based awareness, which stemmed from the therapist's attunement with the client as well as her contact with her own bodily sense, helped move the session forward, revealing another layer of the client's experience. Familiarity with somatic awareness allowed this therapist to recognize her own bodily sense of sadness as well as the imagery that is associated with the client's experience.

## Cultivation of Presence Through Somatic Awareness

Using gentle body movements, stretches, or grounding exercises can invite our inner sensory awareness to awaken and put us in contact with our direct bodily experience. While the brain may dictate what our body responds to, our intention to use the body as a focal cue to arrive from moment to moment helps our brain generate experiences of presence. Repetitive pauses to connect to the body with the intention for presence help to activate neural activity and a bodily memory of presence. Gathering somatic awareness through practices that support interoception, such as grounding and centering, can help to generate somatic awareness and build sustenance of the presence experience.

### Grounding and Centering

Grounding and centering techniques are based in the body. They are both the vehicle to activate somatic presence and a description of key aspects of presence itself. Being ungrounded means feeling disconnected, having scattered attention, and likely a sense of worry or anxiety. To be *uncentered* means to be off balance and easily swayed emotionally and physically.

While grounding includes rooting ourselves in a sense of solidity in self as well as in our beliefs, the focus here is on grounding in the physical body. *Grounding* refers to being present in the moment, in the body, with a sense of inner integration and inner steadiness in self. It includes the skill of connecting through the feeling senses in a visceral way, to the earth or to any other healthy energy source (Scurlock-Durana, 2010). Grounding allows us to maintain a sense of calm and equanimity yet alertness, amidst emotional intensity or chaos. With grounding, we are aware of an unshakeable sense of stability and calm within our self and our being.

*Centering* refers to bringing our somatic awareness internally to the center of the body. Centering is a way of bringing different parts of the body and awareness into one center place in the body to access or return to a sense of equilibrium and inner integration. As described by Silsbee (2008) in his book on presence-based coaching:

> Centering is an internal process of bringing attention into our bodies, connecting with ourselves, and becoming aware and present. It is a living process of reorganization that shifts us from a state of being triggered or responding automatically into being self-generating, resourceful, and creative. When we are centered, we are alert, connected, present, and ready for whatever is next. (p. 155)

Grounding and centering allow therapists to access an inner state of integration and steadiness so that they can open to the fullness of the client's experience without losing a sense of inner stability. This allows the client to rely on the therapist's inner steadiness, which helps to create a sense of safety and trust in the therapeutic relationship and the therapy encounter. Grounding and centering can occur just moments before a client walks into the room, even by simply stopping, placing the feet on the ground, and breathing. A simple grounding exercise is to imagine roots from the bottom of the feet growing into the earth. Yoga postures (e.g., the mountain posture) can also help to create a sense of centering and grounding.

### Body-Centered Practices: Yoga and Dance

Body-centered practices include some gentle yoga postures or moving freely with the body, with the intention of bringing one's awareness into the depth and ground of the body in the moment. This can be especially valuable for therapists in cultivating presence and countering the excessive sitting that they do in their practice, returning calls and writing reports. In therapeutic presence, the body is a gateway for therapists to sense what the client is experiencing as well as to access therapists' own intuition and wisdom that are directly responsive to the moment with the client. Hence, practice with body-centered movement can help to develop that deep and direct relationship with one's own body. Some examples of body-centered practices are yoga and Five Rhythms dance (Roth, 1989, 1997, 2004).

Yoga arose from Indian philosophy and is used to support the mind and body through postures and breath work. Yoga involves a series of postures that invite practitioners to bring their awareness to the breath and the body from moment to moment. Along with positive effects on one's physical health, yoga can have positive psychological benefits, such as a sense of calm and wellness (Schell, Allolio, & Schonecke, 1994; Siegel, 2007; Wood, 1993).

Valente & Marotta (2005) conducted a qualitative study exploring the benefits of yoga for psychotherapists' self-awareness, personal growth, and professional development with six psychotherapists who also practiced yoga. Content analyses revealed four major themes: internal/self-awareness, balance, acceptance of self and others, and yoga as a way of life. The first theme included therapists' reports that yoga enhanced their awareness of what their body was feeling and helped them to let go of rumination and to be more present and focused. The second theme reflected the ability to regulate stimulation and demands to achieve balance and harmony, and to prevent burnout. This included the value of yoga in calming the central nervous system; reducing anxiety, stress, and fatigue; and increasing relaxation and a feeling of being more centered and grounded. The third theme included an acceptance of self and others, without judgment or attachment to outcome. This allowed therapists to be more in the moment and involved in the process of therapy. The fourth theme reflected a sense of integration in their yoga practice, among personal self, professional self, and sense of spirituality, and a sense of how each informed each other. Overall, therapists who practiced yoga in this study suggested that these benefits helped them to be more effective and "increased their ability to be in the 'here and now' and to be truly present with their clients" (Valente & Marotta, 2005, p. 77).

Another way of developing somatic awareness through movement is based in Roth's (1989, 1997, 2004) Five Rhythms, which draws from many indigenous and world traditions using tenets of shamanistic, ecstatic, mystical, and Eastern philosophy as well as Gestalt and transpersonal psychology (Juhan, 2003). Five Rhythms involves moving through a series of self-directed rhythmic movement exercises, accompanied by music, not only to release difficult emotions but also to access a state of presence and joy. Five Rhythms practice can help to release difficult emotions and quiet mental states, as reflected in Roth's work (1989), where she emphasized that the quickest way to still the mind is to move the body.

## EMOTION-FOCUSED APPROACHES TO CULTIVATING PRESENCE (THE HEART)

Another entry point into cultivating presence is through the heart or the emotional body. Opening the heart can also help to generate the second aspect of therapeutic presence, *immersion*, which allows for an absorbed and emotionally connected state to emerge that is unattached to outcome. Connecting emotionally to one's own experience is important in presence as the therapist opens up to the totality of his or her experience to connect and receive the whole of the client's experience. Our research suggests that being in presence supports therapists' receptivity and focus, while emotionally moving toward the client and sensing the client's emotions through one's own emotional world and body (i.e., self as a sensor to the other's experience). Hence, therapists must be aware of their own emotions when clients are expressing themselves emotionally (Greenberg, 2002). Since therapeutic presence involves therapists' emotional presence, the cultivation of presence includes therapists' continued development of their in-the-moment emotional awareness.

Another aspect of emotional approaches to presence involves removing the emotional barriers to presence. The two major barriers are occupation with the future and occupation with the past. Anxiety and worry are future-focused emotions, which prevent us from being fully here now. This can include general anxieties as well as anxieties particular to therapy, such as the underlying fear that we do not know how to help the person one is working with. Modulating anxiety and fear may include going a level deeper to the possible sense of inadequacy, insecurity, or conditioned upbringing (e.g., helping in order to receive love or self-worth), and inner exploration and psychotherapeutic support can help access awareness to work through the subtle pressures we put on ourselves as therapists.

Guilt, shame, and anger are emotions based on the past; they prevent us from being in the moment. A lack of forgiveness of self or others demands intentional forgiveness work, which at the least begins with awareness of unresolved emotions that we carry inside as well as a willingness to work on forgiveness. Forgiveness work (e.g., empty chair work in emotion-focused therapy) results in letting go of the past so that one can be fully present. This is partially attributed to our need to intervene or interfere with a client's process so that we can feel like a helper, which is more about our own issues and the subtle motivations underlying the need to help. In actuality, this subtle motivation, and hence its interference with the client's process through satisfying our need to feel good, can prevent us from being fully present with the client as well as with ourselves. Through the emptying of our unfinished issues and baggage of the past, we have more freedom to allow for the emergence of a deeper immersion and connection with the present.

Although there are different approaches to connecting with one's emotional experiencing in the moment, and to working through unresolved emotional issues, for our purposes we are going to explore focusing and emotion-focused perspectives.

### Focusing and Therapeutic Presence

Eugene Gendlin (1978, 1996), who first described focusing, noticed that there is a flow of experiencing within each person, which that person can reference to discover the meaning of particular experiences for him or her. Focusing emerged from Gendlin's (1978) discovery through research into what made psychotherapy effective, which was one's ability to connect to and symbolize his or her own felt experience. Focusing teaches how experiencing can act as an internal barometer to which the symbolization of experience can be checked against a person's actual experience to determine accuracy.

In Gendlin's terms, focusing involves stages such as clearing a space inside, locating the felt sense, finding a handle (word, phrase, gesture, sound) that seems to fit with the felt sense, resonating or checking that handle with the experience itself, allowing for the revealing of the whole quality of the experience, and allowing a shift to emerge through present-centered contact with the felt sense as well as accepting and nonjudgmental dialogue with one's felt sense and experience (Jordan, 2008). While focusing is often done with another person, it can also be done alone to generate familiarity with one's felt sense of a situation and to learn how to quickly allow that felt sense to reveal an underlying emotional or somatic experience.

The primary assumption in focusing is that there is an experiential felt sense that is separate from our attempt to symbolize it (Gendlin, 1978, 1996; Greenberg et al., 1993). *Felt sense* is a global feeling about the life situations we are in and contains many different aspects of a situation (Welwood, 1985). It is at first experienced as vague or fuzzy, but through attending and dialoguing with the felt sense, its meaning can unfold. After first clearing a space and identifying the felt sense, one can verbally symbolize this feeling and check with his or her bodily experience the accuracy of his or her verbal articulation of the experience.

While focusing is an experiential modality that is primarily used with clients to help connect to their bodily sense of their underlying feelings, experience, and needs, it can also be used to help therapists gain awareness of their own in-the-moment emotional experience as well as the layers of that experience. In fact, therapists who facilitate focusing must be familiar with the language and skill of focusing, which is, at its core, a present-centered way of listening to one's own emotional experience.

Although Gendlin did not initially use the term *presence*, the awareness, sensing, and listening that focusing cultivates are resonant with the presence experience. For example, Leijssen (1990) proposed that focusing is not a technique or a skill but a more general attitude that emerges spontaneously with preparation and a supportive environment. According to Leijssen, the therapist and client clear a space inside to open and quietly remain "present with the not yet speakable, being receptive to the not yet formed" (p. 228). Jordan (2008) described how focusing greatly enhanced her ability to hold clients' experience in the larger space of presence.

Practicing focusing for therapists or therapists in training can help to cultivate therapeutic presence in a few different ways. First, clearing a space inside, which is the beginning of a focusing process, is also part of the preparation therapists can do to cultivate presence. Hence, familiarity with different ways to put aside one's own needs, concerns, issues, and agenda by clearing a space can help to prepare the ground for therapeutic presence.

Second, the language of focusing is based on acceptance and being with what is present without judgment and with compassion. Jordan (2008) noted that this ability to be in presence with a client has emerged in part through learning to be with the felt sense more easily as well as through using presence language. Familiarity with accepting or presence-based language can support therapists in their cultivation of acceptance with their own experience, which will allow them to readily access their experience and their sensory experience of the client in session. Language such as "I am sensing in me," "I am aware right now of," and "I notice in my own body" supports a present and accepting stance.

Third, the in-the-moment somatic and emotional awareness that focusing supports can help the therapist to develop familiarity with his or her inner terrain so that when an experience emerges in session with a client, there is an ability to discern whether it is personally relevant and hence needs to be bracketed or whether it is relevant and an emotional resonance to the client's experience. The more deeply therapists can connect to their own felt sense and cultivate presence, the more their presence and deep listening skills with clients will evolve.

Focusing gives therapists a method and language and technique to gain awareness with their own bodily and emotional experience as well as to work through and clear their own emotional issues. Jordan (2008) noted that focusing (or a focusing attitude) was helpful when she found it difficult to be present with a client because of her own concerns as it allowed her a way to acknowledge the concern with compassion and to return her full presence and immersed awareness back to the client.

A clinical vignette from the first author (S. G.) illustrates the value of her emotional awareness in noticing her own reactions and returning to presence:

> I was with a client who was describing her grief around the death of her brother, and I felt a knot in my stomach. This intensity of tightness began to grow in me and become distracting, as it was physically uncomfortable. A brief moment of checking into my own experience revealed a triggering of an experience of my own loss of a close family member, and I could compassionately acknowledge my pain and grief, and return my full presence and awareness back to the client.

In this example, the internal awareness that was generated through a focusing attitude helped to discern the therapist's grief trigger that was interfering with the ability to be present, and hence to shelve it temporarily and return to presence.

Finally, the ability to discern between therapists' own experience and the sensory or resonant experience of the client's issues is an essential part of therapeutic presence, as noted above. Practice with focusing allows for greater skill and language to connect and dialogue with our inner emotional world and the layers of that inner experience. This check-in and discernment can also reveal that our inner pain, discomfort, and sensation are reflective of the client's experience or of our own issues that need resolving.

## Emotion-Focused Therapy and Presence

Similar to focusing, emotion-focused therapy (EFT) provides therapists a way to become aware of and manage their difficult emotions and generate greater self- and emotional awareness, self-acceptance, and self-empathy. An EFT perspective encourages learning to greet whatever feeling comes up, be it pain, sadness, joy, or anger. This helps us, as therapists, to welcome our client's feelings more easily. Contact with our emotions can be highly therapeutic. The therapist's receptivity, containment, and tolerance to receive whatever emotion the client expresses helps the client in bringing forward seemingly unacceptable parts of the self. One has to fully accept where one is before one can change. The wholeness of the therapist also helps in the acceptance of the client as a whole person without seeing him or her as fragmented or compartmentalized.

In addition, EFT proposes that empathy and compassion toward others are natural extensions of self-empathy and self-compassion. Presence offers a way to change our relationship to suffering by surrendering our need to reject it. This is an act of kindness toward oneself. When we can be really kind to our self, our compassion to others simply arises. When we feel at ease and at peace with our self, we are less likely to find faults with others. The safety of genuine acceptance is thus spontaneously conveyed to our clients.

EFT recommends self-experience as an essential aspect of training. So resolving one's own self-criticism and unfinished business is a part of training and helps to recognize and remove the barriers to presence, hence promoting the ability to be fully present and immersed in the moment with the client.

## EXPRESSIVE ARTS, CREATIVITY, AND NATURE IN CULTIVATING PRESENCE (THE SOUL)

Creativity is a portal to presence. It is the language of the soul and a way to connect to a deeper sense of flow. Opening to the creative realm and a deeper flow helps to connect to the third aspect of therapeutic presence, *expansion*. From this place of expansion our soul or spirit connects to a larger reality and sense of spaciousness that flows from the process of creativity as well as connection to nature. Creative expression is not about the creation of something in particular or an attachment to an outcome. It is purely about the process of expressing what is deeply held inside, without words. When we can get beyond our Grade 8 art or music teacher, who graded us on the right and wrong of what we expressed and squashed our inherent sense of creativity, there is a canvas of opportunity to access and release our deepest essence.

### Art and Therapeutic Presence

Art in various forms, such as painting, drawing, or sculpting, offers opportunities to see and experience the world with presence. When one can experience beginner's mind, an open heart, and trust in the process, then creativity can emerge. Reciprocally, when one is in the flow of an artistic endeavor, not attached to the outcome or a particular product but just immersed in the process of creating, then flow and presence can emerge.

The artistic state of creative flow is similar to psychotherapists' state of therapeutic presence. Epstein (2007) described how the "combination of focused concentration and open, nondiscriminating awareness is one that many artists find essential for the creative process" (p. 184). Like the psychotherapist, it is not an absence of study of technique or strategizing when reflecting on the process, but when engaged in the flow of the creative process there is an emergence of new ideas and a release of attachment to outcome or habitual responding. Therefore, learning to engage in the creative flow of art can provide the canvas for working with clients in a way that is open, trusting of the process and emergence, and deeply centered in the present moment. In this way, art can be a window into the space of presence.

The famous analyst D. W. Winnicott described this state of formless attention and how it is relevant to art and psychoanalysis. Winnicott was "a master of the in-between, of transitional space, of formless experience, intermediate areas, and the worlds between that of inner life and relationships with other people" (Epstein, 2007, p. 187). It is this in-between place of self and other where novel ideas and approaches can emerge. With the artist, it is in the space between the self and connection with the object or canvas, while letting go of preconceptions and attachments, that novel images can emerge. This is much like psychotherapy, where it is in the space between one's self and the client, and the place between the known (about the client and technique) and the unknown, that novel or relevant responses and approaches can emerge from the present-centered connection.

Engaging in the artistic process and finding a way to let go and allow for emergence, without judgment or attachment to outcome, can help therapists to cultivate this state of open and spacious presence. Engaging in the artistic process can help therapists to gain a sense of comfort with the unknown, trust in the process, and understand how the novel and the creative can emerge through that in-between, present-centered state when one is still and empty of thoughts or judgment, without expectations or effort.

## Photography and Being in the Moment

The essence of using photography in the cultivation of therapeutic presence is based on the premise that we can use the lens to see what is present in the moment from different perspectives and angles. Seeing in this way, through the lens of a camera and in the moment, involves being with different aspects of a subject in the moment, without judgment. This means looking at and feeling an aspect of something and taking in the gradient, texture, feel, angles, light, shadow, and aesthetics of an image, without interpretation and with open awareness.

Being aware of the present moment through the lens of a camera does not require technical skill, nor does it require training or expertise as a photographer. Seeing images in this way is not for the purpose of creating a fantastic picture or particular outcome but rather to use the process of sharpening our ability to see, feel, and be with what is in front of us from different angles. Like much of the artistic expression that we are proposing as helpful in the development of presence, it is a process tool rather than a skill-based approach for achieving a particular picture or outcome.

Photography with the intention of being present enhances our awareness of the present moment and allows our self-conscious awareness to subside. In this practice, we let go of the techniques, goals, and expectations of having a good photograph and instead immerse ourselves into the experience of feeling and seeing through the camera. It is a way of allowing experience to come to us, rather than being an objective observer in the way we typically may think of with photography. It involves wandering without a purpose and slowing down when something catches our attention to allow the image to be seen, felt, and experienced from multiple angles.

## Nature and Presence

There is no better place than nature to enhance a sense of presence. For thousands of years, human beings and nature were inseparable, and nature has been a source of art and inspiration across time and cultures. Nature is our greatest teacher when it comes to qualities such as grounding, centering, stillness, change, and flow. Trees can be a great facilitator in grounding and centering. Mountains can teach us to find stillness amidst storms and changing weather. The ocean helps one to connect to the sense of expansion, as does the sky. The river shows us how to flow and move around and through obstacles, such as rocks, and sticks, and our own muck. We can walk along a path to be reminded of taking one step at a time, enjoying the walk and not just the destination. Flowers show us inner beauty. The earth reminds us of what is under our feet. The darkness holds our fears, and the sunlight mirrors our joy. Coleman (2006) described the value of nature in helping to regulate our emotions, gain a larger perspective, and come back to the present:

> When we are distressed, going outside for some fresh air, taking a walk in the park, or wandering deep into the woods quickens our attention, bringing us instantly into the present. Being outdoors provides mental

space and clarity, allowing our bodies to relax and our hearts to feel more at ease. Putting ourselves in the midst of something greater than our personal dramas, difficulties, and pain—as we do when we walk in the open plains, hike in rarefied mountain air, or ramble on an empty beach—can give us a sense of space and openness, lifting us out of our narrow selves. Similarly gazing up at the vast night sky helps us to see our problems and concerns with greater context and perspective. The natural world communicates its profound message: things are okay as they are; you are okay just as you are; simply relax and be present. (p. xvi)

In our world of industrialization, computers, and busyness, we have lost touch with the ability to access, open to, sense, and feel the essence of nature. Schools and training do not emphasize the benefits of nature to help us become comfortable with spaciousness and stillness. It is difficult to keep mind and body still enough amidst the stimulation of the postmodern world without becoming distracted or pulled away from the moment. However, a reminder of returning to an attunement to nature can help tremendously to attune to the moment, a deep inner stillness, and to ourselves. Practicing presence in nature also allows for greater ease in coming into the moment, as the distractions are minimized and the supports for presence are accessible.

One of the founders of psychology, Carl Jung, wrote extensively about the benefits of nature, even equating it to the collective unconscious. A story he told called "The Rainmaker" illustrates the importance of caring for the self through slowing down and allowing for emergence:

> There was a great drought in China and the situation became catastrophic. The Catholics made processions; the Protestants made prayer; the Chinese burned joss sticks, all with no result. Finally, the Chinese said, "Fetch the rainmaker," and from another province an old man appeared. The only thing he asked for was a quiet little house. On the fourth day the clouds gathered, and there was a great storm.
>
> The town was full of wonder. The little man was asked how he did it. He said, "I am not responsible. I come from a country where things are in order. I had to wait 3 days until *I was in order*, and then the rain came." (In Sabini, 2002, p. 211)

The message that Jung was portraying in "The Rainmaker" was that the physician needed to bring himself "in order," and that is all that was needed, which brings to mind the well-known phrase "Physician, heal thyself." The idea is that to help others, we need to help ourselves become balanced, centered, and clear of our own barriers to being relationally present with others, and Jung saw nature as an element or environment that can provide the backdrop for care of the self and opening to a larger context of knowledge.

## RELATIONAL APPROACHES IN THE CULTIVATION OF THERAPEUTIC PRESENCE (CONTACT WITH OTHERS)

While a connection with nature helps to cultivate a larger expansiveness, having healthy and present-centered relationships with others in our daily life can provide the foundation for the cultivation of presence. In particular, the fourth aspect of the experience of therapeutic presence, *being with and for the client,* is supported by attention and care to our personal and everyday relationships.

Many therapists can relate adequately with their clients in the therapy hour but are destructive or withdrawn when it comes to their own personal relationships. A great deal of the pain and the barriers to therapeutic presence emerge from interpersonal suffering. Hence, healing our interpersonal suffering and cultivating relational qualities in our personal relationships are essential.

There are two approaches to cultivating presence in relationship. The first involves facing and working through the barriers to relational connections, such as unresolved anger, hurt, or grief as well as fears of intimacy. This can include forgiveness work that is based on feeling and healing unfinished business. The second approach involves cultivating positive relational qualities in personal, collegial, and everyday relationships; such qualities include respect, love, gratitude, compassion, deep listening, putting aside ego, and sensing and being in the equality of self and other.

### Barriers to Relational Intimacy

A significant aspect of our suffering occurs in relationship to others. An emphasis on facing and removing the relational barriers to presence is essential to finding balance and enhancing the capacity for relational therapeutic presence. The barriers to presence in personal relationships are similar to the barriers noted earlier in the section about emotions as well as those that emerge in relationship to the self. For example, a sense of aloneness is a deep suffering and can act as a barrier to true relational presence. As therapists, we often work in isolation, we feel in isolation, and our individualistic Western society values this separateness. A lack of balance, which includes having an excess of time and energy devoted to work and minimal energy left for family and friends, is another common barrier. Other barriers include unresolved or unfinished business with parents or significant others, a heightened sense of ego, social anxiousness, and interpreting or distancing self from others.

### Cultivating Positive Relational Qualities

Cultivating positive qualities in our everyday relationships is helpful in opening to relational presence. This includes being present and attentive to not only our family and loved ones but also to those in our everyday encounters, for example, with the person at the checkout counter at the grocery store or the gas station attendant. In fact, a personal favorite is challenging my (S. G.) frustration with people who drive carelessly, opening to the possibility that they may have cut me off because they are going to an emergency rather than just being selfish in their action. Paths to cultivating relational presence are presented to us multiple times a day. Whether it be cultivating presence in our interpersonal interactions or cultivating presence in conflict, we need to be open and have a commitment to relational presence. Although there are a number of qualities involved in cultivating relational presence, such as love, gratitude, and connection, for our purpose we are going to focus on a key relational quality, compassion, as well as expand on a model of being in relationship based on Arrien's (1993) Four-Fold Way.

### Compassion

The Tibetan word for compassion is *tsewa* (Dalai Lama in Davidson & Harrington, 2002, p. 98), and it reflects the desire and action to understand and to reduce others' suffering. From this perspective, compassion implies care for alleviation of others' suffering and action to bring about that lessening. There are three aspects of compassion: understanding and caring for another person and that person's suffering, the desire to reduce that suffering, and the action taken to help reduce the other's suffering. Compassion is a naturally occurring by-product of therapeutic presence and is thought to arise naturally from the experience of presence (Geller & Greenberg, 2002; Vivino et al., 2009. However, cultivating compassion can also help presence to arise.

Compassion and love are similar, but love is a feeling and compassion is an action. Compassion is not only a state but also a verb in that how we respond to others and ourselves is with a softness, a tenderness, a strength, and deep love and caring. Sogyal Rinpoche (1992) distinguished compassion from pity as "far nobler" (p. 200). Stephen Levine was quoted by Sogyal Rinpoche as stating, "When your fear touches someone's pain it becomes pity; when your love touches someone's pain, it becomes compassion."

Goleman (2003), in narration with the Dalai Lama, distinguished between afflictive and nonafflictive compassion. *Afflictive compassion* refers to compassion with someone you have an attachment to. *Nonafflictive compassion* involves compassion with someone you do not have an attachment to, for example, an enemy. In this way, cultivating compassion goes beyond the people we feel connected to and extends to those with whom we may have no relationship or an aversive relationship.

Vivino et al. (2009) conducted a qualitative interview of 14 therapists on the value of compassion. A working definition emerged that views compassion as broader and deeper than empathy (i.e., is similar to empathy but allows a deeper engagement), a state of being (including presence), connected to suffering, involving action (i.e., is not simply sitting with others but also involves action to help them reduce their suffering), and hinging on the ability to be compassionate (such that when it is difficult to be compassionate, one must work to facilitate it). The authors also asked about how compassion developed within the participants and found that most believed that it is inborn; however, they also discussed developing compassion through personal work, family influences, having received compassion from an important other (e.g., teacher, therapist), working with clients, spiritual beliefs, and training as a counselor.

Cultivating self-compassion, as well as understanding and healing one's own relational pain and suffering, is essential to cultivating compassion for others (Leary, Tate, Adams, Allen, & Hancock, 2007). Intimacy and compassion in this respect are a kind of attunement to others that begins with an attunement to ourselves. Generating compassion for ourselves and for others helps therapists to generate compassion for clients.

Parallel to self-compassion, developing empathy for and closeness to others is also a preliminary step in developing compassion. This demands that therapists focus their understanding on the pain of those in their personal lives and the intensity of the pain as well as have the intention to help relieve that suffering. This sounds simple on one level, yet many therapists arrive home physically and emotionally exhausted, with little time and energy left for the needs of family, friends, and others. Thus, attention to first cultivating empathy and then compassion needs to go beyond the therapy hour.

Generating compassion includes seeing all people as the same as you, which includes seeing one's own individual concerns as less important than those of others (Dalai Lama, 2001). True compassion then not only comes from wanting to help those less fortunate than ourselves but also from realizing our kinship with all beings. In this vein, service and volunteer work can help to cultivate compassion, as we begin to see the humanness of others on a deeper level. Committing to volunteer work with underprivileged or challenged communities can help in deepening our sense of compassion in a way that goes beyond payment and therapy.

### The Four-Fold Way (of Being in Relationship)

Cultural anthropologist Angeles Arrien (1993, 2010) developed a program, the Four-Fold Way, which is based on four archetypes (warrior, healer, visionary, and teacher) and four ways (principles) developed from cross-cultural research. It is designed to increase our respect for nature and for others and to enhance our ability to work cooperatively and creatively in teams. The Four-Fold Way is based on cross-cultural principles as well as a synthesis of shamanic and contemporary perspectives, and it reflects healthy ways of being in relationships and teams. Each archetype relates to one of the four ways, which are said to encourage ease and peacefulness in self and in relationships. The Four-Fold Way is represented below:

1. *Showing up*. The Way of the Warrior is to show up, or choose to be present. To bring one's self fully to the relationship through appropriate action, right timing, and clear communication.
2. *Paying attention to what has heart and meaning*. The Way of the Healer is to give awareness to what is most poignant and to pay attention to what has heart and meaning.
3. *Telling the truth without judgment or blame*. The Way of the Visionary is to be truthful, authentic, direct, and intentional without blame or judgment, which helps to develop our vision and intuition.
4. *Being open to the outcome, not attached to the outcome*. The Way of the Teacher is to maintain openness and nonattachment to whatever arises from showing up, being authentic, and being truthful, which helps recover resources of wisdom and objectivity.

Translating the Four-Fold Way as an experiential practice of being in relationship can help therapists in their own interactions to be open, receptive, and integral, and to cultivate relational presence. This conscious effort to show up in our relationships, to be connected to that which is most poignant in the heart, and to communicate with honesty and integrity and without judgment or blame while being open and nonattached to the outcome, supports care and presence in our intimate relationships. This includes interactions with our families, colleagues, store clerks, coffee baristas, strangers, and neighbors. Therapeutic presence is greatly enhanced by working on compassion, care, and relational presence in our day-to-day relationships, and presence is compromised by neglecting our personal relationships or by being reactive or noncaring.

## INTEGRATING SOMATIC, EMOTIONAL, CREATIVE, AND RELATIONAL APPROACHES TO PRESENCE: THERAPEUTIC RHYTHM AND MINDFULNESS PROGRAM

The first author (S. G.) developed and facilitates a program called Therapeutic Rhythm and Mindfulness (TRM™), which involves group drumming and percussion, relaxation exercises, mindfulness techniques, and visualization to promote health, wellness, present-moment awareness, and authentic expression while deepening connections with one's own self, intuition, and others. TRM takes elements of two empirically validated techniques, HealthRHYTHMS and mindfulness-based stress reduction, and combines them with a third element: a positive and supportive group environment (Geller, 2009, 2010).

Music and creating rhythm are powerful nonverbal ways to develop deep listening, access intuition, and release stress. Drumming and rhythm making have been used in indigenous cultures to reduce disease and increase harmony with one's self, community, and nature (Clottey, 2004; Diamond, 1999). Drum circles are cross-culturally a part of some of the oldest healing rituals (Bittman et al., 2001, p. 38). Although music, in general, has been linearly defined in Western culture as a performance-based activity, TRM is not performance based but rather a form of self-expression and nonverbal communication.

TRM is a variation of Remo's HealthRHYTHMS and is also referred to as *empowerment drumming*, which is defined as a comprehensive, whole-person, evidence-based therapeutic approach that enriches wellness (Bittman & Bruhn, 2008). TRM involves using drumming and percussion instruments to express nonverbally one's bodily experience and stress and to increase intrapersonal and interpersonal connection as well as a sense of spirituality. Therapeutic rhythm and associated research are explained below. The benefits of mindfulness practice in cultivating presence were discussed in the previous chapter and will not be repeated here.

## Research on Therapeutic Rhythm

Ancient wisdom on drumming has been translated into recent research. For example, a few studies by Bittman and colleagues have demonstrated that the HealthRHYTHMS program, which includes a 6-week composite drumming group, resulted in decreased stress; reduced burnout and fatigue; improvement in mood, anxiety, and depression; increased immune functioning; and an increase in natural cell activity (Bittman et al., 2001; Bittman et al., 2005; Bittman, Bruhn, Stevens, Westengard, & Umbach, 2003; Bittman et al., 2004).

Of particular interest to therapists are two studies on the impact of recreational music making for long-term care workers. Bittman et al. (2003, 2004) demonstrated that a 6-week mind–body wellness recreational music-making program resulted in improved mood disturbance and reduced burnout in long-term health care workers as well as first-year nursing students.

Similarly, Maschi and Bradley (2010) demonstrated that recreational music making (drum/percussion) with social work students, resulted in greater wellbeing, calmness, empowerment, and connectedness. The authors suggest that this positive form of expression can improve social workers wellbeing and, as a result, improve their clinical effectiveness with clients. Overall, group drumming has been demonstrated to balance mood states, combat stress, and increase immune functioning. Releasing the obstacles to presence, such as stress, burnout, and difficult emotions, and increasing self-expression, social connectedness health, vitality, and wellness are all important factors in allowing for contact with presence and hence being more effective clinicians.

The expressive aspect of rhythm making allows for the development of spontaneity, which helps therapists to be more comfortable with moving freely with what is occurring from moment to moment. Openness and flexibility are important qualities of presence because they allow therapists to be with what is arising rather than to impose their agenda or fear of the unknown on the therapeutic process. Research on the improvisation of jazz musicians reflects the development of this quality of spontaneity that can occur in the improvisation of drumming in community. In particular, research using functional magnetic resonance imaging demonstrated that when jazz musicians improvise, "their brains turn off areas linked to self-censoring and inhibition, and turn on those that let self-expression flow" (Melville, 2008). This quality of spontaneity, flow, and self-expression reflects the activation of the medial prefrontal cortex as well as the slowing down of the dorsolateral prefrontal cortex, which is the part of the brain that is linked to planned actions and self-censoring (Melville, 2008). Inferences from Melville's research can be extended to therapeutic drumming since rhythm-based drumming also reflects this spontaneous flow and free self-expression and hence the openness to the rhythm that emerges from being fully open in the moment.

## TRM and the Cultivation of Therapeutic Presence

TRM combines the experiential benefits of drumming and rhythm making (i.e., joy, social connectedness, movement, stress release, attunement with self and others) as well as the value of mindfulness tools (present-moment awareness, emotional regulation) with the meaning making inherent in emotional reflection and processing. TRM has been offered to people living with cancer, depression, anxiety, self-esteem issues, and loneliness, and particularly for our purposes, to health care professionals for self-care and enhancing therapeutic presence. Participants reported experiencing stress-release; deeper relaxation; self-nourishment; enhanced intuition; deeper listening; a feeling of connection with self and others; and increased joy, vitality, and access to presence.

TRM helps to remove some of the obstacles to presence, such as stress and tension. Stress can inhibit therapists' ability to clear a space inside and to access a receptive inner state. Therapeutic drumming supports a reversal in the classic stress response as well as a reduction in burnout (Bittman et. al., 2003, 2005). TRM also allows for the expression of difficult emotions, including the vicarious traumatization and compassion fatigue associated with being a therapist. Reducing stress and increasing self-care and emotional expression and integration are helpful in allowing for the emergence of presence.

TRM also offers an opportunity for therapists to build relationships and a sense of belonging in community with other therapists. This sense of relational connection enhances general wellness and self-care, reduces isolation, and increases inner vitality and a sense of social connectedness.

TRM helps therapists to enhance their own intuition and imagery skills. TRM can support the development of visualization skills (an inherent part of the program), which can be helpful in both emptying one's self of judgment or preconceptions and in opening and preparing to see a client. TRM can also help therapists to increase extrasensory perception, which can support therapists' enhanced listening and sensing skills as they allow for present-based awareness with a client.

Group drumming and imagery also support therapists in general self-care, health, and presence through exercise, connection with self and others, and enhanced joy and vitality. Levitin (2008) described how joy is related to music, as when one experiences joy, "the natural reaction is to sing, jump, dance, shout—all things that are part of standard music-dance in all societies" (p. 83). Neuroscientists have also found that the playing of music can affect dopamine levels, which are the "feel-good" hormones in the brain, and this secretion of feel-good chemicals is involved in the relationship between music and mood (Levitin, 2008, p. 86).

Group drumming can help therapists become more synchronized with their own rhythms as well as the rhythms of others. This fine balance of self and other attunement, as well as the ability to vacillate awareness among all the different present-moment experiences in a session (in self, in other, and in the relationship), is central to therapeutic presence. Therapists must be able to shift awareness from their self to the other and the relationship, depending on what arises in the moment.

In summary, TRM is a novel and poignant way of releasing stress, reconnecting internally and in community, and supporting the emergence of presence. TRM and rhythm making in general can help therapists enhance their own well-being, contact their in-the-moment bodily experience, attune to the rhythm of self and others, release stresses associated with being a therapist, and access their inner potential, all of which help to remove the obstacles to becoming fully present. TRM can help therapists physically express and release some of the stressors associated with work and life. It also allows for self-nourishment and community connection and offers a tool for present-moment awareness and emotional regulation. All of this, in turn, can help to establish a basis for relational presence and reestablishment of internal balance and homeostasis to maintain health and wellness.

## CONCLUSION

In this chapter, we explored four different entry points in the cultivation of presence from an experiential perspective to enhance present-moment awareness and to release the barriers to therapeutic presence. Being present at each entry point (somatic, emotional, creative, and relational) allows for the cultivation of the whole experience of therapeutic presence. In particular, each experiential entry point can also reflect a particular dimension of the experience of therapeutic presence. First, presence in the body and somatic awareness can help to generate a sense of grounding and centering. Second, presence in the heart and emotional awareness can allow for the development of immersion, such as opening to what is poignant or at the heart of the client in a focused, accepting, and nonjudgmental way. Third, being present in the soul through creativity and contact with nature can generate a sense of expansiveness and deeper trust in the unknown. Fourth, being present in relationships and showing up for our loved ones and in our daily encounters can help to cultivate the compassionate stance of being with and for the other.

Experiential practices allow for the emergence of intuition, wisdom, and humanness through taking care of the self and staying in contact with one's self and others and opening to creative expression and sustaining healthy relationships. Taking care of ourselves through direct contact with our own experience and needs, and an enhanced sense of our relational and creative potential, is the best service we can provide in taking care of others. This level of self-care and presence practice also helps to sustain a healthy and alive state for the therapist that transcends the therapy encounter.

# 12

# THERAPEUTIC PRESENCE EXERCISES AND PRACTICES

A therapist has to practice being fully present and has to cultivate the energy of compassion in order to be helpful.
                              —Thich Nhat Hanh (2000, p. 152)

Presence is within us—it is accessible, palpable, and real. However, to cultivate the experience of presence and allow for greater sustainability, there need to be ongoing practice and a commitment to the continued growth and development of our internal, spiritual, and relational selves. Rarely would we see a golf or a tennis professional who has never had any practice. Musicians spend countless hours cultivating their abilities and refining their music. The Dalai Lama spends tens of thousands of hours cultivating presence and inner happiness. Yet some people expect to be present and to be able to sustain an inner receptivity and connection to others and themselves, without practicing or being with others and themselves in this way on an ongoing basis. This illusory belief is partially a consequence of the quick fix, instant messaging, and stressful society that we live in today. This is also partially attributed to our own unwillingness to take time to clear the obstacles and our own personal and relational issues to open fully and completely to the client from a grounded and steady place.

Training in psychotherapy tends to lack emphasis with respect to the focus and skills in knowing and developing our inner terrain as well as with respect to the skill of becoming present in ourselves and in our relationships. Opening to the body, one's self, and others, without judgment and with full awareness, is essential to allow for presence to emerge. This includes, in part, an awareness of the barriers to presence, which is necessary in order to release them, such as busyness, unfinished emotional issues, traumas, distractions, and disconnection. Furthermore, therapeutic presence is about being in direct relationship with another person in an open, grounded, and immersed way with the intention of being with and for the other. Hence, good relationship skills are essential and helpful for the psychotherapist. However, many therapists maintain adequate relationships with their clients, yet their lives are filled with tumultuous personal relationships. Hence, not teaching and including inner and relational work to remove these barriers and to open fully to the moment in a healthy and resourceful way is like not teaching a doctor how to use a stethoscope or not teaching a carpenter how to use a drill.

While practicing presence entails a doing element, it is not the doing of practice that helps presence to emerge. It is the moving toward pausing, slowing down, opening up, and taking time to clear the meadows of our mind and body that allows for a deeper stillness to be revealed. Brown (2005) provided a great illustration of the movement aspect of practice, which is a perceptual shift from outer distraction to inner stillness and includes moving from

> Doing to being.
> Looking to seeing.
> Hearing to listening.
> Pretence to presence.
> Imbalance to balance.
> Separation to oneness.
> Reacting to responding.
> Inauthentic to authenticity.
> Fragmentation to integration.
> Seeking happiness to allowing joy.
> Revenge and blame to forgiveness.
> Incorrect perception to correct perception.
> Complaint and competition to compassion.
> Behaving unconsciously to behaving consciously.
> "Living in time" to experiencing present moment awareness. (p. 52)

This chapter offers a collection of presence exercises to provide easy access to ways of deepening presence. In approaching therapy, we have suggested that one needs to prepare to optimize the emergence of presence. Therefore, we start with a number of presence exercises for preparing the ground for presence. We then present some acronyms for cultivating presence. Finally, we present more general exercises (both individual and classroom/relational exercises) for developing and enhancing the capacity for presence.

# PREPARING THE GROUND FOR THERAPEUTIC PRESENCE

While preparing for presence can occur both in life and in session, some of the pauses and exercises we note here tend to overlap between the two. This way, you can find what works best for you and adapt as feels fit. The most important theme in all aspects of preparing for presence is to pause and slow down and allow the space for a deeper relational presence to emerge.

## In Life

Some basic life practices can help you to cultivate presence. One practice rests on the notion of slowing down. If you take any activity or moment through the day and slow it down, such as walking at half the pace or simply pausing at various moments (e.g., every time you touch a doorknob), you will begin to take greater notice of what is around you in that moment. For example, on a walk to your office, which you do on an almost-daily basis, slow your pace intentionally and notice small things that you must have passed every day but had never noticed before. This present-moment awareness allows you to notice what is right in front of you with a perceptual vividness and acuity, to soften the volume of the running dialogue in your head, and to create a space inside for presence to emerge before arriving at your office.

## Before or During Session

A brief, 5-minute break to pause, breathe, and center before a session with a client can help to optimize being present as well as move the session in the direction of healing. A reminder to bring your attention and bodily senses (back) to presence during sessions can be equally effective in engaging the brain and body in the process of presence quickly, with continued practice. The following are additional awareness exercises for therapists to help deepen presence.

### Starting With the Breath

Generating intimacy with the breath can act as a microcosm for understanding presence as well as a vehicle to touch presence within ourselves in four important ways. First, attention to the breath offers us an experience of the constant change in life. Attachment to a predictable experience from the client or ourselves is a barrier to presence as it is only through our opening to the unknown and allowing for emergence that we can really touch the depth of the moment as it presents itself. Second, attention to a part of the body where we experience the breath, such as at the nostril or on the upper lip, allows us to experience the place where the outside world meets the inside world. From there we can deepen our experience of how we are not separate from others or from the outside world. Instead, we are a part of the flow of the internal and the external, or self and other. Third, the breath is present-time focused. When we attune to our breathing, we are not attuning to what is in the future or the past, we are tuning into the here and now. Fourth, research supports that focus on the breath helps to bring the breath rate to a deeper and slower rhythm, which then calms the nervous system and evokes greater calmness and attention.

*Breathing Deeply Into the Moment.* Another way of using the breath with the intention of calming and bringing your attention to the moment is to deepen the breath. Taking longer and slower breaths allows for a strengthening in heart rate variability and hence can evoke a healthier environment in the body for presence to emerge. A way to begin this exploration is to start with your own experience and explore whether attuning and slowing rhythms of respiration can help to evoke a calmer and more alert and attuned state of being in the moment.

- Pause, get into a comfortable yet upright position and notice what is true in your body and mind right now.
- Relax your body and soften your eyes, with your hands resting on your lap.
- Allow your attention to move to your breath.
- Count to three as you breathe in; count to four as you breathe out.
- Now lengthen the time of each inhalation and exhalation. For example, inhale for 5 seconds, pause briefly, then exhale for slightly longer than your inhale (e.g., 8 seconds).
- Allow yourself to visualize your breath becoming deeper, slower, and more relaxed; continue for 5 minutes.
- Open your eyes and become aware of how you are feeling in this moment.
- Pause and breathe into a more present-centered place with your eyes open and become aware of what is around you in the room. Use those objects of attention as an anchor into the present moment.

*Breathing and Centering.* The following exercise uses the breath as a starting place of awareness before accessing a bodily sense of centering.

- Become aware of your breath. Notice where it is experienced in your body and the rhythm of the inhale and exhale.
- Spend a few minutes paying attention to the flow and rhythm of your natural breath by focusing on the place in the body you experience breathing.

- Become aware of the lower half of your body: your feet, legs, sexual center, buttocks, lower torso. Notice what is true in the lower part of your body.
- Become aware of the upper half of your body: head, neck, shoulders, upper back, chest. Notice the sensations in the upper half of your body.
- Now invite your awareness to where your upper and lower body meet. Become aware of that meeting place at the center of your body, perhaps at your belly or abdomen.
- Allow awareness to rest in the place where you imagine your center is.
- Feel or imagine the stability, strength, and unwavering feeling that is part of your center.
- Invite a symbol, image, or word to emerge that resonates with your center, something to return to when you need to bring yourself back to centeredness.
- Sit in that place of centeredness. Inhale deeply into your core, and exhale out to a larger sense of energy and expansion.

*Moving to Intention*

As noted in Chapter 9, when we set an intention (e.g., to be present), it engages the frontal lobe and creates an integrated state of priming, which is a gearing up of the neural system to be in the mode of that which we are intending (i.e., to be present; Hanson & Mendius, 2009; Siegel, 2007). In a few moments of setting an intention for presence, the neurological underpinnings of the presence experience itself are likely engaged. This also helps the stimulation of the parasympathetic wing of the autonomic nervous system, which in turn invites a greater sense of calm as well as a mild activation of the sympathetic wing, which brings a level of alertness.

Intention for presence can be conducted by taking a few minutes in between sessions, as noted in the following practice:

- Invite yourself to become more fully present to this moment by saying to yourself, "Come into the present moment."
- Take a deep breath, becoming aware of the sensation of the breath in this moment.
- Bring your awareness to your body, starting from your awareness of your feet on the ground and then moving up through your legs, abdomen, torso, midbody, upper body, shoulders, neck, head.
- Be aware of your facial muscles, softening your eyes and facial expression.
- Breathe deeply as you become aware of each body part.

- Take four or five full breaths, repeating quietly to yourself on the inhale, "I arrive into the present moment," and on the exhale, "I let go of the busyness." (Note: Try using briefer words to reflect intentions, such as "arriving" on the inhale and "letting go" on the exhale.)
- Become aware of the feeling in your body now as you invite yourself deeper into the present moment. Attend to and prolong the feeling of becoming present.

Another practice to try before a session is the following:

- Before meeting your next client, take a moment just to be still. Whether seated or standing, feel your feet firmly placed on the ground.
- Begin to pay attention to your breath. Place your hand on your abdomen and feel your belly expand with a full inhalation and contract with a full exhalation. Pay attention to the rise and fall of your belly breath.
- Start to visualize your next client. Be open to the energy of this person, connecting to his or her humanness.
- Open your eyes and walk to the door to greet this person, while connecting to the ground, to your breath, and to the intention for presence.

## ACRONYMS FOR CULTIVATING PRESENCE

While the list of exercises to cultivate presence is endless, the basic foundation is to pause and generate awareness of self and other in the moment. To aid the process of cultivating presence, we developed the acronym PRESENCE, reflecting eight steps for cultivating presence with and for the client:

- Pause.
- Relax into this moment.
- Enhance awareness of your breath.
- Sense your inner body; bring awareness to your physical and emotional body.
- Expand sensory awareness outwards (seeing, listening, touching, sensing what is around you).
- Notice what is true in this moment, both within you and around you. Notice the relationship between the internal and external.
- Center and ground (in yourself and your body).
- Extend and make contact (with client, or other).

A shorter way to allow for presence is to invite a NOW moment:

- Notice what is true in this moment, in your body and experience.
- Open and ground, in your body and your breath, as well as in a larger state of awareness.
- Welcome the other in as you expand your open and grounded self outward.

A helpful acronym that has emerged from the mindfulness and addictions area (Marlatt & Miller, 2009) is SOBER, which has been adapted here as a practice that can help to facilitate the process of presence. This can be used by therapists in session during moments of reactivity.

- Stop—Pause for a moment and step out of the cycle of emotional reactivity.
- Observe—Pay attention to what you are sensing, feeling, and experiencing and what is the primary experience of emotion that underlies that reactivity.
- Breathe—Pause for a few deep breaths to assess your situation in as calm a manner as possible.
- Expand—Expand your awareness and allow yourself to get a larger perspective on what is happening within you and around you.
- Respond—Now respond, rather than react, to the situation at hand so that your response is more effective and comes from an authentic emotional experience rather than just reactivity.

Walking through SOBER helps to calm the sympathetic nervous system and activate a calmer parasympathetic nervous system to respond to a situation with less reactivity and to return one's attention back to the present moment. The idea is that when in a state of emotional reactivity, there is a way to stop and check in with one's own underlying experience both to uncover the barriers to presence and to stop the cycle of reactivity. This is particularly useful in difficult relationships with others and to uncover some of the habitual emotional reactions we engage in that serve to escalate the cycle of reactivity with others.

## GENERAL PRACTICES: INDIVIDUAL EXERCISES

We now provide a set of general exercises that facilitate presence. We encourage you to be creative in using these exercises to find variations that work for you personally or for training purposes, as they are merely suggestions and are not locked to a particular methodology. Because people exhibit a variety of temperaments and attentional capacities, the practices are versatile and can be adapted to integrate with who and where you are as a person, therapist, student, or educator. Also, we encourage you to first experience an exercise that you are naturally drawn toward before offering to others.

## Whole Body Awareness Into Expansion

The first exercise helps to develop the openness and the sense of expansion and sensory awareness that are part of therapeutic presence. This brief exercise can also serve as a practice ground to enhance right hemispheric activity, which is involved in sensing the body and in gestalts, or wholes. This also helps to decrease verbal activity, relax the body, and expand awareness. Ultimately, it helps in sensing the whole of a situation, such as the client's experience or what is occurring in the therapeutic relationship.

- With your eyes closed, allow yourself to pause and move your attention inward to the breath.
- Breathe naturally and see if you can be aware of the breath as a whole.
- Now move your attention to your body. Allow your awareness to be with the interconnectivity of the whole body. Allow your attention to be aware of the body as a whole. If your attention wanders or you become distracted, return your awareness to the moment and allow your awareness to once again be with the whole of the breath or body.
- Now with your eyes open, expand your sensory awareness to notice (see, hear, feel) what is present directly around you in this moment. Take in the details that you are sensing individually and then experience the whole of what is around you.
- You can continue expanding your awareness in stages, such as to notice the building, the street, the community, the town or city, the country, neighboring countries, the other side of the world, the whole of the earth and where it sits in the solar system.

## Clearing a Space

Clearing a space inside involves putting aside one's own needs, concerns, issues, and agenda. Clearing a space allows therapists to be open and accessible to the client and the depth of his or her experience, without assumptions or presuppositions. It is a conscious and intentional practice that is helpful before starting the day, for a few moments before each session, or perhaps after a particularly difficult session.

- Sit or lie down in a comfortable position with your eyes softened or closed.
- Take a few moments to become aware of your breath, becoming aware of the rhythm of the inhalation and the exhalation.
- Begin by asking yourself, "What is between me and feeling fully present and at ease in myself right now?" Wait to see what issues arise. Spend a moment with each issue until you intuitively focus on one particular issue.
- Bring your awareness to how you carry that issue in your body; notice the physical sensations associated with the issue and name them (e.g., tightness in the jaw, butterflies in the stomach, a pit in the chest).
- Ask yourself for the intuitive feel or felt sense of the entire issue, and find words for this (e.g., frightened, scared, confused, frustrated).
- Now visualize putting that issue in a box or on a shelf, putting the whole sense of that issue aside.
- Now ask yourself, "What else is in the way of me feeling fully in the moment and at peace?" See what issues arise.
- Again, just name the issue as it arises, get an intuitive or felt sense of it, notice where it is located in the body, find a word or image that captures its whole quality.
- Now imagine again putting the whole of that issue in a box or on a shelf (or use other images, such as floating the issue down a river).
- Continue this process until all the issues have been named, acknowledged, felt, and put aside temporarily.
- After spending a few moments with this process of acknowledging, naming, feeling, and releasing the barriers to presence, check to see if there is a background sense of presence or a cleared space inside. What does that feel like?
- Take a moment to just feel or be in that sense of presence.

### Mindfulness Meditation Technique

Mindfulness meditation involves sitting straight, following the breath, and letting thoughts and sensations come and go without trying to control or direct them (Goldstein, 1994). When you notice your attention go off, without judgment name the thought with one word (e.g., thinking, planning, worrying) and then gently return your awareness to the breath. Doing this for a period of time each day, such as for 20 minutes, can help to support this practice.

When we let our thoughts arise and fall, we notice our incessant thinking, feelings, and sensations. By observing and opening to our experience without judging or resisting, we gain a more intimate sense of the area of our life where we feel afraid, fixated, or grasping.

### Grounding Walking Practice

Thich Nhat Hanh (1976) has a series of books and tapes that demonstrate the value of walking meditation. The next exercise is a variation of his practice of using a slow walk to focus your attention and intention on grounding. This can be done as a concentrated practice or even incorporated into a walk that you take on a daily basis such as from your car to the office. It can also be done slowly or at normal pace:

- Take two steps in rhythm with your inhale.
- Next, take three steps in rhythm with your exhale.
- On the inhale, gently say the phrase "I feel my feet."
- On the exhale, gently say the phrase "on the ground."
- Continue walking slowly in rhythm with your breath and the phrases intended toward grounding.

### Walking Into the Moment

This practice can help therapists to learn the gentle art of presence, the capacity to return to the moment through movement, listening deeply, opening sensory capacities, grounding, relating to what is around you, inside of you, and sensitivity to the relationship between what is around you and what is inside of you.

Give yourself 20 to 30 minutes to go for a walk. Taking a walk in a quiet environment, such as on a trail or a quiet street, would minimize distractions. When you are ready to begin your walk, pause in a standing position.

1. Stand briefly with your feet firmly planted on the ground. Invite your awareness to your legs, knees, ankles, and the contact place between feet and the ground.
2. Now bring your awareness to the breath, feeling the rise and fall in your abdomen or chest or feeling the brush of air as it passes your upper lip.
3. Now begin walking, synchronizing your breath with your steps. Each step as it touches the ground is your barometer of attention.
4. When you feel connected to your walking and breathing, begin to count with each step, starting with one on the first step and stopping when you reach 100.

5. As you stop at 100, attune to your breath again to ensure that you have not lost contact. Feel your feet on the ground.
6. In this pause, explore different senses in relation to where you are in this moment. Look around and see what is around you, taking a wider view and narrow view, noticing what colors, textures, images, and shapes surround you.
7. When you notice some particular detail, bring your attention there. Notice this tiny image that you would have never noticed had you not stopped.
8. Open your auditory sensory capacity to the sounds that are around you. Listen closely to different levels and pitches of sound and to how the sounds harmonize or perhaps clash.
9. Now check your own body, inviting your awareness to your physical body. First explore your feet, legs, abdomen, torso, arms, hands, fingers, details of the face, head.
10. Move your awareness to the internal terrain of your body. Notice what you feel like, physiologically, emotionally, mentally, relationally. Notice what is true for you.
11. Move your attention outward again, bringing with you your internal awareness and sensory listening capacity while staying connected to the breath. Notice what is around you, what you hear, what you feel, and how you relate to your surroundings.
12. When you are ready, walk until you reach 100 steps again and repeat Steps 5 through 11.

Many variations of walking into the moment can be done. Instead of counting to 100, you can walk until you feel the urge to stop or until something catches your attention. Presence can emerge through this intentional practice of stopping, noticing, feeling, opening, experiencing, and relating in the present moment.

### Noticing and Saying Yes

This exercise was inspired by Tara Brach (2009). The basic practice is to notice all sensations that are present from moment to moment (thinking, feeling, experiencing)—sensing them, naming them, and saying "yes" to each experience. For example, take a few moments to sit quietly and notice the sensations in your body. Each time you experience a sensation, name it and say yes, accepting all aspects of that experience. Let curiosity be there, notice the challenge in really allowing an experience to be in one's bodily awareness.

A variation on noticing is beginning moment-to-moment awareness with "I can sense . . . " or "It is like this . . . " The following practice can help you feel what it is like to first reject and then accept your experience:

- Take a moment to pause and attend to the breath.
- Now become aware of a situation that is difficult. Allow yourself to feel all aspects of this difficulty.
- Sense the whole of the situation, and be aware of any feelings that arise about it.
- First say no to it. Become aware of your bodily response when you close down to your experience.
- Then say yes to all aspects of your experience of that situation.
- Pay attention to what you notice in your body when you say no, rejecting your experience, and when you say yes, allowing all aspects of your experience.

Intentionally pausing and staying present in this way with what you feel around this difficulty also helps in gaining awareness of what difficulties you may be experiencing so that you can attend to and work through whatever is needed. This can be done with a specific situation or a relationship with a client or more generally as a training exercise.

### Observing Without Judgment

The following exercise encourages observing without judgment, which can be done individually or in a training setting. This brief exercise is especially helpful for people who have trouble staying focused for long periods of time.

- Place your hand on the desk or on your lap in front of you, palm open facing in an upward position.
- Now look closely at your hand.
- Notice what you experience in your hand, without describing it; rather experience or sense visually and viscerally the intricacies of your hand without describing it.

Countless variations of this exercise can be used, such as sensing herbs, the breath, a candle, or the taste of a raisin. You can look out the window and activate different senses to experience fully what is in front of you.

### Cultivating Nonjudgment

There are fun ways to work on the quality of being nonjudgmental. For example, Linehan (2009) shared her practice of asking her students in dialectical behavior therapy training to ring a bell whenever they say something with judgment or when they hear a judgment pass from anyone in a training group. A behavioral variation of this, which students or therapists can use by themselves or in groups, is the following:

- Notice judgments while at the same time being aware of not judging yourself or others for being judgmental (i.e., not judging judgments!).
- Count judgments. You can use a clicker or counter. Click it every time you hear a judgment stated or every time you self-judge (in your head or out loud).
- Replace judgments with nonjudgmental statements.

### Facing Attraction and Aversion Through Sound

This is a powerful practice to directly witness our tendency to go toward or move away from the moment when something draws our attention. Rather than create a quiet environment to go within, we invite the opposite. Place yourself in a busy environment or keep your cell phone and any electronic device that calls your attention to someone attempting to contact you. Or do both: Keep your cell phone and devices on and place yourself in a busy environment. However, during the pause described below, try to resist answering or responding to any calls or messages that do come through. This is most poignant when conducted in a group and there are a number of people in the room with their cell phones on. This allows for a direct witnessing not only of the experience of being pulled out of the moment but also of the reaction (aversion) that can come through experiencing other people's phone calls and responses. The intent is to eventually witness and experience these pushes and pulls without reacting to them.

- Close your eyes and pay attention to your breathing.
- Allow your attention to be with the belly breath, feeling the expansion of the belly as you inhale and the contraction as you exhale.
- If you hear a sound in the room, the ring of a cell phone, or a loud voice or sound, use it as a moment to pause, paying attention to what is emerging.
- You may notice a strong negative response if someone's phone has a particular ring or there is a loud and disturbing external noise. Pay attention to aversion, then invite your attention back to the breath, to a new moment.
- If your phone rings, you may likely feel the pull to answer or at least to check the number on the call display. Notice the

sensation of attraction. Then invite your attention back to the moment, back to the breath.

This can be good training for developing focus and attention and for developing a capacity to avoid, or not get stuck in, aversion or attraction. This enables us to see someone as he or she truly is.

### Tonglen: Compassion Practice

Tonglen is a Tibetan Buddhist practice that helps in cultivating the ability to take in the depth of another's suffering and to generate compassion (Sogyal Rinpoche, 1992). It allows us to generate an experience of compassion for self and others. With Tonglen we can experience that we will not fall apart by taking in the other's suffering, and that the other's pain and suffering can be felt in our own body and transmuted into compassion by our breath. The following is a variation of this practice:

1. *Connecting to the breath.* You may want to rest your hands on your belly or pay attention to the flow of air from your nose as it passes your upper lip.

    Inhale a sense of expansion.

    Exhale a sense of releasing or letting go.

2. *Generating compassion.* Remember a moment in your life when you experienced compassion. It could be time spent with a special grandmother who treated you with love and kindness or time spent with a friend who was in deep pain. Remember what it felt like to offer, receive, or witness genuine love and care between strangers or between loved ones, friends, or family.

    What does that experience feel like in the body?

    Allow the feelings of the closeness you experienced with that person to come into the moment.

    Begin to coordinate your breathing with that feeling.

    Inhale taking in the experience of hurting.

    Exhale feeling the experience of care and love from the other.

3. *Befriending pain in close other.* Now think about a deep pain or difficult experience that someone you know is going through (e.g., hurting or struggling from sickness or from sadness). Get a sense of the hard times they are going through.

    Inhale: Feel and expand around the depth of pain of the other.

    Exhale: Let go and send love, compassion, and care to that person.

4. *Befriending pain that is far away.* Next, think about the pain and struggle of someone you do not know. Alternatively, you can think about a global struggle, perhaps about something you read in the news or a conflict in another country or a conflict between people. Offer love, compassion, and care to the object of your thought.

   Inhale: Feel and expand around the pain of this person or community.

   Exhale: Let go of that pain and send that person or community love, care, and compassion.

5. *Befriending your own pain.* Next, think about a pain or struggle you have been experiencing. Allow this giving and receiving to flow through the breath.

   Inhale: Expand and feel the pain, sadness, and suffering that you are experiencing.

   Exhale: Let go and let compassion flow to that pain, breathing out compassion, love, and care to your own pain.

6. *Return to the breath.* Become aware of just breathing. Allow yourself to reconnect to the flow of your own breath. You may bring your hands to your belly or return your awareness to the place in the body where you experience the breath—your chest, belly, nose, or throat; rest your hands on your belly or pay attention to the flow of air from your nose to your upper lip. Rest your attention on your own body. Be aware perhaps of what places in your life need compassion. What did you learn? What steps do you need to take for yourself?

## GENERAL PRACTICES: CLASSROOM AND RELATIONAL EXERCISES

The exercises presented to this point can be used in personal practice or in a group format. The next series of exercises is specifically designed to be conducted in training sessions or in groups.

### Contacting an Experience of Presence

This exercise can be done as a silent reflection for students, where they can begin to get a feel for the qualities of presence. Begin by asking the students to reflect on a time when they felt someone was deeply listening and present to them, really present to their suffering in a time of need. Evoke the experience by asking students to recall the details of that experience, how they felt when that person was really present for them. Then have them jot down some notes (or reflect) addressing the following questions:

- How did you know the person was present for you?
- What did it feel like for you to have that person deeply present?
- What was said or expressed by the person that helped you to feel their presence?
- What was the body posture of that present and helpful person?
- Did that person express this presence through any gestures or facial expressions? Eye contact? What else did you notice?

You can expand this exercise by asking the students to reflect on a time when someone was not present or listening to them when they were in need. Have them evoke that experience and then reflect or write in response to the following questions:

- How did you know the person was *not* present for you?
- What did it feel like for you to have that person not attend or be present for you?
- What was said or expressed by that person who helped you know that they were absent?
- What was the body posture of that absent person?
- Did they express their nonpresence through any gestures or facial expressions? Lack of eye contact? What else did you notice?

This exercise can serve as a good foundation for exploring the concept of presence in a helping relationship and for having students access their own experience of the value of presence. Following individual reflections, students can form pairs for discussion. Students can then return for group discussion and can generate an overall list of qualities of presence and nonpresence.

### Awareness/Mindful Observation

The following gestalt exercise, adapted from Stevens (1971), is helpful in accessing different dimensions of present moment awareness as well as in observing the distinction between present moment awareness and the interpretation or fantasy (middle zone) that takes us out of present-moment awareness.

1. Have participants form pairs and sit facing each other, taking a moment to settle into silence together.
2. Guide participants with the following instructions: I'd like you to come in to the moment and report your present awareness as you become aware of it. It helps to use the sentence, "Now I am aware of . . ." and complete it with whatever comes into awareness.

3. After a few minutes, ask participants, "Pay attention to where your awareness goes. Does it go to the outside, to what you see, touch, or hear, or to the inside, to what you feel inside your skin in your body, sensations or feelings, or do you go to a middle zone, neither inside nor outside but into fantasy where you interpret, imagine, think. A world of construction, illusion, or maya (as referred to in some traditions)."
4. After a few minutes of awareness with their experience, ask participants to take turns (1 minute each) in listening and sharing the following:
   a. Now report only outside awareness.
   b. Now report only inside awareness.
   c. Now middle zone awareness. Be as creative as you wish.
   d. Now link reality with fantasy with statements such as "Now I'm aware of . . ." (inner or outer) and "I imagine (think) that . . . ."
5. Have participants debrief together and then share in the larger group what was learned about how much time they spend in their own present moment and in interpretive awareness, and about the distinction between present-moment awareness and interpretive awareness.

## Listening With the Senses

Pair up with someone, and find a quiet spot to sit together, face to face, a few feet apart. Close your eyes and sit together quietly. Keep your eyes closed to eliminate your vision so that you are forced to use your other senses. Silently get in touch with the experience of having your eyes closed, spend time noticing the sensations of your breath, notice what you feel physically in the body.

Now pick one person to start speaking while the other person listens in a present-centered way, without interruption or feedback. Invite the speaker to tell the listener about the experience of having his or her eyes closed. The listener can focus attention on the voice of his or her partner, being particularly aware of the rhythm and tempo of the voice and what is being expressed by the voice itself. As the listener, see if you can learn to listen as if the other person were speaking a foreign language that you don't understand, so that you only understand the emphasis, tone, hesitations, rhythm, and so on. Do this for about 5 minutes and then switch roles.

Now, express what you notice about your own and your partner's voice. Be very specific about what you are actually aware of in the voice, and say how you feel about it—your response to it and your impression of what it is like.

For instance, "I'm very aware of how softly you speak," "I feel sleepy as I listen to your voice, like listening to a lullaby." Take about 5 minutes to do this.

Now, return to silence together, but this time open your eyes. Take a moment in silence to just look into the other's eyes. Begin to sense what the other person is experiencing, placing close attention to his or her nonverbal body posture, facial expression, and so on. Notice in your own body any sensations that are arising that are unfamiliar; these could be images, pains, tensions, and so on. Now share with each other what you picked up on a sensory level as you connected to the other. Take 5 minutes to do this. After debriefing together, return to the larger group to share what was learned.

### Deep Presence Listening: Listening From the Head, Heart, and Body

As the therapist deepens into presence, he or she listens to the emotional and cognitive (content) of what the client is experiencing. Although the therapist listens from all levels, he or she listens primarily from the bodily sensing levels. This practice can help students to identify the different types of listening and the deepening in relating and expressing that can occur when there is deep sensory listening at the core (personal communication, Ostaseski & Stephens, August 2010).

1. Break into dyads, Persons A and B.
2. Think about an experience that you are coping with right now (at school, work, with clients). Perhaps think about something that is not too personal but is close enough so that it is real for you. Complete each of the exercises in about 3 to 5 minutes. Cognitive listening:
3. Person A speaks about this issue from a cognitive place (the story, the details), while Person B listens (to content, details, assumptions) and perhaps interacts (asks questions) from a cognitive place (e.g., What happened next? What did you say to your boss?).
4. Now switch roles: Person B speaks about his or her issue from a cognitive place (the story, the details), while Person A listens and perhaps interacts (asks questions) from a cognitive place. Emotional listening:
5. Person A speaks about the same issue from an emotional place (feelings about the situation) while Person B listens from his or her emotional body (listens to feelings, mood) and perhaps interacts (reflects feelings, what the other must have felt) from this emotional center.

6. Now switch roles. Person B speaks about his or her issue from his or her emotional body while Person A listens and perhaps interacts (asks questions, provides empathic reflections) from an emotional place.

Bodily sensory listening:

7. Person A now speaks about the same issue from a body-centered place (bodily sensations associated with this experience) while Person B listens from his or her sensory body (listens with his or her own body to what the other is expressing) and perhaps interacts (responds intuitively, reflects bodily empathy) with what the other is expressing in this moment.

8. Now switch roles. Person B speaks about his or her issue from his or her present-centered bodily connection while Person A practices bodily sensory listening.

9. Dyads can take time to debrief about how these types of listening differ as well as their experience in and challenges to listening in a bodily sensory way.

Integrative presence listening:

10. Now return to the dyads and take turns speaking and listening, this time vacillating between listening with the mind (to the content), listening with the heart (to the emotions), and listening with the sensory body (to the somatic expression of the other).

Debrief in dyads and then in the larger group.

## Exploring the Barriers to Contact With Our Experience

The following practices focus on exposing the barriers to presence in ourselves and on touching and resting in our own vulnerability and experience. These are important starting points in allowing clients to experience that opening and vulnerability in session.

### Inquiry Exercise

This exercise is conducted in dyads, with the intention that the speaker be in a place of groundedness and open receptivity, asking questions and listening from a place of nonjudgment. It is important to set the stage by discussing the value of nonjudgmental listening in allowing for the greatest opening and exposure for the speaker in his or her discovery.

- After choosing a partner, dyads should find a place to sit across from each other, so they can have direct eye contact. There will be a series of three questions, asked one at a time by the present-centered questioner (Person A) to the speaker (Person B). Then switch roles. Allow 5 minutes per question with time to pause between each switch.

Question 1: Tell me a way you disconnect from your experience.

Question 2: What is right about disconnecting from your experience?

Question 3: What is it like to be connected to your experience right now?

- Person A asks Person B the first question and just witnesses B's response without judgment. When the first answer is complete, Person A offers an acknowledgment of thanks and then asks the same question again. This process continues until the bell rings.

Pause briefly to connect to presence and then switch roles for Question 1. Repeat this process for Questions 2 and 3. Complete with a return to the larger group and debrief about what was learned and exposed in this exercise.

*Forgiveness Practice*

Forgiveness is central to removing barriers to presence. However, we often do not even recognize the hurts we carry around not only toward others but toward ourselves. This practice, introduced by Frances Vaughan (1978, 2010), can help to identify the places where we carry around guilt, anger, or hurt toward ourselves and to bring to the surface that which is still sitting inside and acting as a barrier to letting others in. This exercise can be conducted in dyads, and the instructions are as follows:

- Sit across from a partner. Look briefly into the eyes of the other, get a feel for that person. Close your eyes and state the intention to be present for the other, to not interfere with his or her process but instead to listen deeply without judgment. Now, allow yourself to be aware of something you have not forgiven yourself for. Reflect on that experience for a moment and allow yourself to feel the associated reactions. Now, open your eyes and silently decide between partners who will first be the listener and who will be speaker.
- Listener: Just listen with presence, witnessing the experience that the speaker will share but listening without interpretation, interruption, or feedback. For 2 to 3 minutes the speaker will share from his or her bodily felt place about this experience that

he or she has not forgiven him- or herself for, being heard and witnessed by the present listener.

- After sharing, both partners close their eyes and connect to their present-moment experience. Then both partners open their eyes. The listener responds by looking the speaker in the eyes and saying, "You are forgiven," as many times as it takes for the speaker to begin to receive this forgiveness. Close eyes and pause. Then switch roles and repeat the process. When both partners have completed sharing, listening, and a quiet pause for reflection and feeling, take a few minutes to debrief. Come back and share and discuss in the larger group about both your experience and how this lack of forgiveness may have been a barrier to being present.

### Drumming Practices

Drumming is ideally practiced in a group context as it encourages personal expression as well as community connection, which are valuable for therapists in cultivating presence, in promoting health and well-being, and in releasing the stresses that can act as obstacles to presence. Group drumming has also been used in team building, in personal and professional development, and in complementary care for people with various health-related conditions (Friedman, 2000). Furthermore, drumming in a group, either together or in a talking pattern (one person or group plays and the other person or group responds), promotes nonverbal expression and increases a sense of connection internally and with others.

Drumming and rhythm practices can also be adapted to be done individually. For example, drumming along with music can provide an opportunity to use rhythm awareness to synchronize emotions or experience and cognition, as well as enhance the synchronicity of the left and right brain hemispheres, eliciting a clearer sense of focus, concentration, and inner harmony. As noted in Chapter 11, listening and playing in this way help to cultivate the qualities of presence listening, which requires vacillating attention and contact between self and other.

Although the following drumming exercises can be done individually, they are particularly powerful when done in a group because the experience of entrainment emerges in that context. Entrainment is a physics phenomenon of resonance, which occurs when independent rhythms (or oscillating bodies) that are interacting begin to join (one speeds up while the other slows down) to come into sync with each other. Powerful experiences and lessons can emerge from this experience, reflecting the process of presence and being in contact with one's self, others, and a larger collective wisdom.

*Drumming Your Bodily Rhythms*

This exercise can help therapists to connect to their internal bodily terrain, first by attuning to their bodily rhythm in the moment and then by externalizing those rhythms through movement and sound. In a group context, the experience of first connecting to one's own rhythm and then in resonance with others can help therapists develop this dual awareness of self and other that is a part of the presence process. Also by slowing down the rhythm, there is more opportunity for the emergence of underlying emotions, helping to generate awareness of what is true in the emotional body as well as in the physical body. Slowing down external rhythm also supports the body in slowing down in sync with the playing, hence creating a calmer and more stable place inside, despite what else is being felt. Playing one sound for a time also shifts the state of consciousness to a more expansive place, and hence a sense of joy and calm can be experienced. In addition, the repetition of playing, in coordination with both hands and with the heart and breath bodily rhythms, helps to syncopate right and left hemispheric activity, which helps to create greater balance and mental acuity.

This practice can be done on a hand drum (i.e., djembe or ashiko) or even on the top of a desk or on your lap. A large empty jug turned upside down also makes a useful rhythm tool.

- Put your nondominant hand on your heart, neck, or wrist to sense your heartbeat or pulse. Try and connect to the rhythm of your heart or pulse as it is right now. Notice what it feels like. Is it fast, slow, deep, or narrow? Feel and experience the rhythm of your heartbeat.
- With your dominant hand, play the rhythm of your heartbeat with a soft tap on the drum, desk, or table.
- When that feels comfortable and natural, allow yourself to tune into the rhythm of your breath. Feel and experience the rhythm of your breath.
- Play the rhythm of your breath with your nondominant hand by tapping at the beginning of each inhale and at the start of each exhale. Begin to distinguish the rhythm of your breath from your heartbeat or pulse and feel how these rhythms relate to each other.
- If alone or in a group, keep playing the rhythm of your heart and breath for 10 to 15 minutes, at times inviting yourself to slow down and continue the same rhythms but at a slower pace. Notice your experience as your external rhythms slow.
- When you are ready to come to close, rest with your hands on your drum (table, lap) and sit in silence for a moment, sensing what is true in your bodily rhythms and in your experience, in this moment.

*Drumming Out Stress*

Drumming can also be used in an intentional way to express some of the personal or professional challenges that are experienced throughout the day and to release the associated stress so that one can become more present. The following is a brief description of an exercise that can help in accessing barriers to presence and in expressing and releasing them in an intentional way.

- Begin by attuning to the breath.
- Become aware of any stress or unresolved issue in your life or therapy work.
- Begin to tap out this feeling on the instrument, while keeping the focus on expression as opposed to performance.
- Allow this expression to come to full crescendo and then return to gentle tapping and then breathe.

When this exercise is used in a group context, individuals can take turns expressing and releasing stress while others resonate and reflect the individual's experience through sound by playing in resonance together. This can help to develop a sense of empathy and attunement as well as create a sense of safety and community connection.

*Heartbeat Rhythm*

A simple yet powerful therapeutic drumming exercise is to create a simple rhythm, which could be a heartbeat (hitting the center of the drum twice and then repeating) or another variation of a simple rhythm. Keeping focused on this simple yet repetitive rhythm for 10 minutes, while being aware of breathing, can help to increase focus, deepen listening, and increase contact with self and the moment. This simple exercise can also help to connect to present-based emotions as well as provide an opportunity for synchronization of mind and heart. When the exercise is done in a group, entrainment can ensue, offering the group a direct experiential sense of how awareness and bodily sensations can shift in resonance with others (i.e., clients). It can also help to strengthen therapists' simultaneous awareness of self and other that the process of being in presence demands.

## CONCLUSION

There are multiple avenues for cultivating therapeutic presence, with most based on the premise of pausing, facing and removing the obstacles to presence, and cultivating the various qualities of presence. In this chapter, we provided an array of exercises to access different aspects of therapeutic presence. A variety of exercises can also be found throughout this book. With a commitment to presence in one's daily life as well as in psychotherapy training, the cultivation of this essential therapeutic stance becomes possible. It is not just talking about the value of presence in psychotherapy that is helpful, but more so a commitment to practice that can allow therapeutic presence to emerge. These practices can be used not just in psychotherapy training but also in a variety of careers and circumstances in which one wishes to cultivate health, wellness, and a present-moment awareness.

# EPILOGUE

When we honestly ask ourselves which person in our lives means the
most to us, we often find that it is those who, instead of giving much
advice, solutions, or cures, have chosen rather to share our pain and
touch our wounds with a gentle and tender hand.

—Henri J. M. Nouwen

In this book, we presented an empirically grounded model of therapeutic presence and a theory of what makes relationships therapeutic. We argued
that presence is a precondition of Rogers's therapist-offered conditions (communicating empathy, unconditional positive regard, and congruence) and
that presence leads to attuned responsiveness and to the forming of an
alliance and, through them, to a positive therapeutic outcome. In addition,
we discussed the role of different levels of presence, challenges to therapeutic presence, and the neurobiology of presence. This was followed by a discussion of practical approaches to cultivating presence, including mindfulness
and experiential approaches.

This book invites therapists to risk entering the moment with their
clients, to actualize the opportunity for healing. This involves working
through potential barriers to relational therapeutic presence to be aware in
the moment of what is occurring in one's self, in others, and between self and
others, such that one can optimize the "now moments" (kairos) in the therapy relationship. Therapeutic presence and the types of encounters this pro-
duces demand a level of openness and intimacy that can leave therapists
feeling vulnerable, and this can be frightening. It can be challenging to rely
less on an exact plan or a technique and more on using one's self and the

deepest levels of one's humanness to reach out and respond from the fertile ground of the present moment to another's present experience of joy or suffering. It is this ability, however, that can be most helpful and lead to responses, interventions, or techniques that fit the moment in a manner that can change the course of the next moment in highly therapeutic ways. Therapy thus unfolds in the direction of healing, as within the experience of being relationally connected, clients are guided in a way that is attuned to their current state.

## PRESENCE AS A TRANSTHEORETICAL CONCEPT

We have suggested that presence and the relationship are necessary as the backdrop for any therapeutic encounter, even those that are purely technique oriented. Humanistic traditions have always seen the genuine interaction as important, and presence is an attempt to capture the essence of what is proposed in these approaches. Presence also is highly relevant in psychodynamic and psychoanalytic approaches. It is what facilitates therapists in becoming aware of their own interpersonal reactions and their ability *in the moment* to rapidly discriminate whether these reactions are a function of their own issues or an aspect of the interpersonal dynamics. Although therapeutic presence and the deepening into relational presence are conceptually the central aspects of humanistic and psychodynamic relational treatments, they are also important in manual-based therapies, where it is the combination of the therapeutic relationship and technique that optimizes outcome.

In psychodynamic interpersonal treatments, presence promotes the ability to separate one's own emotional reactivity, to put it aside, and to be aware of what is happening between self and other. Notions of countertransference in relational treatments have come to be viewed more as an aspect of the relationship that needs to be understood as such than as a therapist's overreaction to the client on the basis of his or her own unresolved issues. Practice in presence and self-awareness thus helps therapists to discern the source of their reactions to the client and to work with these reactions effectively. Therapists who cultivate presence will develop an ease in rapidly discriminating whether a reaction is a difficulty in personal emotion regulation versus interpersonal information that is clinically useful to explore. If a reaction is identified as one's own feeling of being threatened, one notices it as soon as it happens, breathes, and is able to bracket it for later processing. If one's reaction is felt in the moment to be more about the relationship than a personal overreaction, then one sees what is emerging within and in between as interpersonally useful.

Although adherence to a manual is seen as essential in approaches such as cognitive–behavioral therapy, competence is equally important and requires therapists to attend to clients and where they are at in the moment, so that responses, tasks, and homework are attuned to what they need. When therapists provide an intervention to clients that is purely technical and not attuned or responsive to the client's in-the-moment experience, or when it is detached from a person-to-person encounter, it will be limited in its efficacy. How therapists intervene is as important as what they do. Offering an intervention with therapeutic presence, grounded in an attunement to the moment and the readiness of the client, optimizes the efficacy of the intervention and provides a feeling of resonance for both the therapist and the client that strengthens the relational bond. What is needed is the utilization of technique with full presence to bring about the type of responsive attunement that ensures that each step of the procedure fits the client's current state.

Presence also supports therapists' well-being, as it involves an attunement and opening within as well as ongoing awareness of therapists' own barriers, needs, and energy levels so that there is a balance between giving and receiving. This in turn helps therapists to sustain their own energy and mitigate burnout. Therapists across different traditions who value and practice presence have more energy for their own well-being and in turn offer a calm, healing, and effective approach and relational environment for the client, which is healing in and of itself (Scurlock-Durana, 2007, 2010). Furthermore, the self-awareness that is called upon in cultivating presence can help to reduce reactive states in the therapist, as openness to one's own feelings has been shown to be associated with less countertransference behavior (Robbins & Jolkovski, 1987).

## THERAPEUTIC PRESENCE AS A RELATIONAL CONSTRUCT

When we first began recognizing presence as a core therapeutic stance, we primarily saw it as a within-self variable, a grounded and open place within the therapist. Through our years of studying, researching, and exploring our own and others' experience of presence, we now view presence as having a relational component: the therapist in relation to the client and to a larger wisdom.

Relational therapeutic presence, then, is viewed as a triad of relationships: with self, with others, and with a larger sense of expansion or spirituality. The session is guided by this dance of awareness and attunement with self and other, pausing between what is known and what is not known, and listening deeply from that still place that exists between self and other. This develops into a sense of relational copresence that promotes emergence of the novel and facilitative healing.

The four aspects of the experience of presence, as reflected in our model, can be seen as the four experiential doorways to a deeper shared relational therapeutic presence. *Grounding* is enhanced through the *body* and somatic awareness, steady and centered, firmly held to the ground. *Immersion* is focused in the *heart*, open and absorbed into the moment with the other. *Expansion* is expressed in relationship with spirituality and the soul and is experienced in *creativity and nature. Being with and for the client* is experienced relationally, while staying connected to the body, heart, and a spacious awareness. Relational therapeutic presence includes contact between the therapist and the client on multiple levels including cognitive, bodily/sensory, emotional, transcendental, and relational.

Although presence begins in the self of the therapist (through an ongoing commitment to cultivating self-care, balance, and presence in self and in relationships), the transformation emerges through the therapist's offering of presence to the client and the depth of meeting that can occur between the two. As therapists receptively and nonjudgmentally attune to their clients, clients experience their therapists as present and become present within and with their therapists, and relational presence emerges. This shared relational presence creates a higher level of connectedness between therapist and client, which includes a reverberatory attunement that is expressed as flow in the therapeutic encounter.

The following may explain how relational therapeutic presence emerges: Therapists approach their clients from a place of presence, which reflects an integrated state of receptivity to the moment. When clients receive their therapist's presence and experience their therapist as receptively attuned and being with and for them, they experience a sense of safety. The brain is always monitoring the environment for signs of danger or safety (D. J. Siegel, 2010) in a process Porges (2009) termed *neuroception* (see Chapter 9, this volume, for details). Clients' neuroception of safety when feeling fully met by their therapist allows them to become more open to their own experience and to their therapists. The hormone oxytocin releases with this neuroception of safety (Porges, 2009), which allows for a positive and caring bond to arise between therapist and client. This positive relationship invites the client to feel safe to access and work through his or her pain, as well as to feel trusting and open to the therapist and the interventions offered. The therapist continues to respond in attunement with the moment and their neural firings (i.e., mirror neurons) becomes in sync with their client's experience, which allows for a shared sense of intersubjective consciousness. The client opens in response to this attunement, and a reciprocal opening and connection unfolds between both, which further deepens the mutual sense of therapeutic presence. The meeting in relational therapeutic presence creates a larger expanse of energy and wisdom than that of any individual and accessed by both. A state of inner and relational integration begins to arise.

The part of this theory of what may occur from a neurobiological perspective in therapeutic presence and the emergent relational therapeutic presence stems from the evolving theory of neuroplasticity and the role of presence and relational bonding in interpersonal neurobiology (D. J. Siegel, 2007, 2010). Although the scientific literature is limited, the theory existing to date reflects the experiential aspect we have noted with therapeutic presence.

## DIRECTIONS FOR FUTURE RESEARCH

Future research should explore presence as a key underlying aspect of the therapeutic relationship. We have proposed that although therapeutic presence is a powerful curative agent in and of itself, it also promotes a positive therapeutic alliance and allows for optimal efficacy when accompanied by modality-specific techniques.

Another important future direction is the exploration of factors related to clients' perception of therapeutic presence (e.g., as measured by the Therapeutic Presence Inventory-client [TPI-C]; see Chapter 2). Just as client-perceived empathy is more predictive of good outcome than is therapist-reported empathy, it appears that client-perceived presence is more predictive of a good outcome than is therapist-reported presence (Geller et al., 2010). More research on client perception of presence is thus indicated. The two studies of TPI-C—one involving a three-item measure developed by us (Geller et al., 2010) and the other an 18-item questionnaire developed by Vinca and Hayes (2007), a translation of the therapist measure into a set of items measuring client's perception of therapists' presence—provide a good starting point for future research on the validity and usefulness of these measures. Future research could also include the development of an observation-based rating scale of therapeutic presence. This would allow more understanding of how therapists communicate their presence in a way that is optimal for clients to receive it.

Future investigation should also focus on understanding clients' experience of presence within themselves and how it may be facilitated by therapists' presence, as we theorized in Chapter 3. Clients' presence includes a sense of deepening in their own self-experience and may be an important factor in developing a therapeutic relationship and working alliance, as well as good therapy process and outcome. Finally, clinical practice would benefit from research exploring TRP and how the shared reality and connection between therapist and client are heightened through presence encounters and affect therapy outcome.

# DIRECTIONS FOR FUTURE THERAPIST TRAINING

We propose that the cultivation of presence be incorporated into psychotherapy training programs. Currently, programs often train students in intervention and techniques without attention to their state of being. Therapeutic presence, which includes accessing one's own natural resources and somatic awareness as a tool for facilitation of technique, is rarely taught in manualized therapies. Presence, however, is teachable, as indicated by the brain changes that reflect the occurrence of enhanced presence during training. Practice in presence enhances neuronal integration, which can lead to greater access of the presence experience in session.

For example, training in self-attunement creates a neural state of integration that forms the basis for receptive awareness and attunement to the other. Further, interoception (i.e., perceiving inwardly the experience of the other) is possible through practices of self-attunement (i.e., mindfulness). Training, however, also needs to include relational practices (e.g., group drumming, relational mindfulness) to help therapists remove the barriers to meeting another with presence as well as to deepen the ability to be fully open with another while in contact with their own experience, the foundation for relating with presence.

Rather than minimizing the value of intervention, we are strongly suggesting that the cultivation of therapeutic presence of the person and his or her personal and relational growth should be an equal adjunct in psychotherapy training and can enhance the efficacy of therapeutic technique. It is essential to balance the *doing* mode of therapy with the *being* mode for greatest efficacy in the client's healing.

Training in presence optimally includes the cultivation of present-moment awareness, as well as the recognition and working through of the barriers to presence. These barriers include attachment and aversion from a mindfulness perspective, unresolved issues in relationships, and lack of contact with one's body, emotions, and needs. Working through self- and other forgiveness from an experiential perspective, we can open up to greater intimacy in self and with others. Cultivating positive qualities such as love, compassion, equanimity, receptivity, and healthy intimacy is an important part of cultivating presence. Hence, recognizing and mastering one's inner terrain as well as skillful and compassionate relationships are a central aspect of cultivating relational therapeutic presence. The ongoing practice of presence also helps to enhance therapists' own emotional health, relationships, and well-being, which further supports sustainability in the profession.

For the psychotherapy trainee to truly experience the fruits of presence, it is important that the relational connection between supervisor and supervisee also be infused with presence. When supervisors are committed to the value of presence in their own life and practice being fully in presence with their trainees, then deep learning and wisdom can ensue. This requires supervisors to be open to what emerges in the supervisory relationship, with acceptance, nonjudgment, and attunement to the present moment.

From this perspective, supervision is recognized as emerging from the present interaction between supervisor and trainee (Smythe, MacCulloch, & Charmley, 2009). Although being in therapeutic presence may stem from the supervisor, this stance allows for an environment for therapeutic presence and relational presence to emerge and for the trainee to feel open and safe in expressing the issues that need addressing. Nichols (2007) described supervision as Socratic yet present based, where the supervisor works to help trainees to find the answers that are already within themselves. This is made possible by the supervisor creating a safe environment that allows for both support and challenge (Gazzola & Theriault, 2007).

Supervisors also benefit by having a structure or theory of practice and supervision and then being able to let that go when in the room with the trainee and be open to emergence. Smythe et al. (2009) wrote the following:

> Increased reliance on evidence-based practice convinces us that there can be certainty in what we seek to do. And yet the real mark of excellence can only come when we allow ourselves to become lost in the unfolding of each unique moment of a supervision relationship . . . Deep and reverent trust in oneself, the other, and the process enables both to be moved and changed. (p. 19)

With therapeutic presence, the supervisor puts aside preconceived plans and directions and instead listens deeply to the trainee's experience, being attuned to the moment, resting comfortably in the unknown, with an openness to trust in the process.

Acknowledging the humility of equality is also important in the supervisory relationship. Both the nature of the human-to-human encounter of training and the supervisor's modeling and being with the trainee in a present-centered way will help cultivate therapeutic presence in the trainee. Through the supervisor's presence, willingness to be there as a whole person, and deep listening with and for the trainee, wisdom and direction can emerge.


## FINAL THOUGHTS

Although presence is valuable within a psychotherapy context, we also need to go beyond therapy to see presence as fundamental for optimal personal and professional relationships in general. Other disciplines have recognized presence as a key process in facilitating their work in an effective manner. Presence has been described as important in teaching (Farber, 2008; Hart, 2004; Kessler, 1991; Meijer, Korthagen, & Vasalos, 2009; Miller, 2005; Rodgers & Raider-Roth, 2006; Tremmel, 1993); medicine (Epstein, 1999, 2001, 2003a, 2003b; Zoppi & Epstein, 2002); nursing (Gilje, 1993; Hines, 1992; Liehr, 1989; McDonough-Means, Kreitzer, & Bell, 2004; McKivergin & Daubenmire, 1994; Osterman & Schwartz-Barcott, 1996); psychiatric care (Torre, 2002); manual therapies, including craniosacral therapy (Blackburn & Price, 2007; Scurlock-Durana, 2007, 2010); coaching and leadership (Halpern & Lubar, 2003; Silsbee, 2004, 2008); public speaking (Kimball, 2003); and business and organizations (Kahn, 1992; Scharmer, 2006, 2009; Senge, 2008; Senge, Jaworski, Scharmer, & Flowers, 2004; Tolbert and Hanafin, 2006).

The lessons in recognizing this essential way of being across disciplines involves opening to a paradigm shift from emphasizing doing to recognizing the importance of being (and back to doing again from the foundation of what emerges in presence). We need to be actively aware of the fears, busyness, and distractions from being in the moment so that we can bring our receptive awareness, with others and ourselves, to create the best conditions for efficacy and fullness in our personal and professional encounters. When we engage with others from our own inner terrain of receptive awareness, nonjudgment, nonreaction, and grounding, in the service of the other's healing, there emerges the possibility of being at peace and effectively evolving from a place of deeper wisdom into a relational and collective movement toward growing with and from each other. Presence is not just a therapeutic principle but a way of being that involves commitment to ourselves, to others, to living fully, and to trust in the process. The result is an abundance of growth and an understanding as individual and relational beings who together can make changes toward living more fully with presence and in alignment with deeper wisdom, which promotes sustainable, successful, and mutually fulfilling professional relationships.

# REFERENCES

Ackerley, G. D., Burnell, J., Holder, D. C., & Kurdek, L. A. (1988). Burnout among licensed psychologists. *Professional Psychology: Research and Practice, 19*, 624–631. doi:10.1037/0735-7028.19.6.624

American Psychiatric Association. (2000) *Diagnostic and statistical manual of mental disorders* (4th ed., text rev.). Washington, DC: Author.

Aponte, H., & Winter, J. E. (2000). The person and practice of the therapist: Treatment and training. In M. Baldwin (Ed.), *The use of self in therapy* (pp. 127–165). New York, NY: Haworth Press.

Arrien, A. (1993). *The four-fold way: Walking the paths of the warrior, teacher, healer, and visionary*. San Francisco, CA: HarperCollins.

Arrien, A. (2010, August). *The four-fold way*. Symposium conducted at the Metta Institute Conference, San Rafael, CA.

Baer, R. A. (2003). Mindfulness training as a clinical intervention: A conceptual and empirical review. *Clinical Psychology: Science and Practice, 10*, 125–143. doi:10.1093/clipsy/bpg015

Baer, R. A. (Ed.) (2006). *Mindfulness-based treatment approaches*. Oxford, England: Academic Press.

Baker, E. K. (2002). *Caring for ourselves: A therapist's guide to personal and professional well-being*. Washington, DC: American Psychological Association.

Baldwin, M. (2000). Interview with Carl Rogers on the use of the self in therapy. In M. Baldwin (Ed.), *The use of self in therapy* (2nd ed., pp. 29–38). New York, NY: Haworth Press.

Barrett-Lennard, G. T. (1961, August). *Dimensions of a therapeutic relationship*. Paper presented at the British Psychological Society, University of Sydney, Australia.

Barrett-Lennard, G. T. (1973). *Relationship inventory*. Unpublished manuscript, University of Waterloo, Ontario, Canada.

Barrett-Lennard, G. T. (1981). The empathy cycle: Refinement of a nuclear concept. *Journal of Counseling Psychology, 28*, 91–100. doi:10.1037/0022-0167.28.2.91

Barrett-Lennard, G. T. (1986). The relationship inventory now: Issues and advances in theory, method, and use. In L. S. Greenberg & W. M. Pinsof (Eds.), *The psychotherapeutic process: A research handbook* (pp. 439–476). New York, NY: Guilford Press.

Basch, M. F. (1983). Empathic understanding: A review of the concept and some theoretical considerations. *Journal of the American Psychoanalytic Association, 31*(1), 101–126. doi:10.1177/000306518303100104

Beeli, G., Casutt, G., Baumgartner, T., & Jancke, L. (2008). Modulating presence and impulsiveness by external stimulation of the brain. *Behavioral and Brain Functions, 4*(33). doi:10.1186/1744-9081-4-33

Begley, S. (2007). *Train your mind, change your brain: How a new science reveals our extraordinary potential to transform ourselves.* New York, NY: Ballantine Books.

Beitman, B. D., Viamontes, G. I., Soth, A. M., & Nitler, J. (2006). Toward a neural circuitry of engagement, self-awareness and pattern search. *Psychiatric Annals, 36,* 272–280.

Benson, H., Beary, J., & Carol, M. (1974). The relaxation response. *Psychiatry: Journal for the Study of Interpersonal Processes, 37,* 37–46.

Beutler, L. E., Malik, M., Alimohamed, S., Harwood, T. M., Talebi, H., Nobel, S., & Wong, E. (2004). Therapist variables. In M. J. Lambert (Ed.), *Bergin and Garfield's handbook of psychotherapy and behaviour change* (5th ed., pp. 227–306). New York, NY: Wiley.

Bien, T. (2006). *Mindful therapy: A guide for therapists and helping professionals.* Boston, MA: Wisdom.

Bien, T. (2008). The four immeasurable minds: Preparing to be present in psychotherapy. In S. F. Hick & T. Bien (Eds.), *Mindfulness and the therapeutic relationship* (pp. 37–54). New York, NY: Guilford Press.

Bishop, S. R., Lau, M., Shapiro, S. L., Carlson, L., Anderson, N. D., Carmody, J., … Devins, G. (2004). Mindfulness: A proposed operational definition. *Clinical Psychology: Science and Practice, 11,* 230–241. doi:10.1093/clipsy.bph077

Bittman, B. B., Berk, L., Felten, D., Westengard, J., Simonton, O., Pappas, J., & Ninehouser, M. (2001). Composite effects of group drumming music therapy on modulation of neuroendocrine-immune parameters in normal subjects. *Alternative Therapies in Health and Medicine, 7,* 38–47.

Bittman, B., Berk, L., Shannon, M., Sharaf, M., Westengard, J., Guegler, K. J., & Ruff, D. W. (2005). Recreational music-making modulates the human stress response: A preliminary individualized gene expression strategy. *Medical Science Monitor, 11,* 31–40.

Bittman, B., & Bruhn, K. (2008). Recreational music making defined [Web post]. Retrieved from http://www.remo.com/portal/pages/hr/learnmore/Recreational+Music+Making.html

Bittman, B., Bruhn, K. T., Stevens, C., Westengard, J., & Umbach, P. O. (2003). Recreational music-making: A cost-effective group interdisciplinary strategy for reducing burnout and improving mood states in long-term care workers. *Advances in Mind-Body Medicine, 19,* 4–15.

Bittman, B. B., Snyder, C., Bruhn, K. T., Liebfried, F., Stevens, C. K., Westengard, J., & Umbach, P. O. (2004). Recreational music-making: An integrative group intervention for reducing burnout and improving mood states in first year associate degree nursing students. Insights and economic impact. *International Journal of Nursing Education Scholarship, 1,* e12–29.

Blackburn, J., & Price, C. (2007). Implications of presence in manual therapy. *Journal of Bodywork and Movement Therapies, 11,* 68–77. doi:10.1016/j.jbmt.2006.05.002

Boerstler, R. W., & Kornfield, H. S. (1995). *Life to death, harmonizing the transition: A holistic and meditative approach for caregivers and the dying.* Rochester, VT: Healing Arts Press.

Bohart, A., & Greenberg, L. S. (Eds.). (1997). *Empathy reconsidered: New directions in psychotherapy.* Washington, DC: American Psychological Association. doi:10.1037/10226-000

Bohart, A. C., & Tallman, K. (1998). The person as active agent in experiential therapy. In L. S. Greenberg, J. C. Watson, & G. Lietaer (Eds.), *Handbook of experiential psychotherapy* (pp. 178–200). New York, NY: Guilford Press.

Bordin, E. S. (1976, September). *The working alliance: Basis for a general theory of psychotherapy.* Paper presented at a symposium of the American Psychological Association, Washington, DC.

Bordin, E. S. (1979). The generalizability of the psychoanalytic concept of the working alliance. *Psychotherapy: Theory, Research & Practice, 16,* 252–260. doi:10.1037/h0085885

Bordin, E. S. (1980, June). *Of human bonds that bind or free.* Presidential address delivered at the meeting of the Society for Psychotherapy Research. Washington, DC.

Bozarth, J. D. (2001). Congruence: A special way of being. In G. Wyatt (Ed.), *Rogers' therapeutic conditions: Evolution, theory and practice.* Volume 1: Congruence (pp. 184–199). Herefordshire, England: PCCS Books.

Brach, T. (2003). *Radical acceptance: Embracing your life with the heart of a Buddha.* New York, NY: Bantam Dell.

Brach, T. (2009, April). *Practices and applications of mindfulness in psychotherapy.* Symposium conducted at the Faces Conference, San Diego, CA.

Brown, K. W., & Ryan, R. (2003). The benefits of being present: Mindfulness and its role in psychological well being. *Journal of Personality and Social Psychology, 84,* 822–848. doi:10.1037/0022-3514.84.4.822

Brown, M. (2005). *The presence process: A healing journey into present moment awareness.* Vancouver, Ontario, BC: Namaste.

Buber, M. (1958). *I and thou* (2nd ed.). New York, NY: Scribner.

Buber, M. (1965). *Between man and man.* New York, NY: Macmillan.

Buber, M. (1988). *Eclipse of God.* Atlantic Highlands, NJ: Humanities Press.

Bugental, J. F. T. (1978). *Psychotherapy and process.* Menlo Park, CA: Addison-Wesley.

Bugental, J. F. T. (1983). The one absolute necessity in psychotherapy. *The Script, 13,* 1–2.

Bugental, J. F. T. (1986). Existential-humanistic psychotherapy. In I. L. Kutash & A. Wolf (Eds.), *Psychotherapist's casebook: Theory and technique in the practice of modern therapies* (pp. 222–236). San Francisco, CA: Jossey-Bass.

Bugental, J. F. T. (1987). *The art of the psychotherapist.* New York, NY: Norton.

Bugental, J. F. T. (1989). *The search for existential identity.* San Francisco, CA: Jossey-Bass.

Cahn, B. R., & Polich, J. (2006). Meditation states and traits: EEG, ERP, and neuroimaging studies. *Psychological Bulletin, 132,* 180–211. doi:10.1037/0033-2909.132.2.180

Castonguay, L. G., Schut, A. J., Aikins, D., Constantino, M. J., Laurenceau, J., Bologh, L., & Burns, D. (2004). Integrative cognitive therapy for depression: A preliminary investigation. *Journal of Psychotherapy Integration, 14,* 4–20. doi:10.1037/1053-0479.14.1.4

Chung, C. Y. (1990). Psychotherapist and expansion of awareness. *Psychotherapy and Psychosomatics, 53,* 28–32. doi:10.1159/000288336

Clark, A. (1979). On being centered. *Gestalt Journal, 2,* 35–49.

Clarkson, P. (1997). Variations on I and thou. *Gestalt Review, 1,* 56–70.

Clottey, K. (2004). *Mindful drumming: Ancient wisdom for unleashing the human spirit and building community.* Oakland, CA: Sankofa.

Cole, J. D., & Ladas-Gaskin, C. (2007). *Mindfulness centered therapies: An integrative approach.* Seattle, WA: Silver Birch Press.

Coleman, M. (2006). *Awake in the wild: Mindfulness in nature as a path of self-discovery.* Maui, HI: Inner Ocean.

Cooper, M. (2003). *Existential therapies.* Glasgow, Scotland: University of Strathclyde. Sage.

Cooper, M. (2005). Therapists' experiences of relational depth: A qualitative interview study. *Counselling & Psychotherapy Research, 5*(2), 87–95.

Cornell, A. W. (1994). The attitude of not knowing. *The focusing connection, XI*(1). Retrieved from http://www.focusingresources.com/articles/notknowing.html

Cornell, A. W. (1996). *The power of focusing: A practical guide to emotional self-healing.* Oakland, CA: New Harbinger.

Corsini, R. J., & Wedding, D. (Eds.). (1989). *Current psychotherapies* (4th ed.). Itasca, IL: Peacock.

Coster, J. S., & Schwebel, M. (1997). Well-functioning in professional psychologists. *Professional Psychology: Research and Practice, 28,* 5–13. doi:10.1037/0735-7028.28.1.5

Craig, P. E. (1986). Sanctuary and presence: An existential view of the therapist's contribution. *The Humanistic Psychologist, 14,* 22–28. doi:10.1080/08873267.1986.9976749

Csikszentmihalyi, M. (1990). *Flow: The psychology of optimal experience.* New York, NY: HarperCollins.

Cummings, N. A., & VandenBos, G. R. (1981). The twenty years of Kaiser-Permanente experience with psychotherapy and medical utilization: Implications for national health policy and national health insurance. *Health Policy Quarterly, 1*(2), 159–175.

Cunningham, I. (1992). The impact of leaders: Who they are and what they do. *Leadership & Organization Development Journal, 13*(2), 7–10.

Dalai Lama. (2001). *An open heart: Practicing compassion in everyday life*. Boston, MA: Little, Brown.

Davidson, R. J. (2000). Affective style, psychopathology, and resilience: Brain mechanisms and plasticity. *American Psychologist, 55*, 1196–1214.

Davidson, R. J. (2004). Well-being and affective style: Neural substrates and biobehavioural correlates. *Philosophical Transactions of the Royal Society of London. Series B, Biological Sciences, 359*, 1395–1411. doi:10.1098/rstb.2004.1510

Davidson, R. J., & Harrington, A. (Eds.). (2002). *Visions of compassion: Western scientists and Tibetan Buddhists examine human nature*. New York, NY: Oxford University Press.

Davidson, R. J., Kabat-Zinn, J., Schumacher, J., Rosenkranz, M., Muller, D., Santorelli, S. F., . . . Sheridan, J. F. (2003). Alterations in brain and immune functioning produced by mindfulness meditation. *Psychosomatic Medicine, 65*, 564–70. doi:10.1097/01.PSY.0000077505.67574.E3

Davidson, R. J., & Lutz, A. (2008). Buddha's brain: Neuroplasticity and meditation. *IEEE Signal Processing Magazine, 25*, 176–174. doi:10.1109/MSP.2008.4431873

Deatherage, G. (1975) The clinical use of mindfulness meditation technique in short term psychotherapy. *Journal of Transpersonal Psychotherapy, 6*, 133–42.

Decety, J., & Chaminade, T. (2003). When the self represents the other: A new cognitive neuroscience view on psychological identification. *Consciousness and Cognition: An International Journal, 12*, 577–596. doi:10.1016/S1053-8100(03)00076-X

Deci, E., L., & Ryan, R. M. (1985). *Intrinsic motivation and self-determination in human behavior*. New York, NY: Plenum.

Delmonte, M. M. (1984). Physiological responses during meditation and rest. *Biofeedback & Self Regulation, 9*, 181–200. doi:10.1007/BF00998833

Diamond, J. (1999). *The way of the pulse: Drumming with spirit*. Bloomingdale, IL: Enhancement Books.

Dimidjian, S., & Linehan, M. M. (2003). Defining an agenda for future research on the clinical application of mindfulness practice. *Clinical Psychology: Science and Practice, 10*, 166–171.

Doidge, N. (2007). *The brain that changes itself*. New York, NY: Penguin Books.

Duncan, B. L., & Moynihan, D. W. (1994). Applying outcome research: Intentional utilization of the client's frame of reference. *Psychotherapy: Theory, Research, Practice, Training, 31*, 294–301. doi:10.1037/h0090215

Elliott, R., Watson, J., Goldman, R. N., & Greenberg, L. S. (2004). *Learning emotion-focused therapy: The process-experiential approach to change*. Washington, DC: American Psychological Association.

Engler, J. (1986). Therapeutic aims in psychotherapy and meditation. In K. Wilber, J. Engler, & D. Brown (Eds.), *Transformations of consciousness* (pp. 17–51). Boston, MA: Shambhala.

Epstein, M. (1995). *Thoughts without a thinker: Psychotherapy from a Buddhist perspective*. New York, NY: Basic Books.

Epstein, M. (2007). *Psychotherapy without the self: A Buddhist perspective*. London, England: Yale University Press.

Epstein, R. M. (1999). Mindful practice. *JAMA, 282*, 833–839. doi:10.1001/jama.282.9.833

Epstein, R. M. (2001). Just being. *The Western Journal of Medicine, 174*, 63–65. doi:10.1136/ewjm.174.1.63

Epstein, R. M. (2003a). Mindful practice in action 1: Technical competence evidence based medicine and relationship-centered care. *Families, Systems, & Health, 21*, 1–9. doi:10.1037/h0089494

Epstein, R. M. (2003b). Mindful practice in action 2: Cultivating habits of mind. *Families, Systems, & Health, 21*, 11–17. doi:10.1037/h0089495

Evans, K. R. (1994). Healing shame: A gestalt perspective. *Transactional Analysis Journal, 24*, 103–108.

Farber, J. (2008). Teaching and presence. *Pedagogy, 8*, 215–225. doi:10.1215/15314200-2007-038.

Fasko, D., Jr., Osborne, M. R., Hall, G., Boerstler, R. W., & Kornfeld, H. (1992). Comeditation: An exploratory study of pulse and respiration rates and anxiety. *Perceptual and Motor Skills, 74*, 895–904. doi:10.2466/PMS.74.3.895-904

Fodor, I., & Hooker, K. E. (2008). Teaching mindfulness to children. *Gestalt Review, 12*(1), 75–91.

Fogel, A. (2009). *The psychophysiology of self-awareness: Rediscovering the lost art of body sense*. New York, NY: Norton.

Fosshage, J. L. (1997). Listening/experiencing perspectives and the quest for a facilitating responsiveness. *Progress in Self Psychology, 13*, 33–55.

Fraelich, C. B. (1989). A phenomenological investigation of the psychotherapist's experience of presence. *Dissertation Abstracts International, 50*(04), 1643B.

Freud, S. (1912). *Recommendations to physicians practicing psychoanalysis. Standard edition, 12*. London, England: Hogarth Press.

Freud, S. (1930). *Civilization and its discontents. Standard edition*. (J. Strachey, Trans.) New York, NY: Norton.

Friedman, M. (1985). *The healing dialogue in psychotherapy*. New York, NY: Aronson.

Friedman, M. (1996). Becoming aware: A dialogical approach to consciousness. *The Humanistic Psychologist, 24*, 203–220. doi:10.1080/08873267.1996.9986851

Friedman, R. L. (2000). *The healing power of the drum: A psychotherapist explores the healing power of rhythm*. Reno, NV: White Cliffs Media.

Fulton, P. R. (2005). Mindfulness as clinical training. In C. K. Germer, R. D. Siegel, & P. R. Fulton (Eds.), *Mindfulness and psychotherapy* (pp. 55–72). New York, NY: Guilford Press.

Gabbard, G. O. (2001). A contemporary model of countertransference. *Journal of Clinical Psychology, 57*, 983–991.

Garske, G. G. (2000). The significance of rehabilitation counselor job satisfaction. *Journal of Applied Rehabilitation Counseling, 31*, 10–13.

Gazzola, N., & Theriault, A. (2007). Super- (and not-so-super-) vision of counsellors-in-training: Supervisee perspectives on broadening and narrowing process. *British Journal of Guidance & Counselling, 35*, 189–204.

Gehart, D., & McCollum, E. E. (2008). Inviting therapeutic presence: A mindfulness based approach. In S. F. Hick & T. Bien (Eds.), *Mindfulness and the therapeutic relationship* (pp. 176–194). New York, NY: Guilford Press.

Geller, S. M. (2001). *Therapeutic presence: The development of a model and a measure.* (Unpublished doctoral dissertation). York University, Toronto, Canada.

Geller, S. M. (2003). Becoming whole: A collaboration between experiential psychotherapies and mindfulness meditation. *Person-Centered and Experiential Psychotherapies, 2*, 258–273.

Geller, S. M. (2009). Cultivation of therapeutic presence: Therapeutic drumming and mindfulness practices. *Dutch Tijdschrift Clientgerichte Psychotherapie (Journal for Client Centered Psychotherapy), 47*, 273–287.

Geller, S. M. (2010). *Clearing the path of therapeutic presence to emerge: Therapeutic rhythm and mindfulness practices.* Unpublished manuscript.

Geller, S. M., & Greenberg, L. S. (2002). Therapeutic presence: Therapists' experience of presence in the psychotherapeutic encounter. *Person-Centered and Experiential Psychotherapies, 1*, 71–86.

Geller, S. M., Greenberg, L. S., & Watson, J. C. (2010). Therapist and client perceptions of therapeutic presence: The development of a measure. *Psychotherapy Research, 20*, 599–610. doi:10.1080/10503307.2010.495957

Gelso, C. J. (2011). *The real relationship in psychotherapy: The hidden foundation of change.* Washington, DC: American Psychological Association. doi:10.1037/12349-000

Gelso, C. J., & Hayes, J. A. (2007). *Countertransference and the therapists inner experience: Perils and possibilities.* Mahwah, NJ: Erlbaum.

Gendlin, E. T. (1978). *Focusing.* New York, NY: Everest House.

Gendlin, E. T. (1986). *Let your body interpret your dreams.* Wilmette, IL: Chiron.

Gendlin, E. T. (1996). *Focusing oriented psychotherapy: A manual of the experiential method.* New York, NY: Guilford Press.

Germer, C. K. (2005). Mindfulness: What is it? What does it matter? In C. K. Germer, R. D. Siegel, & P. R. Fulton (Eds.), *Mindfulness and psychotherapy* (pp. 3–27). New York, NY: Guilford Press.

Germer, C. K., Siegel, R. D., & Fulton, P. R. (2005). *Mindfulness and psychotherapy.* New York, NY: Guilford Press.

Gilje, F. L. (1993). A phenomenological study of patients' experiences of the nurse's presence (Doctoral dissertation, University of Colorado Health Sciences Center, 1993). *Dissertation Abstracts International, 54*(08), 4078B. (UMI No. 9401784).

Gladwell, M. (2008). *Outliers: The story of success.* New York, NY: Little, Brown.

Goldfried, M. R., & Davila, J. (2005). The role of relationship and technique in therapeutic change. *Psychotherapy: Theory, Research, Practice, Training, 42*, 421–430. doi:10.1037/0033-3204.42.4.421

Goldman, R., Greenberg, L. S., & Angus, L. (2006). The effects of adding emotion focused interventions to the therapeutic relationship in the treatment of depression. *Psychotherapy Research, 16*, 537–549. doi:10.1080/10503300600589456

Goldstein, J. (1994). *Insight meditation: The practice of freedom.* Boston, MA: Shambhala.

Goleman, D. (2003). *Destructive emotions: How can we overcome them? A scientific dialogue with the Dalai Lama.* New York, NY: Bantam Dell.

Goleman, D. J., & Schwartz, G. (1976). Meditation as in intervention in stress reactivity. *Journal of Consulting and Clinical Psychology, 44*, 456–466. doi:10.1037/0022-006X.44.3.456

Gormally, J., & Hill, C. E. (1974). Guidelines for research on Carkhuff's training model. *Journal of Counseling Psychology, 21*, 539–547.

Grafanaki, S. (2001). What counselling research has taught us about the concept of congruence: Main discoveries and unresolved issues. In G. Wyatt (Ed.), *Rogers' therapeutic conditions: Evolution, theory and practice. Volume 1: Congruence* (pp. 18–35). Herefordshire, England: PCCS Books.

Greenberg, L. S. (2002). *Emotion-focused therapy: Coaching clients to work through their feelings.* Washington, DC: American Psychological Association. doi:10.1037/10447-000

Greenberg, L. S. (2007). Emotion in the therapeutic relationship in emotion focused therapies. In P. Gilbert & R. L. Leahy (Eds.), *The therapeutic relationship in the cognitive behavioural therapies* (pp. 43–62). New York, NY: Routledge.

Greenberg, L. S., & Geller, S. M. (2002). Congruence and therapeutic presence. In G. Wyatt (Ed.), *Congruence.* London, England: PCCS Books.

Greenberg, L. S., Rice, L., & Elliott, R. (1993). *Facilitating emotional change: The moment-by-moment process.* New York, NY: Guilford Press.

Greenberg, L. S., & Rosenberg, R. (2002). Therapist experience of empathy. In J. C. Watson, R. N. Goldman, & M. Warner (Eds.), *Client-centered and experiential psychotherapy in the 21st century: Advances in theory, research, and practice* (pp. 221–234). Ross-on-Wye, Herefordshire, England: PCCS Books.

Greenberg, L. S., & Watson, J. C. (2005). *Emotion-focused therapy for depression.* Washington, DC: American Psychological Association.

Greenberg, L., Watson, J., & Lietaer, G. (Eds). (1994). *Handbook of experiential therapy.* New York, NY: Guilford Press.

Grepmair, L., Mitterlehner, F., Loew, T., Bachler, E., Rother, W., & Nickel, M. (2007). Promoting mindfulness in psychotherapists in training influences the treatment results of their patients: A randomized double-blind control study. *Psychotherapy and Psychosomatics, 76*, 332–338. doi:10.1159/000107560

Hahn, T. N. (1976). *The miracle of mindfulness: A manual of meditation.* Boston, MA: Beacon Press.

Hahn, T. N. (2000). *The path of emancipation: Talks from a 21-day mindfulness retreat.* Berkeley, CA: Parallax Press.

Hanh, T. N. (2007). *Living Buddha, living Christ.* New York, NY: Penguin.

Hanh, T. N. (2008). *Mindful movements: Ten exercises for well-being.* Berkeley, CA. Parallax Press.

Hanh, T. N. (2011). Mindfulness makes us happy. In B. Boyce (Ed.), *The mindfulness revolution* (pp. 65–67). Boston, MA: Shambhala.

Halifax, J. (2009). *Being with dying: Cultivating compassion and fearlessness in the presence of death.* Boston, MA: Shambhala.

Halpern, B. L., & Lubar, K. (2003). *Leadership presence: Dramatic techniques to reach out, motivate, and inspire.* New York, NY: Gotham Books.

Hannigan, B., Edwards, D., & Burnard, P. (2004). Stress and stress management in clinical psychology: Findings from a systematic review. *Journal of Mental Health, 13,* 235–245. doi:10.1080/09638230410001700871

Hanson, R. (2007). *Train your brain # 6: Mindful presence.* Unpublished manuscript.

Hanson, R., & Mendius, R. (2009). *Buddha's brain: The practical neuroscience of happiness, love, & wisdom.* Oakland, CA: New Harbinger.

Hanson, R., & Mendius, R. (2010). *Meditations to change your brain: Rewire your neural pathways to transform your life* [CD]. Boulder, CO: Sounds True.

Hariri, A. R., Bookheimer, S. Y., & Maziotta, J. C. (2000). Modulating emotional responses: Effects of neocortical network on the limbic system. *NeuroReport: For Rapid Communication of Neuroscience Research, 11,* 43–48. doi:10.1097/00001756-200001170-00009

Hart, T. (2004). Opening the contemplative mind in the classroom. *Journal of Transformative Education, 2,* 28–46. doi:10.1177/1541344603259311

Hayes, S. C., Strosahl, K. D., & Wilson, K. G. (1999). *Acceptance and commitment therapy: An experiential approach to behaviour change.* New York, NY: Guilford Press.

Heard, W. G. (1993). *The healing between: A clinical guide to dialogic psychotherapy.* San Francisco, CA: Jossey-Bass.

Hebb, D. O. (1949). *The organization of behavior.* New York, NY: Wiley.

Henry, W. P., Schacht, T. E., & Strupp, H. H. (1990). Patient and therapist introject, interpersonal process, and differential psychotherapy outcome. *Journal of Consulting and Clinical Psychology, 58,* 768–774. doi:10.1037/0022-006X.58.6.768

Hick, S. F. (2008). Cultivating therapeutic relationships: The role of mindfulness. In S. F. Hick & T. Bien (Eds.), *Mindfulness and the therapeutic relationship* (pp. 3–18). New York, NY: Guilford Press.

Hines, D. R. (1992). Presence: Discovering the artistry in relating. *Journal of Holistic Nursing, 10,* 294–305. doi:10.1177/089801019201000403

Hoffman, L. (2004–2005). *Jim Bugental tribute.* Retrieved from http://www.depthpsychotherapynetwork.com/Professional_Section/Bugental_Tributes/Louis_Hoffman.html

Holtforth, M. G., & Castonguay, L. G. (2005). Relationship and technique in cognitive-behavioral therapy—A motivational approach. *Psychotherapy: Theory, Research, Practice, Training. 42*, 443–445. doi:10.1037./0033-3204.42.4.443

Horvath, A. O. (1994). Empirical validation of Bordin's pantheoretical model of the alliance: The working alliance inventory perspective. In A. O. Horvath & L. S. Greenberg (Eds.), *The working alliance: Theory, research, and practice* (pp. 109–128). New York, NY: Wiley.

Horvath, A. O., & Greenberg, L. (1986). The development of the Working Alliance Inventory. In L. S. Greenberg & W. M. Pinsof (Eds.), *The psychotherapeutic process: A research handbook* (pp. 529–556). New York, NY: Guilford Press.

Horvath, A. O., & Greenberg, L. (1989). Development and validation of the Working Alliance Inventory. *Journal of Counseling Psychology, 36*, 223–233.

Horvath, A. O., & Greenberg, L. S. (1994). *The working alliance: Theory, research, and practice.* New York, NY: Wiley.

Horvath, A. O., & Luborsky, L. (1993). The role of the therapeutic alliance in psychotherapy. *Journal of Consulting and Clinical Psychology, 61*, 561–573. doi:10.1037/0022-006X.61.4.561

Hunter, B. (2007). Comeditation & cross-breathing: Healing applications in hospice, grief, and trauma. *Ministry, 14*(1), 13–16.

Hycner, R. (1993). *Between person and person: Toward a dialogical psychotherapy.* New York, NY: Gestalt Journal Press.

Hycner, R., & Jacobs, L. (1995). *The healing relationship in gestalt therapy: A dialogical/self psychology approach.* New York, NY: Gestalt Journal Press.

Jacobson, L. (2007). *Journey into now: Clear guidance on the path of spiritual awakening.* La Selva Beach, CA: Conscious Living.

Jha, A. P., Krompinger, J., & Baime, M. J. (2007). Mindfulness training modifies subsystems of attention. *Cognitive, Affective & Behavioral Neuroscience, 7*, 109–119. doi:10.3758/CABN.7.2.109

Jordan, S. (2008). *Practicing presence: Focusing, Buddhist understanding and core process psychotherapy.* Retrieved from http://www.focusing.org.uk/practising_presence.html

Juhan, A. (2003). *Open floor: dance, therapy, and transformation through the 5Rhythms.* Retrieved from http://www.openfloor.org/

Jung, C. (1959). *Archetypes and the collective unconscious.* Princeton, NJ: Princeton University Press.

Kabat-Zinn, J. (1990). *Full catastrophe living: Using the wisdom of your body and mind to face stress, pain, and illness.* New York, NY: Dell.

Kabat-Zinn, J. (1994). *Wherever you go, there you are.* New York, NY: Hyperion.

Kabat-Zinn, J. (2005). *Coming to our senses: Healing ourselves and the world through mindfulness.* New York, NY: Hyperion.

Kahn, W. A. (1992). To be fully there: Psychological presence at work. *Human Relations, 45*, 321–349. doi:10.1177/001872679204500402

Kanter, J. W., Rusch, L. C., Landes, S. J., Holman, G. I., Whiteside, U., & Sedivy, S. K. (2009). The use and nature of present-focused interventions in cognitive and behavioral therapies for depression. *Psychotherapy: Theory, Research, Practice, Training, 46*, 220–232. doi:10.1037/a0016083

Keefe, T. (1975). Meditation and the psychotherapist. *American Journal of Orthopsychiatry, 45*, 484–489. doi:10.1111/j.1939-0025.1975.tb02560.x

Kempler, W. (1970). The therapist's merchandise. *Voices: The Art & Science of Psychotherapy, 5*, 57–60.

Kessler, S. (1991). The teaching presence. *Holistic Education Review, 4*, 4–15.

Killackey, N. A. (1998). *Mindfulness meditation: Getting to the heart of psychotherapy.* Unpublished doctoral dissertation, Widener University, Chester, PA.

Kimball, C. (2003). *The art of presence in public speaking.* Retrieved from http://www.riverways.com/articles.tao-8a.htm

Korb, M. P. (1988). The numinous ground: I–thou in gestalt work. *The Gestalt Journal, XI*, 97–106.

Kramer, G. (2007). *Insight dialogue: The interpersonal path to freedom.* Boston, MA: Shambhala.

Kramer, G., Meleo-Meyer, F., & Turner, M. L. (2008). Cultivating mindfulness in relationship: Insight dialogue and the interpersonal mindfulness program. In S. F. Hick & T. Bien (Eds.), *Mindfulness and the therapeutic relationship* (pp. 195–214). New York, NY: Guilford Press.

Krug, O. T. (2009). James Bugental and Irvin Yalom: Two masters of existential therapy cultivate presence in the therapeutic encounter. *Journal of Humanistic Psychology, 49*, 329–354. doi:10.1177/0022167809334001

Kvale, S. (1996). *InterViews: An introduction to qualitative research interviewing.* London, England: Sage.

Lambert, M. J., & Barley, D. E. (2002). Research summary on the therapeutic relationship and psychotherapy outcome. In J. C. Norcross (Ed.), *Psychotherapy relationships that work: Therapist contributions and responsiveness to patients* (pp. 17–32). New York, NY: Oxford University Press.

Lambert, M. J., & Bergin, A. E. (1994). The effectiveness of psychotherapy. In A. E. Bergin & S. L. Garfield (Eds.), *Handbook of psychotherapy and behavior change* (4th ed., pp. 143–189). New York, NY: Wiley.

Lambert, M. J., Hansen, N. B., Umphress, V., Lunnen, K., Okiishi, J., Burlingame, G., . . . Reisinger, C. W. (1996). *Administration and scoring manual for the Outcome Questionnaire (OQ-45.2).* Wilmington, DE: American Professional Credentialing Services.

Lambert, M. J., & Ogles, B. M. (2004). The efficacy and effectiveness of psychotherapy. In M. J. Lambert (Ed.), *Bergin and Garfield's handbook of psychotherapy and behavior change* (5th ed., pp. 139–193). New York, NY: Wiley.

Lambert, M. J., & Simon, W. (2008). The therapeutic relationship: Central and essential in psychotherapy outcome. In S. F. Hick & T. Bien (Eds.), *Mindfulness and the therapeutic relationship* (pp. 19–33). New York, NY: Guilford Press.

Lanyado, M. (2004). *The presence of the therapist: Treating childhood trauma*. New York, NY: Brunner-Routledge.

Lazar, S. W. (2005). Mindfulness research. In C. K. Germer, R. D. Siegel, & P. R. Fulton (Eds.), *Mindfulness and psychotherapy* (pp. 220–238). New York, NY: Guilford Press.

Lazar, S. W., Bush, G., Gollub, R., Fricchione, G., Khalsa, G., & Benson, H. (2000). Functional brain mapping of the relaxation response and meditation. *Neuro-Report: For Rapid Communication of Neuroscience Research, 11*(7), 1581–1585. doi:10.1097/00001756-200005150-00041

Lazar, S. W., Kerr, C. E., Wasserman, R. H., Gray, J. R., Greve, D. N., Treadway, M. T., . . . Fischl, B. (2005). Meditation experience is associated with increased cortical thickness. *NeuroReport: For Rapid Communication of Neuroscience Research, 16,* 1893–1897. doi:10.1097/01.wnr.0000186598.66243.19

Leahy, R. L. (2001). *Overcoming resistance in cognitive therapy*. New York, NY: Guilford Press.

Leahy, R. L. (2003). *Cognitive therapy techniques: A practitioner's guide*. New York, NY: Guilford Press.

Leary, M. R., Tate, E. B., Adams, C. E., Allen, A. B., & Hancock, J. (2007). Self-compassion and reactions to unpleasant self-relevant events: The implications of treating oneself kindly. *Journal of Personality and Social Psychology, 92,* 887–904. doi:10.1037/0022-3514.92.5.887

Leijssen, M. (1990). On focusing and the necessary conditions of therapeutic personality change. In G. Leitaer, J. Rombauts, & R. Van Balen (Eds.), *Client-centered and experiential psychotherapy in the nineties* (pp. 225–250). Leuven, Belgium: Leuven University Press.

Lejuez, C. W., Hopko, D. R., Levine, S., Gholkar, R., & Collins, L. M. (2005). The therapeutic alliance in behavior therapy. *Psychotherapy: Theory, Research, Practice, Training, 42,* 456–468. doi:10.1037/0033-3204.42.4.456

Levinas, E. (1985). *Ethics and infinity, conversations with Philippe Nemo* (R. A. Cohen, Trans.). Pittsburgh, PA: Duquesne University Press.

Levitin, D. J. (2008). *The world in six songs: How the musical brain created human nature*. New York, NY: Dutton/Penguin Books.

Lewin, K. (1951). *Field theory in social science: Selected theoretical papers*. D. Cartwright (Ed.). New York, NY: Harper & Row.

Liehr, P. R. (1989). Core of true presence: A loving center. *Nursing Science Quarterly, 2,* 7–8. doi:10.1177/089431848900200105

Lietaer, G. (1993). Authenticity, congruence, and transparency. In D. Brazier (Ed.), *Beyond Carl Rogers* (pp. 17–46). London, England: Constable.

Linehan, M. M. (1993a). *Cognitive behavioral treatment for borderline personality disorder*. New York, NY: Guilford Press.

Linehan, M. M. (1993b). *Skills training manual for treating borderline personality disorder*. New York, NY: Guilford Press.

Linehan, M. M. (2009, April). *Mindfulness skills and dialectical behavior therapy (DBT)*. Symposium conducted at the Faces Conference, San Diego, CA.

Lutz, A., Dunne, J. D., & Davidson, R. J. (2007). Meditation and the neuroscience of consciousness. In P. D. Zelazo, M. Moscovitch, & E. Thompson (Eds.), *The Cambridge handbook of consciousness* (pp. 499–551). Cambridge, England: Cambridge University Press.

Lutz, A., Greischar, L., Rawlings, N., Ricard, M., & Davidson, R. J. (2004). Long-term meditators self-induce high amplitude gamma synchrony during mental practice. *Proceedings of the National Academy of Sciences of the United States of America, 101*, 16369–16373. doi:10.1073/pnas.0407401101

Mace, C. (2008). *Mindfulness and mental health: Therapy, theory and science*. New York, NY: Routledge.

Marlatt, G. A., Bowen, S., Chawla, N., & Witkiewitz, K. (2008). Mindfulness-based relapse prevention for substance abuse: Therapist training and therapeutic relationships. In S. F. Hick & T. Bien (Eds.), *Mindfulness and the therapeutic relationship* (pp. 107–121). New York, NY: Guilford Press.

Marlatt, G. A., & Kristeller, J. L. (1999). Mindfulness and meditation. In W. R. Miller (Ed.), *Integrating spirituality into treatment* (pp. 67–84). Washington, DC: American Psychological Association.

Marlatt, G. A., & Miller, L. D. (2009, April). *Mindfulness-based relapse prevention*. Symposium conducted at the Faces Conference, San Diego, CA.

Martin, D. J., Garske, J. P., & Davis, M. K. (2000). Relation of the therapeutic alliance with outcome and other variables: A meta-analytic review. *Journal of Consulting and Clinical Psychology, 68*, 438–450. doi:10.1037/0022-006X.68.3.438

Maschi, T., & Bradley, C. (2010). Recreational drumming: A creative arts intervention strategy for social work teaching and practice. *The Journal of Baccalaureate Social Work, 15*(1), 53–66.

Maslach, C. (1986). *Burn-out: The cost of caring*. NJ: Prentice-Hall.

May, R. (1958). Contributions to existential therapy. In R. May, E. Angel, & H. Ellenberger (Eds.), *Existence: A new dimension in psychiatry and psychology* (pp. 37–91). New York, NY: Basic Books. doi:10.1037/11321-002

May, R. (1994). *The discovery of being: Writings in existential psychology*. New York, NY: Norton.

May, R., & Yalom, I. (2005). Existential psychotherapy. In R. J. Corsini & D. Wedding (Eds.), *Current psychotherapies* (7th ed., pp. 269–298). Belmont, CA: Brooks/Cole.

May, S., & O'Donovan, A. (2007). The advantages of the mindful therapist. *Psychotherapy in Australia, 13*, 46–53.

McCollum, E. E., & Gehart, D. R. (2010). Using mindfulness meditation to teach beginning therapists therapeutic presence: A qualitative study. *Journal of Marital and Family Therapy, 36*, 347–360.

McCullough, J. P. (2000). *Treatment for chronic depression: Cognitive behavioral analysis system of psychotherapy* (CBASP). New York, NY: Guilford Press.

McDonough-Means, S. I., Kreitzer, R. N., & Bell, I. R. (2004). Fostering a healing presence and investigating its mediators. *Journal of Alternative and Complementary Medicine, 10,* S25–S41. doi:10.1089/1075553042245890

McKay, M., Brantley, J., & Wood, J. (2007). *The dialectical behavior therapy skills workbook: Practical DBT exercises for learning mindfulness, interpersonal effectiveness, emotion regulation, and distress tolerance.* Oakland, CA: New Harbinger.

McKivergin, M. J., & Daubenmire, M. J. (1994). The healing process of presence. *Journal of Holistic Nursing, 12,* 65–81. doi:10.1177/089801019401200111

Meijer, P. C., Korthagen, F. A. J., & Vasalos, A. (2009). Supporting presence in teacher education: The connection between the personal and professional aspects of teaching. *Teaching and Teacher Education, 25,* 297–308. doi:10.1016/j.tate.2008.09.013

Melville, K. (2008). *This is your brain on jazz.* Retrieved from Science a Go Go website: http://www.scienceagogo.com/news/20080127203614data_trunc_sys.shtml

Messer, S. B., & Warren, C. S. (1995). *Models of brief psychodynamic therapy: A comparative approach.* New York, NY: Guilford Press.

Miller, J. J. (1993). The unveiling of traumatic memories and emotions through mindfulness and concentration meditation: Clinical implications and three case reports. *The Journal of Transpersonal Psychology, 25,* 169–180.

Miller, J. P. (2005). Enhancing teaching presence through mindfulness. *The Holistic Educator, 16,* 1–4.

Mitchell, S. (2003). *Relationality: From attachment to intersubjectivity.* Hillsdale, NJ: Analytic Press.

Morgan, W. D., & Morgan, S. T. (2005). Cultivating attention and empathy. In C. K. Germer, R. D. Siegel, & P. R. Fulton (Eds.), *Mindfulness and psychotherapy* (pp. 73–90). New York, NY: Guilford Press.

Mountain Dreamer, O. (2006). *The call: Discovering why you are here.* New York, NY: HarperCollins.

Moustakas, C. (1969). *Personal growth.* Cambridge, MA: Howard A. Doyle.

Moustakas, C. (1985). *A conceptual-methodological model of existential Dasein analytical psychotherapy.* Unpublished manuscript.

Nichols, J. (2007). Clinical supervision in mental health nursing. In D. Wepa (Ed.), *Clinical supervision in Aotearoa/New Zealand, a health perspective* (pp. 62–71). Auckland, New Zealand: Pearson.

Niedenthal, P. M. (2007, May 18). Embodying emotion. *Science, 316,* 1002–1005. doi:10.1126/science.1136930

Norcross, J. C. (2002). *Psychotherapy relationships that work: Therapists' contributions and responsiveness to patients.* New York, NY: Oxford University Press.

Norcross, J. C. (2011). *Psychotherapy relationships that work: Evidence-based responsiveness* (2nd ed.). New York, NY: Oxford University Press.

Ochsner, K. N., Bunge, S. A., Gross, J. J., & Gabrieli, J. D. E. (2002). Rethinking feelings: An fMRI study of the cognitive regulation of emotion. *Journal of Cognitive Neuroscience, 14,* 1215–1229. doi:10.1162/089892902760807212

Oghene, J. E., Pos, A. E., & Geller, S. M. (2010). *Therapist presence, empathy and the alliance in experiential treatment for depression.* Unpublished honors thesis, York University, Toronto, Canada.

O'Leary, A. (1990). Stress, emotion and human immune function. *Psychological Bulletin, 108,* 363–382. doi:10.1037/0033-2909.108.3.363

Orlinsky, D. E., & Rønnestadt, M. H. (2005). *How psychotherapists develop: A study of therapeutic work and personal growth.* Washington, DC: American Psychological Association. doi:10.1037/11157-000

Ostaseski, F. (n.d.) *The five precepts.* Retrieved from http://www.peacemaker.ch/pdf/FivePrecepts.pdf

Osterman, P., & Schwartz-Barcott, D. (1996). Presence: Four ways of being there. *Nursing Forum, 31*(2), 23–30. doi:10.1111/j.1744-6198.1996.tb00490.x

Pagnoni, G., & Cekic, M. (2007). Age effects on gray matter volume and attentional performance in Zen meditation. *Neurobiology of Aging, 28,* 1623–1627. doi:10.1016/j.neurobiolaging.2007.06.008

Pemberton, B. (1977). *The presence of the therapist.* Unpublished doctoral dissertation, Georgia State University, School of Education, Atlanta, GA.

Perls, F. S. (1969). *Gestalt therapy verbatim.* Lafayette, CA: Real People Press.

Perls, F. S. (1970). Four lectures. In J. Fagan & I. L. Shepherd (Eds.), *Gestalt therapy now: Theory, techniques, and applications* (pp. 14–38). New York, NY: Harper Colophon.

Phelon, C. (2001). Healing presence: An intuitive inquiry into the presence of the psychotherapist. (Doctoral dissertation, Institute of Transpersonal Psychology, 2001) *Dissertation Abstracts International, 62*(04), 2074B. (UMI No. 3011298).

Phelon, C. (2004). Healing presence in the psychotherapist. *The Humanistic Psychologist, 32,* 342–356. doi:10.1080/08873267.2004.9961759

Polster, E., & Polster, M. (1973). *Gestalt therapy integrated: Contours of theory and practice.* New York, NY: Brunner/Mazel.

Polster, E., & Polster, M. (1999). *From the radical center: The heart of gestalt therapy.* Cambridge, MA: GIC Press.

Porges, S. W. (1998). Love: An emergent property of the mammalian autonomic nervous system. *Psychoneuroendocrinology, 23,* 837–861. doi:10.1016/S0306-4530(98)00057-2

Porges, S. (2009). Reciprocal influences between body and brain in the perception and expression of affect: A polyvagal perspective. In D. Fosha, D. J. Siegel, & M. Solomon (Eds.), *The healing power of emotion: Affective neuroscience, development and clinical practice* (pp. 27–54). New York, NY: Norton.

Purcell-Lee, C. R. (1999, June). *Some implications of the work of Martin Buber for psychotherapy.* Paper presented to the Society for Psychotherapy Research, Braga, Portugal.

Reich, A. (1951). On counter-transference. *The International Journal of Psychoanalysis, 32*, 25–31.

Reik, T. (1948). *Listening with the third ear*. New York, NY: Farrar Straus.

Robbins, A. (Ed.). (1998). *Therapeutic presence: Bridging expression and form*. London, England: Jessica Kingsley.

Robbins, S. B., & Jolkovski, M. P. (1987). Managing countertransference feelings: An interactional model using awareness of feelings and theoretical framework. *Journal of Counseling Psychology, 34*, 276–282. doi:10.1037/0022-0167.34.3.276

Rodgers, C. R., & Raider-Roth, M. B. (2006). Presence in teaching. *Teachers and Teaching: Theory and Practice, 12*, 265–287. doi:10.1080/13450600500467548

Roemer, L., & Orsillo, S. M. (2009). *Mindfulness- and acceptance-based behavioral therapies in practice*. New York, NY: Guilford Press.

Rogers, C. R. (1951). *Client-centered therapy: Its current practice, implications, and theory*. Boston, MA: Houghton Mifflin.

Rogers, C. R. (1957). The necessary and sufficient conditions of therapeutic personality change. *Journal of Consulting Psychology, 21*, 95–103. doi:10.1037/h0045357

Rogers, C. R. (1961). *On becoming a person*. Boston, MA: Houghton Mifflin.

Rogers, C. R. (1979). The foundations of the person-centered approach. *Education, 100*, 96–107.

Rogers, C. R. (1980). *A way of being*. Boston, MA: Houghton Mifflin.

Rogers, C. R. (1986). Client-centered therapy. In I. L. Kutash & A. Wolf (Eds.), *Psychotherapist's casebook: Theory and technique in the practice of modern therapies* (pp. 197–208). San Francisco, CA: Jossey-Bass.

Rogers, C. R., Gendlin, D. J., Kiesler, D. J., & Truax, C. (1967). *The therapeutic relationship and its impact: A study of psychotherapy with schizophrenics*. Madison, WI: University of Wisconsin Press.

Rogers, C. R., & Truax, C. B. (1976). The therapeutic conditions antecedent to change: A theoretical view. In C. R. Rogers, E. T. Gendlin, D. J. Kiesler, & C. B. Truax (Eds.), *The therapeutic relationship and its impact: A study of psychotherapy with schizophrenics* (pp. 97–108). Westport, CT: Grennwork.

Rosenberg, L. (1998). *Breath by breath: The liberating practice of insight meditation*. Boston, MA: Shambhala.

Rotenstreich, N. (1967). *The philosophy of Martin Buber*. In P. A. Schlipp & M. S. Friedman (Eds.), *The library of living philosophers, vol. XXII* (pp. 97–132). Chicago, IL: Open Court.

Roth, G. (1989). *Maps to ecstasy*. Novato, CA: Nataraj.

Roth, G. (1997). *Sweat your prayers*. New York, NY: Jeremy P. Tarcher/Penguin.

Roth, G. (2004). *Connections*. New York, NY: Jeremy P. Tarcher/Penguin.

Rubin, J. B. (1996). Meditation and psychoanalytic listening. In G. Stricker (Ed.), *Psychotherapy and Buddhism* (pp. 115–127). New York, NY: Plenum Press.

Rueda, M. R., Posner, M. I., & Rothbart, M. K. (2005). The development of executive attention: Contributions to the emergence of self-regulation. *Developmental Neuropsychology, 28,* 573–594. doi:10.1207/s15326942dn2802_2

Sabini, M. (2002). *The Earth has a soul: Nature writings of C. G. Jung.* Berkeley, CA: North Atlantic Books.

Safran, J. D. (2003). *Psychoanalysis and Buddhism.* Boston, MA: Wisdom.

Safran, J. D., Crocker, P., McMain, S., & Murray, P. (1990, June). *The therapeutic alliance rupture resolution and nonresolution events.* Paper presented at the annual meeting of the Society for Psychotherapy Research, Berkeley, CA.

Safran, J. D., & Muran, J. C. (1996). The resolution of ruptures in the therapeutic alliance. *Journal of Consulting and Clinical Psychology, 64,* 447–458. doi:10.1037/0022-006X.64.3.447

Safran, J. D., Muran, J. C., Samstag, L. W., & Stevens, C. (2002). Repairing alliance ruptures. In J. C. Norcross (Ed.), *Psychotherapy relationships that work: Therapists' relational contributions to effective psychotherapy* (pp. 235–254). New York, NY: Oxford University Press.

Safran, J. D., & Reading, R. (2008). Mindfulness, metacommunication, and affect regulation in psychoanalytic treatment. In S. Hick & T. Bien (Eds.), *Mindfulness and the therapeutic relationship* (pp. 122–140). New York, NY: Guilford Press.

Salzberg, S. (1999). *A heart as wide as the world: Stories on the path of lovingkindness.* Boston, MA: Shambhala.

Santorelli, S. (1999). *Heal thyself: Lessons on mindfulness in medicine.* New York, NY: Bell Tower.

Scharmer, C. O. (2006). *Presence in action: An introduction to theory U* [DVD]. Cambridge, MA: Society for Organizational Living (SoL).

Scharmer, C. O. (2009). *Theory U: Leading from the future as it emerges. The social technology of presencing.* San Francisco, CA: Berrett-Koehler.

Schell, F. J., Allolio, B., & Schonecke, W. (1994). Physiological and psychological effects of hatha-yoga exercise in healthy women. *International Journal of Psychosomatics, 41,* 46–52.

Schmid, P. F. (1998). "Face to face": The art of encounter. In B. Thorne & E. Lambers (Eds.), *Person-centered therapy: A European perspective* (pp. 74–90). London, England: Sage.

Schmid, P. F. (2002). Presence—Im-media-te co-experiencing and co-responding. Phenomenological, dialogical and ethical perspectives on contact and perception in person-centred therapy and beyond. In G. Wyatt & P. Sanders P. (Eds.), *Contact and perception* (pp. 182–203). Ross-on-Wye, England: PCCS Books.

Schneider, K., & Krug, O. T. (2010). *Existential-humanistic therapy.* Washington, DC: American Psychological Association.

Schneider, K. J., & May R. (1995). *The psychology of existence. An integrative, clinical perspective.* New York, NY: McGraw-Hill, Inc.

Schure, M. B., Christopher, J., & Christopher, S. (2008). Mind-body medicine and the art of self-care: Teaching mindfulness to counseling students through yoga, meditation, and qigong. *Journal of Counseling & Development, 86,* 47–56.

Schwaber, E. (1983). Psychoanalytic listening and psychic reality. *The International Journal of Psychoanalysis, 10,* 379–392.

Schwaber, E. A. (1981). Empathy: A mode of analytic listening. *Psychoanalytic Inquiry, 1,* 357–392.

Scurlock-Durana, S. (2007). The gift of therapeutic presence. *Massage Today.com, 7*(1), pp. 1–3. Retrieved from http://www.massagetoday.com/mpacms/mt/article.php?id=13546&no_paginate=true&no_b=true

Scurlock-Durana, S. (2010). *Full body presence: Learning to listen to your body's wisdom.* Novato, CA: Nataraj.

Segal, Z. V., Williams, J. M. G., & Teasdale, J. D. (2002). *Mindfulness-based cognitive therapy for depression.* New York, NY: Guilford Press.

Segrera, A. (2000, June). *Necessary and sufficient conditions.* Paper presented at ICCEP Conference in Chicago, IL.

Senge, P. (2008). *The power of presence: Shifting your awareness to transform your business, your life, and our future* [CD]. Boulder, CO: Sounds True.

Senge, P., Scharmer, C. O., Jaworski, J., & Flowers, B. S. (2004). *Presence: human purpose and the field of the future.* New York, NY: Doubleday.

Shapiro, S. L., Brown, K. W., & Biegel, G. M. (2007). Teaching self-care to caregivers: Effects of mindfulness based stress reduction on the mental health of therapists in training. *Training and Education in Professional Psychology, 1,* 105–115. doi:10.1037/1931-3918.1.2.105

Shapiro, S. L., & Carlson, L. E. (2009). *The art and science of mindfulness: Integrating mindfulness into psychology and the helping professions.* Washington, DC: American Psychological Association. doi:10.1037/11885-000

Shepherd, I., Brown, E., & Greaves, G. (1972). Three-on-oneness (presence). *Voices, 8,* 70–77.

Siegel, D. J. (2007). *The mindful brain: Reflection and attunement in the cultivation of well-being.* New York, NY: Norton.

Siegel, D. J. (2010). *Mindsight: The new science of personal transformation.* New York, NY: Bantam Books.

Siegel, R. D. (2010). *The mindfulness solution: Everyday practices for everyday problems.* New York, NY: Guilford Press.

Silsbee, D. (2008). *Presence-based coaching: Cultivating self-generative leaders through mind, body, and heart.* San Francisco, CA: Jossey-Bass.

Silsbee, D. K. (2004). *The mindful coach: Seven roles for helping people grow.* Marshall, NC: Ivy Press.

Smythe, E., MacCulloch, T., & Charmley, R. (2009). Professional supervision: Trusting the wisdom that comes. *British Journal of Guidance & Counselling, 37*(1), 17–25. doi:10.1080/03069880802535903

Sogyal Rinpoche (1992). *The Tibetan book of living and dying*. New York, NY: Harper & Row.

Sonneman, V. (1959). *Existence and therapy: An introduction to phenomenological psychology and existential analysis*. New York, NY: Grune & Stratton.

Stern, D. (1985). *The interpersonal world of the infant*. New York, NY: Basic Books.

Stern, D. (2004). *The present moment in psychotherapy and everyday life*. New York, NY: Norton.

Stevens, J. O. (1971). *Awareness: Exploring, experimenting and experiencing*. Palo Alto, CA: American West.

Stevens, J. O. (1977). Hypnosis, intention, wakefulness. In J. O. Stevens (Ed.), *Gestalt is* (pp. 258–269). New York, NY: Bantam Books.

Stiles, W. B., & Snow, J. S. (1984). Counseling session impact as viewed by novice counselors and their clients. *Journal of Counseling Psychology, 31*, 3–12.

Stolorow, R., Brandchaft, B., & Atwood, G. (1987). *Psychoanalytic treatment: An intersubjective approach*. Hillsdale, NJ: Analytic Press.

Surrey, J. L. (2005). Relational psychotherapy, relational mindfulness. In C. K. Germer, R. D. Siegel, & P. R. Fulton (Eds.), *Mindfulness and psychotherapy* (pp. 91–110). New York, NY: Guilford Press.

Suzuki, S. (2006). *Zen mind, beginner's mind*. Boston, MA: Shambhala.

Sweet, M., & Johnson, C. (1990). Enhancing empathy: The interpersonal implications of a Buddhist meditation technique. *Psychotherapy: Theory, Research, Practice, Training, 27*, 19–29. doi:10.1037/0033-3204.27.1.19

Thera, N. (1973). *The heart of Buddhist meditation*. New York, NY: Samuel Weiser.

Thomson, R. F. (2000). Zazen and psychotherapeutic presence. *American Journal of Psychotherapy, 54*, 531–548.

Thorne, B. (1992). *Carl Rogers*. London, England: Sage.

Thorne, B. (1996). Person-centered therapy: The path to holiness. In R. Hutterer, G. Pawlowsky, P. F. Schmid, & R. Stipsits (Eds.), *Client-centered and experiential psychotherapy: A paradigm in motion* (pp. 107–116). Frankfurt, Germany: Peter Lang.

Tolbert, M. A. R., & Hanafin, J. (2006). Use of self in OD consulting: What matters is presence. In B. B. Jones & M. Brazzel (Eds.), *The NTL handbook of organization development and change: Principles, practices and perspectives* (pp. 69–82). San Francisco, CA: Pfeiffer.

Torre, M. A. L. (2002). Integrated perspectives: Enhancing therapeutic presence. *Perspectives in Psychiatric Care, 38*(1), 34–36.

Tremlow, S. W. (2001). Training psychotherapists in attributes of "mind" from Zen and psychoanalytic perspectives, part I. *American Journal of Psychotherapy, 55*, 1–21.

Tremmel, R. (1993). Zen and true art of reflective practice in teacher education. *Harvard Educational Review, 63*, 434–458.

Trop, J. L., & Stolorow, R. D. (1997). Therapeutic empathy: An intersubjective perspective. In A. Bohart & L. Greenberg (Eds.), *Empathy reconsidered: New directions in psychotherapy* (pp. 279–294). Washington, DC: American Psychological Association. doi:10.1037/10226-012

Trungpa, C. (1984). *Shambhala: The sacred path of the warrior* (p. 71). New York, NY: Bantam Books.

Tsang, H. W. H., Cheung, L., & Lak, D. C. C. (2002). Qigong as a psychosocial intervention for depressed elderly with chronic physical illness. *International Journal of Geriatric Psychiatry, 17*, 1146–1154.

Valente, V., & Marotta, A. (2005). The impact of yoga on the professional and personal life of the psychotherapist. *Contemporary Family Therapy: An International Journal, 27*(1), 65–80. doi:10.1007/s10591-004-1971-4

Valentine, E., & Sweet, P. (1999). Meditation and attention: A comparison of the effects of concentrative and mindfulness meditation on sustained attention. *Mental Health, Religion & Culture, 2*, 59–70. doi:10.1080/13674679908406332

Vanaerschot, G. (1993). Empathy as releasing several microprocesses in the client. In D. Brazier (Ed.), *Beyond Carl Rogers* (pp. 47–71). London, England: Constable.

Van Wagoner, S. L., Gelso, C. J., Hayes, J. A., & Diemer, R. A. (1991). Countertransference and the reputedly excellent therapists. *Psychotherapy: Theory, Research, Practice, Training, 28*, 411–421. doi:10.1037/0033-3204.28.3.411

Vaughan, F. (2002). What is spiritual intelligence? *Journal of Humanistic Psychology, 42*(2), 16–33. doi:10.1177/0022167802422003

Vaughan, F. (2010, August). *Dimensions of self.* Symposium conducted at the Metta Institute Conference, San Rafael, CA.

Vinca, M. (2009). *Mindfulness and psychotherapy: A mixed methods investigation.* Unpublished dissertation, Pennsylvania State University.

Vinca, M., & Hayes, J. (2007, June). *Therapist mindfulness as predictive of empathy, presence and session depth.* Presentation at the annual meeting for the Society for Psychotherapy Research, Madison, WI.

Vivino, B. L., Thompson, B. J., Hill, C. E., & Ladany, N. (2009). Compassion in psychotherapy: The perspective of therapists nominated as compassionate. *Psychotherapy Research, 19*(2), 157–171. doi:10.1080/10503300802430681

Waddington, L. (2002). The therapy relationship in cognitive therapy: A review. *Behavioural and Cognitive Psychotherapy, 30*, 179–192. doi:10.1017/S1352465802002059

Wallace, R. K., Benson, H., & Wilson, A. (1971). A wakeful hypometabolic physiological state. *The American Journal of Physiology, 221*, 795–799.

Wallner Samstag, L. Muran, C., Zindel, V., Segal, Z., & Schuman, C. (1992, June). *Patient pretreatment interpersonal problems and therapeutic alliance in short-term cognitive therapy.* Paper presented at the annual meeting of the Society for Psychotherapy Research, Berkeley, CA.

Watson, J. C., & Geller, S. M. (2005). The relation among the relationship conditions, working alliance, and outcome in both process–experiential and cognitive–behavioral psychotherapy. *Psychotherapy Research, 15,* 25–33. doi:10.1080/10503300512331327010

Watson, J. C., Gordon, L. B., Stermac, L., Kalogerakos, F., & Steckley, P. (2003). Comparing the effectiveness of process-experiential to cognitive-behavioural psychotherapy in the treatment of depression. *Journal of Consulting and Clinical Psychology, 71,* 773–781. doi:10.1037/0022-006X.71.4.773

Watson, J. C., Greenberg, L. S., & Lietaer, G. (1998). The experiential paradigm unfolding: Relationship and experiencing in therapy. In L. S, Greenberg, J. C. Watson, & G. Lietaer (Eds.), *Handbook of experiential psychotherapy* (pp. 3–27). New York, NY: Guilford Press.

Watson, J. C., Shein, J., & McMullen, E. (2009). An examination of clients' in-session changes and their relationship to the working alliance and outcome. *Psychotherapy Research, 4,* 1–10.

Webster, M. (1998). Blue suede shoes: The therapist's presence. *Australian and New Zealand Journal of Family Therapy, 19,* 184–189.

Weil, G. M. (2003). Qigong as a portal to presence: Cultivating the inner energy body. *Oriental Medicine Journal, 2*(2), 1–8.

Welwood, J. (1992). The healing power of unconditional presence. In J. Welwood (Ed.), *Ordinary magic: Everyday life as spiritual path* (pp. 159–170). Boston, MA: Shambhala.

Welwood, J. (1996). Reflection and presence: The dialectic of self-knowledge. *Journal of Transpersonal Psychology, 28,* 107–128.

Welwood, J. (2000). *Toward a psychology of awakening: Buddhism, psychotherapy, and the path of personal and spiritual transformation.* Boston, MA: Shambhala.

Wiens, S. (2005). Interoception in emotional experience. *Current Opinion in Neurology, 18,* 442–447. doi:10.1097/01.wco.0000168079.92106.99

Wilson, K. G., & DuFrene, T. (2008). *Mindfulness for two.* Oakland, CA: New Harbinger.

Witkiewitz, K., & Marlatt, G. A. (2007). *Therapists guide to evidence-based relapse prevention.* New York, NY: Elsevier.

Witkiewitz, K., Marlatt, G. A., & Walker, D. D. (2005). Mindfulness-based relapse prevention for alcohol use disorders: The meditative tortoise wins the race. *Journal of Cognitive Psychotherapy, 19,* 221–228.

Wood, C. (1993). Mood change and perception of vitality: A comparison of the effects of relaxation, visualization, and yoga. *Journal of the Royal Society of Medicine, 86,* 254–258.

Wyatt, G. (2000, June). *Presence: Bringing together the core conditions.* Paper presented at ICCEP Conference in Chicago, IL.

Yalom, I. (2008). *Staring at the sun: Overcoming the terror of death.* San Francisco, CA: Jossey-Bass.

Yinger, R. J. (1990). The conversation of practice. In R. T. Clift, W. R. Houston, & M. C. Pugach (Eds.), *Encouraging reflective practice in education: An analysis of issues and programs* (pp. 73–94). New York, NY: Teachers College Press.

Yontef, G. (1998). Dialogic gestalt therapy. In L. S. Greenberg, J. C. Watson, & G. Lietaer (Eds.), *Handbook of experiential psychotherapy* (pp. 82–102). New York, NY: Guilford Press.

Yontef, G. (2005). Gestalt therapy theory of change. In A. L. Woldt & S. M. Toman (Eds.), *Gestalt therapy: History, theory, and practice* (pp. 81–100). Thousand Oaks, CA: Sage.

Zoppi, K., & Epstein, R. M. (2002). Is communication a skill? Communication behaviors and being in relation. *Family Medicine, 34,* 319–324.

Zylowska, L., Ackerman, D. L., Yang, M. H., Futrell, J. L., Horton, N. L., Hale, T. S., . . . Smalley, S. L. (2007). Mindfulness meditation training in adults and adolescents with ADHD: A feasibility study. *Journal of Attention Disorders, 11,* 737–746. doi:10.1177/1087054707308502

# INDEX

Coflow, 28
Cognitive–behavioral therapy (CBT)
    competence with presence in, 257
    in empirical research on presence,
        44–45, 47
    mindfulness in, 32–34
    therapeutic relationship in, 8–9
    therapeutic stance in, 34–35
    uncertainty in, 148
Cognitive processes, 19–20
Cognitive understanding, 77–78
Cole, J. D., 30
Coleman, M., 221–222
Collective unconscious, 62
Comeditation, 203–204
Commitment, 39, 77–78
Communication
    attuned, 164
    extrasensory level of, 99–100
    of presence, by therapist, 52
    technology-based, 149
Compassion
    in being with and for client, 126, 128
    brain changes with, 163
    in cultivating presence, 224–225
    in Dalai Lama, 77
    defined, 194
    with end-of-life care, 156–157
    meditation, 199–200
    and mindfulness practice, 192,
        194–195
    for self, 195
    for suffering, 224, 245–246
    in therapist, 194
    Tonglen practice for, 244–245
Compassionate action, 156
Concentrative meditation, 194
Conceptual self-awareness, 209
Conceptual understanding, 78
Congruence
    and inwardly attending, 103–104
    in relationship theory, 68
    and therapeutic presence, 26, 67
    transparency in, 67, 103–104, 107
Connection
    and communication, 99–100
    emotions with, 151
    inner, 62
    practicing for, 231
    in preparing the ground for presence,
        75–76

in process of therapeutic presence,
    93
in relationship theory, 59
with sense of client, pre-session, 138
in spaciousness, 124
Consciousness
    dual level of, 55–56
    expansion of, 120
    intersubjective, 63, 64
    introspective, 63–64
    perceiving the whole with, 168
    phenomenal, 63
    reflective, 63–64
    verbal, 63
Contact
    between client and therapist, 20
    in cultivating presence, 223–226
    with experience of presence,
        245–246
    physical, 139
    preliminary, 138
    in process of presence, 94, 105–108
    within self, 135
Control, 117
Cooper, M., 28, 62
Copresence, 28, 62
Core body centering, 113–114
Core values, 83
Cornell, A. W., 29–30
Cortex
    prefrontal, 196
    sensory, 196
Countertransference
    as challenge to presence, 144–147
    and inwardly attending, 104–105
    misunderstood energy in, 152
    relational approach to, 256
Creative flow, 220
Creativity
    in cultivating therapeutic presence,
        219–222, 226–229
    as entry point for presence, 208
    increase in, 102
    in model of therapeutic presence,
        258
Cross-breathing, 203
Csikszentmihalyi, M., 122–123
Cultivation of therapeutic presence.
    See also Exercises and practices
    acronyms for, 236–237

Emotion-focused therapy (EFT), 29, 218–219
Emotion regulation
    and inwardly attending, 170–171
    mindfulness approaches to, 189, 195
    in session, 256
Emotions
    in affect attunement, 71
    and bodily rhythms, 252
    connecting with bodily sense of, 217
    with connection, 151
    difficult, 115
    in expansion state, 120
    letting go of, 87–88
    openness to, 146–147
    primary, 28–29
    reactions to, 197–198, 256
    of therapist and client, 215–216
    therapist management of, 218–219
Empathy
    and affect attunement, 71
    brain structures in, 172–174
    and compassion, 225
    and inclusion, 114–115
    in mindsight, 188
    prefrontal cortex activity with, 164
    and presence, 26–27
    in relationship theory, 68
    and self-empathy, 219
    as therapist-offered condition, 65–66
Empirical research, 37–49
    and pause moments, 37–38
    previous models of presence, 39–41
    qualitative study, 41–42
    quantitative study, 42–48
    related studies, 48–49
Empowerment drumming, 227
Empty mind, 90
End-of-life, 156, 203
Energy
    in expansion state, 123
    flowing from therapist to client, 28
    misunderstood by therapist, 151–152
Enfolding, 39
Enhanced attunement, 70–71
Enhanced awareness, 99, 124–125
Entrainment, 251
Environmental suffering, 183
Environments, 243
Epstein, M., 18–20, 220

Equanimity, 112
Escape, 185
"Evenly suspended attention," 18, 20
Executive attention, 172
Exercises and practices, 231–262
    for absorption, 116–117
    for acceptance, 97
    for affect regulation, 195
    for attention, 119–120
    body-centered, 168, 214–215
    for calm alertness, 167
    classroom exercises, 245–253
    for core body centering, 113–114
    for cultivation of presence, 198–204
    for daily life, 78–80
    drumming, 252–253
    for expansion state, 121–122, 238
    facing attraction and aversion, 243
    for grounding, 111–112
    for holding suffering with love, 123–124
    for immersion state, 119–120
    individual exercises, 237–245
    for meditation, 80–82
    for mindfulness, 182, 194–195, 201–203
    for preparing the ground, 90–91, 233–237
    relational exercises, 245–253
    for relationships, 78–80
    seeing inner nobility, 129
    for self-compassion, 126–127
    spiritual, 80–82
    tai chi, 151, 152, 201
    walking mediation, 240–241
Existential therapy, 25–26
Expanded awareness, 99
Expansion
    and creativity, 219
    as experience of presence, 120–126
    in model of therapeutic presence, 258
    and right brain hemisphere, 168
    in therapeutic presence, 109–110
    whole body awareness exercise for, 238
Expectation, 59
Experience of therapeutic presence, 109–131
    expansion state, 120, 120–126

Painful experiences, *continued*
  therapist nonattachment to,
    117–118
  traumatic, 158–159
Parasympathetic nervous system (PNS)
  activation of, 237
  and intention for presence, 235
  in neurobiology of presence,
    166–167, 169
  in neuroception of safety, 174
Partial presence, 137, 139, 140
*Patthana*, 31, 180
Pause moments, 37–38, 77, 81–82, 90,
    94–95, 106, 110, 144, 150–151,
    210
Pemberton, B., 39, 40
Perceptions, 43–48, 124–125
Percussion, 227
Perls, F. S., 21
Personal growth, 11, 82–83
Personal issues, 87–88, 138
Personality disorders, 152–155
Personal needs and concerns, 83–84
Person-centered approach, 189
PET (positron emission tomography),
    162
PET (process experiential therapy),
    44–45, 47
Phelon, C., 40
Phenomenal consciousness, 63
Philosophical commitment, 77–78
Photography, 220–221
Phowa, 203
Physical body, 213
Physical contact, 139
Physical health, 212
Physical presence, 136–137, 139
Pleasure, 185
PNS. *See* Parasympathetic nervous
    system
Polster, E., 21
Polster, M., 21
Porges, S. W., 174
Pos, A. E., 48, 49
Positron emission tomography (PET),
    162
*The Practical Neuroscience of Buddha's
    Brain* (R. Hanson & R. Mendius),
    167
Practices. *See* Exercises and practices

Preconceptions, 88–89, 138
Prefrontal cortex
  functions associated with, 164–165
  in mindfulness practice, 196
  in therapeutic presence, 171–172
Preliminary contact, 138
Preparing the ground, 75–91
  as component of presence, 42
  in daily life, 75–84, 233
  exercises and practices for, 233–237
  meditation for, 80–82
  personal growth in, 82–83
  personal needs and concerns in,
    83–84
  philosophical commitment in, 77–78
  prior to or in session, 84–91
  in relationships, 78–80
  self-care in, 76–77
  spiritual practice for, 80–82
Presence, 4. *See also* Therapeutic presence
  cultivating. *See* Exercises and practices
  defined, 17–18
  emotional, 139, 140
  full, 137
  full body, 209–210
  interpersonal, 136
  intrapersonal, 136
  light, 139
  mutual, 20
  in nursing duties, 136, 137
  partial, 137, 139, 140
  physical, 136–137, 139
  psychological, 139, 140
  self-conscious, 104
  as therapeutic, 56–61
  therapeutic presence vs., 109–110
  transpersonal, 136, 139–141
PRESENCE (acronym), 236
Presence of mind, 32–34
Present-centered psychotherapy,
    148–149
Present moment
  awareness of, 77
  breathing deeply into, 234
  in Buddhist mindfulness, 180
  direct engagement with, 195–196
  exercise for, 246–247
  in Gestalt therapy approach, 21
  in immersion state, 118–119
  and multiple roles, 150

Relationship theory, *continued*
    therapeutic relationship in, 51–52
    therapist-offered conditions in,
        64–68
Relaxation, 162, 199
Reliability, 44–46
Remo's HealthRHYTHMS, 227
Resonance
    entrainment in, 251
    present-centered experience of,
        59–61
    in process of therapeutic presence,
        93–94
    sensory awareness in, 173
    with trauma, 158
Resources, inner, 32
Response flexibility, 164
Responses
    authenticity of, 71
    to client experiences, 57
    flexibility of, 164
    of self to Other, 57
    and theoretical approaches, 88–89
Responsibility, 24
Responsiveness, 53, 57–59
Rhythm, therapeutic, 227–229
Rhythm practices, 251–253
RI (Relationship Inventory), 65
Right brain hemisphere, 168
Rinpoche, Sogyal, 224
Risk taking, 102–103
Robbins, A., 29, 55
Roemer, L., 33, 34
Rogers, C. R., 4, 17–18, 26–28, 47, 51,
    64, 65, 68, 115, 141, 189, 255
Rønnestadt, M. H., 76
Rotenstreich, N., 22
Roth, G., 215
Ryan, R., 195

Safety, 69, 174, 258
Safran, J. D., 69, 189
Santorelli, S., 31–32
*Sati*, 31, 180
*Satipatthana*, 31, 180
Scan, body, 138
Schacht, T. E., 10
Schema, body, 210
Schmid, P. F., 28, 59, 62, 64–65
Schneider, K., 25–26, 61–62

Schwaber, E., 71
Schwartz, G., 167, 196
Schwartz-Barcott, D., 136–138
Scurlock-Durana, S., 209–210
Sedentary tasks, 208, 214
Self
    groundedness in, 66
    as instrument, 101
    oneness with, 39
    sense of, 210
    as sensor or indicator, 145
    transcending of, 120–121
Self-attunement, 260
Self-awareness
    in balanced life, 209
    and burnout, 11
    conceptual, 209
    and countertransference, 145–147
    embodied, 209–210
Self-care
    bodily experience in, 211–212
    in personal growth, 82–83
    in preparing the ground, 76–77
    in therapeutic presence, 11
    of therapist, 212
Self-coaching, 86
Self-compassion
    and compassion for others, 225
    in emotion-focused therapy, 219
    lack of, 195
    practices for cultivation of, 126–127
Self-concerns, 87–88
Self-consciousness, 130–131
Self-conscious presence, 104
Self-development, 76, 82–83
Self-empathy, 219
Self-healing, 78–79
Self-identity, 185
Self-knowing awareness, 164
Sensory cortex, 196
Sensory experience
    in access to client experience, 173
    enhanced awareness of, 124–125
    listening with, 208
    noticing and saying yes to, 241–242
    receptivity to, 97
    in therapeutic presence, 211
Serotonin, 162, 197
Sexual abuse, 158
Sexual energy, 151–152

Shame, 216
Shapiro, P., 193, 195
Shapiro, S. L., 182, 194
Shared reality, 63
Sharing space, 106–107
Siddartha Gautama, 182
Siegel, D. J., 113, 164–165, 169, 188, 195, 197
Siegel, R. D., 186
Silence, 148
Silsbee, D., 113, 211, 213
Smythe, E., 261
SNS. *See* Sympathetic nervous system
SOBER (acronym), 237
Social suffering, 183
Socratic method, 261
Somatic approaches
    to cultivating presence, 208–215, 226–229
    entry points for, 208
Somatic awareness
    cultivation of presence with, 213–215
    in focusing state, 216–218
    lack of, 209
    and presence, 211–212
Somatic practices, 151, 152
The soul, 219–222
Sound, 243–244
Spaciousness
    and art, 220
    and expansion state, 120, 124
    in mindfulness, 31
    in preparing the ground, 76
    in psychoanalytic approach, 19
Spiritual dimension
    in deepening into presence, 139–141
    in expansion state, 121
    in grounding state, 111
    in immersion state, 115
    in preparing the ground, 76–77, 80–82
    in presence, 23
    in process of therapeutic presence, 27–28
    in spaciousness state, 124
Spontaneity, 102, 228
Steadiness, 112–113
Stern, D., 20, 63, 64, 142, 210
Stevens, J. O., 21, 246–247

Stolorow, R. D., 71
Stress
    and bodily awareness, 208–209
    as challenge to presence, 149–151, 228
    drumming practices for, 253
    mindfulness meditation for, 199
    with multiple roles, 149–151
    in therapist life, 183
    TRM for release of, 229
Strupp, H. H., 10
Suffering
    being with and for client during, 126–131
    causes of, 184, 185
    cessation of, 184–185
    of client, 153
    compassion for, 224, 245–246
    eightfold path for, 186–187
    in four noble truths, 179, 182–184
    practice for holding with love, 123–124
    in Tonglen practice, 200
Supervisor relationship, 260–261
Surrey, J. L., 13
Survivors of trauma, 158–159
Suspension, 88
Sustainability, 194
Suzuki, Shunryu, 75
Sweet, P., 194
Sympathetic nervous system (SNS)
    calming exercises for, 237
    in neurobiology of presence, 166–167, 169
    in neuroception of safety, 174
Synaptic connections, 198
Synergy, 93–94, 107

Tai chi practice, 151, 152, 201
Taoist tai chi practice, 201
Technique
    and bracketing, 88–89
    in existential approaches, 25
    focus on, in psychotherapy training, 7, 76
    implementation of, 59
    mindfulness as, 181
    for mindfulness meditation, 239–240
    and presence, 9, 153–154, 257
    therapeutic alliance facilitation of, 69
    and therapist personal growth, 11

TPI-T. *See* Therapeutic Presence
      Inventory-therapist
Traditional Chinese medicine, 201
Training in psychotherapy. *See*
      Psychotherapy training
Traits, 163
Transcendental Meditation, 162
Transcending self, 120–121
Transparency, 67, 103–104, 107
Transpersonal presence, 136, 139–141
Transtheoretical approach, 256–257
Trauma, 158–159
Traumatization, vicarious, 10
Tree meditation, 111–112
TRM (Therapeutic Rhythm and
      Mindfulness), 226–229
Trop, J. L., 71
Trungpa, C., 109
Trust
      and anxiety, 12
      and ease, 115
      in intuitions, 102–103, 108
      in process of presence, 147–149
      in relationship theory, 59, 61
*Tsewa*, 224
Turner, M. L., 199

Unavailability, 23
Uncenteredness, 213
Uncertainty, 147–149
Unconditional positive regard, 26,
      66–68
Unconscious, collective, 62
Ungroundedness, 213
Unknown, 90
Unresolved issues, 82

Valente, V., 214
Valentine, E., 194

Validity, 44–46
Values, 83
Vanaerschot, G., 29
VanWagoner, S. L., 146
Vaughan, F., 250–251
Verbal consciousness, 63
Vicarious traumatization, 10
Vinca, M., 48–49, 192–193
*Vipassana*, 80
Virtual reality, 165
Visualization, 138
Vitality, 12
Vivino, B. L., 224–225
Vulnerability, 26, 255–256

Walking meditation, 201, 240–241
Warmth, 128
Watson, J. C., 32, 48, 49
Way of the Healer, 226
Way of the Teacher, 226
Way of the Visionary, 226
Way of the Warrior, 226
Well-being, 9–12, 257
Welwood, J., 30, 62
Whole body awareness, 238
Wholeness, 112–113, 128
Wilson, K. G., 33
Winnicott, D. W., 220
Wonder, 128
Working alliance, 55

Yoga, 151, 152, 214–215
Yontef, G., 21

Zen Buddhism, 187, 193
Zen Hospice Project, 156
Zen meditation, 197
Zen mind, 90

# ABOUT THE AUTHORS

**Shari M. Geller, PhD,** is a registered clinical psychologist with a commitment to mindfulness practices and a passion for rhythm and drumming. Dr. Geller has a 20-year mindfulness practice and weaves Buddhist philosophy and rhythm-based work into her life and clinical practice. She has a private practice in Toronto and Grey-Bruce County, where she sees individuals and couples with a variety of issues as well as a desire for personal growth and/or emotional, psychological, and spiritual integration. She is also a contract faculty member at York University and the University of Toronto, where she teaches counseling skills, mindfulness, and therapeutic presence practices. Dr. Geller developed Therapeutic Rhythm and Mindfulness (TRM), a group program integrating mindfulness and rhythm-based technologies to facilitate emotional healing. Her research interests include the relationship of therapeutic presence to effective therapy and the health benefits of the TRM program for cancer survivors.

**Leslie S. Greenberg, PhD,** is a Distinguished Research Professor of Psychology at York University in Toronto, Ontario. He is a leading authority on working with emotion in psychotherapy and the developer of emotion-focused therapy, an evidence-based approach. He has authored the major texts on emotion-focused approaches to treatment of individuals and couples. He has received the Distinguished Research Career Award of the Society for Psychotherapy Research, the Carl Rogers Award of the American Psychological Association's Society for Humanistic Psychology, the Canadian Council of Professional Psychology Programs' Award for Excellence in Professional Training, and the Canadian Psychological Association's Award for Distinguished Contributions to Psychology as a Profession. Dr. Greenberg is a founding member of the Society for the Exploration of Psychotherapy Integration and a past president of the Society for Psychotherapy Research. He conducts a private practice for individuals and couples and trains people in emotion-focused therapy.